America's Wetland

America's Wetland

*An Environmental
and Cultural History
of Tidewater Virginia
and North Carolina*

Roy T. Sawyer

University of Virginia Press   *Charlottesville and London*

University of Virginia Press
© 2010 by the Rector and Visitors of the University of Virginia
All rights reserved
Printed in the United States of America on acid-free paper

First published 2010

9 8 7 6 5 4 3 2 1

Library of Congress Cataloging-in-Publication Data
Sawyer, Roy T.
    America's wetland : an environmental and cultural history of tidewater Virginia
and North Carolina / Roy T. Sawyer.
        p.   cm.
    Includes bibliographical references and index.
    ISBN 978-0-8139-2921-7 (cloth : alk. paper) — ISBN 978-0-8139-2969-9 (e-book)
    1. Wetland ecology—Virginia—Atlantic Coast. 2. Wetland ecology—North
Carolina—Atlantic Coast. 3. Drainage—Environmental aspects—Virginia—Atlantic
Coast. 4. Drainage—Environmental aspects—North Carolina—Atlantic Coast.
5. Climate change—Virginia—Atlantic Coast. 6. Climate change—North Carolina—
Atlantic Coast. 7. Atlantic Coast (Va.)—Environmental conditions. 8. Atlantic Coast
(N.C.)—Environmental conditions. I. Title.
    QH105.V8S27 2010
    508.755′1—dc22

                                                                        2009039565

CONTENTS

ACKNOWLEDGMENTS

A book of this kind is a synthesis of the work of many others who have contributed through remarkably diverse disciplines. The challenge has been to integrate these disparate studies into a meaningful story. Any failure to do so in the following pages is mine alone and in no way reflects on the countless scholars without whom this ecohistory would not be possible.

The assistance given by numerous institutions is hereby acknowledged with gratitude. These include the North Carolina Office of Archives and History, Department of Cultural Resources, Raleigh; J. Y. Joyner Library and Department of Anthropology, East Carolina University, Greenville; John D. Rockefeller Jr. Library, Colonial Williamsburg; New Bern-Craven County Public Library; Tyrrell County Genealogical and Historical Society and Tyrrell County Public Library, Columbia, North Carolina; Hyde County Genealogical Society, Englehard; Pasquotank County Public Library, Elizabeth City; Charleston County Public Library, Charleston, South Carolina; Zoology Department, U.S. National Museum of Natural History, Washington, DC; Zoology Department, British Museum (Natural History), London; Buckridge Preserve, North Carolina Division of Coastal Management; Pettigrew State Park; Somerset Place, Creswell; North Carolina Museum of Natural Sciences, Raleigh; J. C. Raulston Arboretum, North Carolina State University, Raleigh; U.S. Environmental Protection Agency, Washington, DC; North Carolina Division of Water Quality, Raleigh; North Carolina Division of Marine Fisheries, Elizabeth City; and U.S. Geological Survey, Lakewood, Colorado. The generosity of many helpful individuals at these institutions is acknowledged and greatly appreciated.

The faith in this ambitious project expressed throughout by the University of Virginia Press is gratefully acknowledged. In particular I thank Boyd Zenner, Angie Hogan, Mark Mones, Mark Saunders, and Andrew Katz for their continued support and encouragement. The contributions made by three anonymous referees were invaluable and gratefully received.

Personal thanks are extended especially to Etta W. A. Ward, Chris Meekins, Woody Webster, Zelda Pledger, Hattie Mae Cowell, Buddy Brickhouse, William Moser, Rus Wheeler, Fred Hechtel, Patrick Pattison and many others not singled out here. I take special pride in recognizing those deceased individuals who shared with me over many years their extensive knowledge of the history and natural history of the Alligator River (Gum Neck): Kizzie Langley Sawyer (1884–1964), Lennie Jones Christianson (1903–2006), Walter Basnight (1913–2001), Edison Weatherly (1929–2008), and Dimple Jones Taylor (1933–2007). Finally, I must recognize my grandmother Carrie Jones Weatherly (1896–1969), an extraordinary lady who instilled in me the harmony of nature and history in this beautiful swampland.

America's Wetland

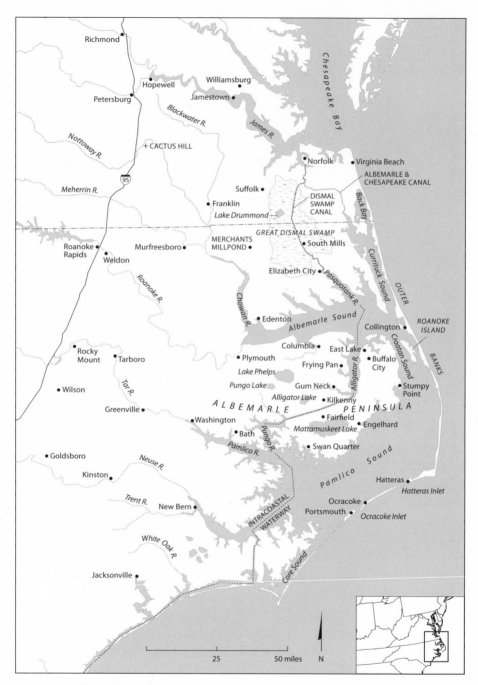

Map of the Albemarle-Pamlico region of Virginia and North Carolina.

Introduction

At one critical period in America's history the Albemarle region of southeastern Virginia and northeastern North Carolina was the absolute center of the non-Spanish New World. It was here in the 1580s that England chose to locate its first colony in the Western Hemisphere. This "lost colony" disappeared under mysterious circumstances, still one of the unsolved questions of the Age of Exploration. Nonetheless, this was just the beginning of the successful Jamestown era of English colonization. Migrating from the expanding Virginia colony, settlers soon returned to the Albemarle region. It was the earliest region of both North and South Carolina to be settled, a full generation before Charleston. The first colonial and state capitals of North Carolina were here; in fact, this immense coastal lowland is a region of many historic firsts.

The Albemarle region contains America's most historic wetland for another reason, perhaps of even greater significance. During the last ice age, and perhaps earlier, this region was a center of human habitation surviving at the northern end of a warm coastal strip. This wetland abounded in overwintering waterfowl, fish, and game, a rich oasis at the southern end of a tundralike region. The very early Clovis people had a tool factory (Williamson quarry) in the Albemarle watershed during the late ice age, over ten thousand years ago. Furthermore, recent evidence is emerging here of an earlier pre-Clovis people of the ice age itself, fifteen thousand years ago (Cactus Hill). Finally, Pleistocene Albemarle may present an environmental context for the contentious hypothesis discussed in chapter 1 that ice-age man may have migrated to America from Europe (Solutrean).

The early settlements of the Albemarle region both by the pre-Clovis and Clovis peoples and millennia later by the Roanoke/Jamestown settlers are linked to a common environmental feature unique in the world. Although the coastline has moved erratically westward due to rising sea levels following the Pleistocene, this swampy region has remained for thousands of years at the northern end of a warm coastal strip, a freshwater wetland abounding in food and waterways naturally conducive to early human habitation.[1]

This book is an ecohistory of the Albemarle watershed, an ancient, resilient wetland ecosystem that has featured disproportionately in America's history and prehistory. It is an account of a unique environment and its interface with man over a lengthy period of time, starting when people first arrived here some fifteen thousand years ago, or earlier. This land of rivers and swamps created an Albemarle "tidewater culture" in much the same way that the Berbers of the Sahara adapted to life deprived of water or the Inuits of the Arctic to life on frozen water.

In addition, this book is an account of how man has affected this wetland environment. Examples abound elsewhere of how deforestation brought droughts to Saharan Africa, how overfishing has depleted fish stocks in the North Sea, and how release of fossil fuels may be contributing to melting ice in the Arctic. The following pages show that humans' exploitation of natural resources in this region has been remarkably short-sighted, leaving each subsequent generation that much more impoverished.

Humans have been altering the Albemarle environment with unprecedented intensity only over the past one hundred years or so, but this is not just a modern phenomenon. In fact, human alteration of this environment goes back tens of thousands of years, well into prehistory, when it was not done with such intensity but continued for a far, far greater period of time. Thus, early humans probably contributed to extinction of the mammoth and other megafauna, brought domesticated dogs with them into the New World, burned immeasurable quantities of underbrush and firewood, contributed to forest fires, and cleared land for maize cultivation.

The final lesson, however, is that humanity is not central to determining the Albemarle's long-term environmental future, in spite of current appearances. Humans are only part of a much larger picture in this region. Overpowering environmental events have occurred here independently of humanity with a kind of regularity barely discernible over the short term. Warming periods, land submergences, droughts, prolonged freezes, mini ice ages, lightning-caused forest fires, great storms and floods are normal themes here, over the long term. They only become disasters when humans are affected, but human activities have significantly increased the severity and frequency of such disasters. This eco-history examines the causes and extent of humans' contribution to environmental changes. These are best, or perhaps only, understood over the very long term.

On a personal note, there is another dimension to this particular eco-history. The Albemarle region has been my homeland for more than half a century and for ten generations before me, not to mention the Native American blood so common in old families throughout this region. I grew up on the Alligator River (Gum Neck) at the peninsular heartland of this swampy region. Naturally, I became fascinated with the animals and plants around me, resulting in my becoming a biologist with a specialty in leeches. As an inquisitive child I was surrounded by aging kinfolk who shared glimpses into a bygone age. For me this book has been a personal journey into the past, not just into the biology and history of my youth but toward an understanding of what happened here since people first arrived in this pivotal part of the world.[2]

World Unique Ecosystem

What makes the massive swamps and lakes of southeastern Virginia and northeastern North Carolina so intriguingly special? The short answer is because this region lies on top of the Appalachian Mountains. More accurately, it lies on top of thousands of feet of sediment eroded from those very mountains over millions of years. What sets this vast region apart from the coastal plain is its near-sea-level elevation, such that much of this wetland is subject to primarily wind-driven tides, hence the "tidewater" epithet.

Waters of the northern strip of this tidewater region around Norfolk and Portsmouth flow northward into the James River and Chesapeake Bay (Virginia tidewater). However, most of this wetland flows southward ultimately into the Albemarle and Pamlico sounds of North Carolina. For brevity, the term *Albemarle region* is used in this book to describe this watershed, in the knowledge that a significant portion, including the Great Dismal Swamp, actually lies in southeastern Virginia.

Extending approximately 150 miles from north to south and 100 miles east to west, the Albemarle tidewater contains one of the largest freshwater wetlands in the nation, fully comparable in scale and biological wonder to the Everglades, the Okefenokee Swamp, and the Mississippi Delta.

A unique feature of this wetland lies in its physical geography. Like nowhere else on earth, the Albemarle region juts abruptly into the Atlantic Ocean, deflecting the warm Gulf Stream away from the mainland toward Europe. Thus, this region is the last, northernmost point on the American continent warmed by the Gulf Stream. For this reason winters here are significantly milder than those on the American mainland at this latitude.

In its entirety the Albemarle ecosystem encompasses the Albemarle and Pamlico sounds and their respective river drainage basins (totaling about 28,000 square miles). The basically freshwater Albemarle Sound receives water from the Roanoke River (drainage basin of 8,900 square miles, extending as far as the Appalachian Mountains) and the Chowan-Meherrin-Nottoway-Blackwater River system (4,800 square miles). Both drainage systems lie primarily in Virginia. The more brackish Pamlico Sound receives water from the Neuse River (6,200 square miles), and the Tar-Pamlico River (5,400 square miles). Both the Neuse and Tar-Pamlico rivers lie entirely in North Carolina. The Outer Banks, a series of sandy barrier islands, bound this region to the east and south. This narrow island archipelago supports very limited freshwater systems and is not considered in this book as part of the Albemarle tidewater.

This huge, but little known, wetland is made up of dismal swamps, mysterious Carolina bays and lakes, sluggish blackwater rivers, plus large freshwater and brackish sounds (one so large that in 1524 an early explorer thought he had discovered the Pacific Ocean). All this surface water contributes to a maritime climate, further tempering winter extremes.

The improbable warmth of the Albemarle region explains why this region is the northern limit of a number of plant and animal species. The heart of this region is the Albemarle peninsula, sometimes called the Great Alligator Swamp because it is the northernmost home of the American alligator. In fact, this region is amazingly rich in reptiles, with over forty species of snakes, turtles, and lizards already recorded from these swamps.[3] Similarly, this wetland supports prodigious numbers of over-wintering waterfowl, migratory fish, and other species, including relict populations of the black bear. More recently the red wolf has been re-introduced to this region.

In the primeval condition of these swamps they comprised hundreds of thousands of acres of undisturbed bald cypress, black gum (tupelo), Atlantic white cedar, and other water-loving hardwood forests unsur-passed in the eastern United States. The rich, damp soil and warm climate created a canopy of trees of truly gargantuan size and age. Some of these trees still survive and represent the oldest living things east of the Rocky Mountains, in some cases over sixteen hundred years old.

As befitting a landscape of ancient water-saturated forests, the Albe-marle region has the greatest accumulation of swamp peatlands (poco-sins) in the United States. For eons, leaves and other organic matter have fallen into water-saturated swamps where, under anaerobic conditions, they were preserved as peat. Unlike a normal forest where decomposition ultimately returns its carbon back into the atmosphere in a generation or so, these pocosins lock carbon away indefinitely, literally for thousands of years. In other words, the Albemarle tidewater is a significant "car-bon sink."

This freshwater swampland is kept saturated by bountiful rainfall from passing hurricanes and nor'easters. Its geographical position is for-tuitous in that its eastward projection into the Atlantic exposes this re-gion to an unusual number of such storms. Not surprisingly, the Albe-marle tidewater has been drenched by more hurricanes than anywhere else in the United States, a veritable hurricane alley. The energy in the greatest of these storms periodically opens and closes inlets on the nearby Outer Banks and scours pocosin lakes. Lesser storms regularly fell weak, insect-ridden trees. As they slowly rot, these vital logs generate food and homes for amphibians, reptiles, birds, and other insectivorous animals, including at one time the ivory-billed woodpecker.

The term *Albemarle region* as used in this book is for the most part interchangeable with *Albemarle tidewater, wetland,* or *basin.* Where ap-propriate, *Albemarle-Pamlico region* is used for contextual emphasis. In its entirety the Albemarle region extends roughly from Suffolk, Vir-ginia, in the north to White Oak River in Carteret County, North Car-olina, in the south, and includes the Albemarle peninsula and the Tar-

Neuse peninsula. Within this once-continuous wetland there are today four biologically disparate swamp systems, disjunct relics of a bygone primeval past.

At the northern end of this wetland, and remarkably close to Norfolk, is the Great Dismal Swamp, most of which is located in Virginia. At the heart of this pocosin swamp is Lake Drummond, the largest natural lake in Virginia. The Dismal Swamp has captivated public imagination since colonial days, when it was linked directly to young George Washington. Its significance as a wildlife preserve was recognized officially in 1974 as the Great Dismal Swamp National Wildlife Refuge, under jurisdiction of the U.S. Fish and Wildlife Service. Encompassing 196 square miles in all, the Dismal Swamp refuge is greatly reduced from the original size of this swamp system (about 2,000 square miles). Its fabulous history and rich wildlife are relatively well known.[4]

Toward the west is the quite different river swamp system of the Roanoke River, which has the widest flood plain in North Carolina, up to five miles across. This bottomland of cypress and gum/tupelo trees includes the Roanoke River National Wildlife Refuge (about 24,000 acres, in five tracts along 70 miles of the lower river).

At the southern end of the Albemarle-Pamlico region lies still another type of preserve, the Croatan National Forest (about 160,000 acres). Ecologically diverse, this coastal forest predominates in pines and encompasses several small "Carolina bay" lakes generally characteristic of coastal wetlands. It contains more insectivorous plants, including Venus flytrap, than any other national forest in America.

At the geographical center of the Albemarle region lies the vast Albemarle peninsula (70 by 50 miles). Sandwiched between two of the largest sounds in the United States, this remote peninsula receives special attention throughout this book. A little-known wildlife wonderland, this swampland is the most isolated and least populated part of the Albemarle wetland. This watery land of bears, wolves, and alligators contains the nation's greatest peat swamps (pocosins), interspersed among which are four large enigmatic lakes (including the largest and second-largest natural lakes in North Carolina). Fittingly, the Albemarle peninsula contains nearly 70 percent of the vast wildlife refuge land found in the Albemarle-Pamlico region.

1 Ice-Age Enclave

The Albemarle region holds a unique place in prehistory of the Americas. Just as this region today is the northernmost warm strip along the Atlantic coast, it was also a thermal strip during the last ice age (late Pleistocene). Glaciers and winter ice came close to, but did not encompass, this unglaciated coastal enclave whose relative warmth and abundance of food was amenable to early human habitation. Its nearest ice-age counterpart across the Atlantic, near the other end of the Gulf Stream, was southern France, where a cultural enclave renown for Clovis-type tools is well documented at about the same time or a bit earlier (see, for example, the Solutrean culture in Lascaux, France).

The contentious Solutrean Hypothesis that ice-age man migrated from Europe to North America lies outside the scope of this book. However, Pleistocene Albemarle may become relevant to this debate in that this ancient warm ecosystem represents the northernmost Solutrean counterpart in the New World during the last glacial maximum. On both sides of the Atlantic the sea level was much lower than today, resulting in coastlines extending farther into the Atlantic. Furthermore, during the last ice age the Albemarle Sound, the Pamlico Sound, and even the Chesapeake Bay did not exist. Instead, they were represented by the paleo-Roanoke River, the paleo-Pamlico River, and the paleo-James/paleo-Susquehanna River, respectively, each discharging independently into the ocean at the continental slope. Thus, ten thousand years ago, when the sea level was about four hundred feet below its present level, the main channel of the Roanoke River was located at what is now the bottom of the Albemarle

TABLE 1. Cold-tolerant animals and plants at southern limits of distribution in the Albemarle region

At the time of the ice ages, cold-tolerant animals and plants of the Albemarle region lived along a steep thermal gradient in proximity to a warm coastal strip warmed by the Gulf Stream. Most of the following species are vaguely reminiscent of such relicts in that their southern limits of distribution along the East Coast occur at or near the Albemarle ecosystem. A fossil ancestor of the great auk was found in a phosphate mine in Beaufort County, North Carolina, indicating that conditions in the Albemarle region were boreal during the Pliocene epoch, two to five million years ago (S. Olson 1977). The recently extinct great auk, a flightless, penguinlike seabird, was reportedly a winter visitor to this general region in the early eighteenth century (Gaskell 2000). Its near relatives the razorbill and the dovekie are both species of auk typically found in the Arctic, but they return irregularly this far south as winter visitors. Geese and swans return annually from subarctic regions to overwinter here.

COMMON NAME	SCIENTIFIC NAME
Great auk (Pliocene ancestor)	*Pinguinus alfrednewtoni*
Great auk (historical)	*Pinguinus impennis*
Razorbill auk	*Alca torda*
Dovekie (little auk)	*Alle alle*
Atlantic brant goose	*Branta bernicla hrota*
Trumpeter swan (historical)	*Cygnus buccinator*
Tundra swan (whistling swan)	*Cygnus columbianu*
River herring (alewife)	*Alosa pseudoharengus*
Redback salamander	*Plethodon cinereus*
Redbelly turtle	*Pseudemys rubriventris*
Southern bog lemming	*Synaptomys cooperi*
Intermediate woodfern	*Dryopteris intermedia*
Eelgrass	*Zostera marina*

Sound, and it emptied into the ocean between fifteen and sixty miles east of Nags Head.[1]

In the Albemarle enclave of the last ice age the nearby tundralike climate supported mastodons and mammoths and other megafauna, which could have served as food for skilled hunters. The southern bog lemming *Synaptomys cooperi* is a Pleistocene relict that is still living in the Dismal Swamp and other parts of northeastern North Carolina (see table 1).[2]

Perhaps the most remarkable mammal once living along the coastal strip was the giant (seventeen-foot-long) ground sloth (*Eremotherium eomigrans*), an intact skeleton of which was found recently near Wilmington. No direct evidence exists that early humans in the Albemarle killed these or other megafauna now extinct in this area, but based on evidence elsewhere, such a supposition is reasonable. (In this context, the Page-Ladson pre-Clovis site of northern Florida is particularly significant.)

Recent archaeological research in the Albemarle basin has presented tantalizing evidence that a site on the Chowan-Nottoway River (Cactus Hill, Virginia) is one of the oldest inhabited parts of North America, dating to at least 15,000 BP (i.e., before the last ice age receded). In other words, humans were living in this freshwater ecosystem, free from permanent ice cover, more than five thousand years before humans first occupied Ireland.

Cactus Hill is one of a handful of archaeological sites in North and South America that, at this writing, challenges the traditional view ("Clovis First") that the first inhabitants of America came about 12,000 BP from Asia via the Bering Strait. In any case, the Albemarle-Pamlico region is unusually rich in Clovis and other Paleo-Indian artifacts, indicating that these people were unquestionably thriving here about the time the ice was finally receding.

This ancient center of population, if it could be described as such, is attributable to the ecological richness of the Albemarle-Pamlico region from time immemorial. Then, as now, this relatively warm freshwater ecosystem was an abundant source of overwintering waterfowl, spring migrating fish, summer and autumnal game, and edible plants.

Superimposed on this picture was a slow rise in sea level that encroached inexorably on potentially habitable land. When the last glacial ice started receding more than ten thousand years ago, these wetlands extended well east of today's Outer Banks. The rising water no doubt submerged many artifacts waiting to tell the full story of humans' earliest prehistory here.[3]

Then, a major environmental event, called the Younger Dryas episode, struck the Clovis people here and elsewhere. Twelve thousand nine hundred years ago the temperature dropped abruptly about seven degrees Celsius in twenty years and continued cold for another thirteen hundred years. Recent research is focusing on the possibility that some extraterrestrial impact struck somewhere in North America, heralding a mini ice age of great significance, including extinctions of megafauna. This cold period was a major setback for the Clovis culture throughout North America. Without speculating too much, one wonders if the warm thermal enclave of the southeastern United States might have developed a notable pre-Columbian civilization had it not been for this accident of nature (as opposed to the flourishing uninterrupted culture that developed in the climatically similar southeastern China).[4]

Overwintering Waterfowl

Waterfowl, more than any other animal group, offer tangible insight into the ancient relationship between the peculiar features of the Albemarle-Pamlico wetland and human settlement in this area.

Since the last ice age marsh vegetation of this freshwater wetland afforded food for various species of plant-eating waterfowl, such as ducks, geese, and swans. Over millennia, as the climate warmed, these birds flew farther and farther north for summer food and breeding grounds. As winter approached, however, they returned precisely back to the same wetland so reliably rich in winter vegetation. In turn, bountiful numbers of overwintering waterfowl afforded an unusually rich and reliable source of food for the earliest human hunter-gatherers, of special importance during the lean winter months.

There is reason to believe that overwintering waterfowl constituted the single most important factor in explaining the very early, intensive human settlement during the mid-Archaic Period (7000–3500 BP) in this region. In fact, compelling, indirect evidence indicates that waterfowl populations significantly exceeded those of today. As the last ice age receded the sea level gradually rose, leading to open expanses of unwooded marshes.

That these freshwater marshes were occupied by large numbers of waterfowl is indicated by the unusual preponderance of the one major hunting tool (bola) found in this area relating to that time frame. Bolas are two or more rounded stones connected by rawhide, a sort of archaic but deadly slingshot. When thrown at waterfowl the stones separate in flight, one hitting the bird and the other wrapping around the victim to the point of immobilization. Bolas were only effective in open country, such as a marsh, and were impractical in a forest. Thus, as the freshwater marshes progressed into cypress-gum swamps, after 3500 BP, the bola was replaced by the stone arrow as the main hunting weapon. Concomitantly, many waterfowl habitats were replaced by forested swamps.

Archaeological data from more recent prehistory confirm that Indians along the coastal region subsisted on a number of different species of ducks and other waterfowl. At the time of first contact with Europeans the Carolina Algonquins controlled this vital winter resource in the Albemarle-Pamlico region. Arguably, it was the existence of these over-wintering waterfowl, more than anything else, that brought the Algonquins to their southernmost limit.[5] Historical and biological aspects of these waterfowl are discussed in detail in the next chapter.

Pocosin Lakes: Inhabited before the Egyptian Pyramids

The Albemarle peninsula, at the geographical center of the Albemarle-Pamlico region, is dominated by four mysterious lakes, including the largest and second-largest natural lakes in North Carolina. Across the Albemarle Sound to the north in the Great Dismal Swamp is a similar lake, Lake Drummond, the largest natural lake in Virginia. To the south, in Craven County, North Carolina, is a group of five smaller lakes, associated with the Croatan National Forest. These shallow bodies of water, together called the "pocosin lakes," are peculiar to this region. The formation of these lakes by means of powerful hurricanes and the early settlement and drainage of these lakes are discussed in detail in chapters 3 and 7, respectively.

The four lakes of the Albemarle peninsula—namely, Lake Mattamuskeet, Lake Phelps, Alligator Lake (New Lake), and Pungo Lake—are set individually among a vast expanse of water-saturated swamp pocosin, the largest in the world. Each lake has a distinctive elliptical shape and an improbable raised ridge along one rim. These four lake ridges constitute the highest land in the pocosin, and each is associated with prehistoric

Indian activity, some truly ancient. Satellite images reveal the existence of other, earlier pocosin lakes on this peninsula. The most recent was Stumpy Point Lake, which has been eroded in historic times into Stumpy Point Bay on the eastern side of mainland Dare County.

For many hundreds of years, if not significantly more, the means of transportation throughout these wetlands was by dugout canoe. We know this because a severe drought in 1985 led to the discovery in Lake Phelps of "the largest *in situ* collection of canoes in Southeastern United States."[6] Submerged in the lake were about thirty rot-resistant cypress canoes, the largest of which was thirty-seven feet long. A smaller number of similar canoes had been found earlier in nearby Alligator Lake.

Nineteen canoes in the Lake Phelps collection were radiocarbon tested. The oldest dated to 3095 BC, and furthermore, this remarkable collection of canoes spanned a period of nearly forty-five hundred years. Four of the canoes dated to a very early period (3095 BC to 1120 BC), but by far the majority (eleven) dated to a much later time (193 BC to AD 432). Then, there is an apparent gap of nearly eight hundred years before the next set of only three canoes (AD 1225 to AD 1361). Only one of the canoes (number 227, dated to 1120 BC) could be independently dated, in that it was associated with fragments of net-impressed pottery interpreted as "Deep Creek" (Early Woodland). Parenthetically, the radiocarbon data prove decisively that this area in the vicinity of Lake Phelps has been a land of cypress swamps for more than five thousand years.

Significantly, Lake Phelps, as with all the pocosin lakes, did not have a direct outlet to its nearest river. A tributary of the Scuppernong River was linked to the lake itself only by a swampy morass of at least a mile, which received spillover at times of excessive rains. In this context, it is unimaginable that Indians, in search of seasonable food (wildfowl), would have dragged their heavy canoes through a nearly impenetrable morass to reach the lake, which was elevated a good ten feet above the river. Instead, the Indians would have made dugout canoes at the lake itself (and would have left them there for future use).

These dugouts indicate that three disparate groups of Native Americans canoed on Lake Phelps, commencing at the very beginning of the Late Archaic Period, that is, even before the period of sedentary lifestyle and pottery (i.e., pre-agriculture). The most intensive group occurred in the earlier part of the Woodland Period. Surprisingly, the pocosin lakes appear to have been relatively uninhabited in recent prehistory (Late Woodland, possibly relating to the Algonquin period).

At first intimate contact with Europeans (AD 1584) the Carolina Algonquins here were already advanced masters at building dugout canoes, some of which held twenty people. These dugouts were the means of transportation, fishing, and hunting throughout the Albemarle region. The Roanoke colonists described and illustrated in some detail how these people crafted their fine dugouts from individual trees, using only fire and scrapers.

Their close relatives to the north, the Virginia Algonquins (Powhatan Indians of the Jamestown period), also depended on such dugouts in the Chesapeake region. The largest were "about four feet deep and up to fifty feet long, with a carrying capacity of some forty men,"[7] but most dugouts were smaller. Helen Rountree, an authority on Powhatan Indian culture, observed that in terms of labor the dugout canoe was the most expensive object in their possession (like a family car is today). In this context, it is especially enigmatic that thirty dugout canoes were "lost" in Lake Phelps.[8]

$\mathcal{2}$ *Relict Fauna*

The Albemarle-Pamlico region is one of America's most remarkable wildlife habitats. Where else in the world could a tundra swan be attacked by an alligator? Where else could seals, dolphins, or indeed sharks be found in a blackwater river? Where were terrapins hunted commercially with specially trained dogs? Where has the oldest known pond cypress in America lived for fourteen hundred years? Where is the northern limit of the alligator, eastern diamondback rattlesnake, Carolina pigmy rattlesnake, marsh rabbit, Venus flytrap, Spanish moss, and so many other animals and plants?[1]

Why is the Albemarle ecosystem so biologically unique? The answer lies in its climate and geography. It juts into the Atlantic at the very point that the warming water of the Gulf Stream is deflected away from the American mainland, creating a sharp demarcation of northern and southern saltwater species at Hatteras. The inland sounds grade imperceptibly from fresh water through brackish to salty, allowing broad overlap of freshwater and marine species, and at one time an incomparable abundance of anadromous fish such as herring, shad, and sturgeon.

This improbably warm strip of wetland allows the intrusion of southern species far north of what latitude alone would dictate (see table 2). Summers in these water-saturated swamps are hot and wet, almost subtropical, the water table replenished annually with tropical rains. Winters are maritime tempered, such that the bears do not hibernate. No wonder the food-rich wetlands of this region attract one of the largest populations of overwintering waterfowl in North America, migrating since prehistory from as far away as the tundra of northwest Canada and even Alaska.

With the notable exceptions of the bison, Carolina parakeet, passenger pigeon, and ivory-billed woodpecker, nearly all the colonial fauna of the Albemarle wetland have (just) survived humans' impact. This remarkable achievement is attributable to the region's sheer remoteness and impene-

TABLE 2. Notable animal and plant species at northern limits of distribution in the Albemarle region

The following are notable animal and plant species whose northern limits of distribution along the East Coast occur at or near the tidewater ecosystem of southeastern Virginia and northeastern North Carolina. In general, these species thrive under the moist conditions of a warm thermal strip influenced by the Gulf Stream. The unique salamander called the Neuse River waterdog is confined to the Neuse and Tar rivers, a reflection of the geological antiquity of these isolated rivers.

COMMON NAME	SCIENTIFIC NAME
American alligator	*Alligator mississipiensis*
Eastern cottonmouth moccasin	*Agkistrodon piscivorus piscivorus*
Eastern diamondback rattlesnake	*Crotalus adamanteus*
Carolina pigmy rattlesnake	*Sistrurus miliarius miliarius*
Carolina swamp snake	*Seminatrix pygaea paludis*
Banded water snake	*Nerodia fasciata fasciata*
Glossy crayfish snake	*Regina rigida rigida*
Florida cooter	*Pseudemys floridana floridana*
Green anole lizard	*Anolis carolinensis*
Eastern glass lizard	*Ophisaurus ventralis*
Southern toad	*Bufo terrestris*
Oak toad	*Bufo quercicus*
Squirrel treefrog	*Hyla squirella*
Southern cricket frog	*Acris gryllus gryllus*
Lesser siren	*Siren intermedia*
Dwarf waterdog	*Necturus punctatus*

continued

Common name	Scientific name
Neuse River waterdog	*Necturus lewisi*
Ivory-billed woodpecker (historical)	*Campephilus principalis*
Marsh rabbit	*Sylvilagus palustris palustris*
Cotton mouse	*Peromyscus gossypinus*
Rafinesque's big-eared bat	*Corynorhinus rafinesquii*
Seminole bat (nests in Spanish moss)	*Lasiurus seminolus*
Spanish moss	*Tillandsia usneoides*
Pond cypress	*Taxodium ascendens*
Live oak	*Quercus virginiana*
Red bay	*Persea borbonia*
Gordonia	*Gordonia lasianthus*
Southern red cedar	*Juniperus silicicola*
Pond pine	*Pinus serotina*
Long-leaf pine	*Pinus palustris*
Dwarf palmetto	*Sabal minor*
Venus flytrap	*Dionaea muscipula*
Yellow pitcher plant	*Sarracenia flava*

trability. Humans have managed to intrude only so far, begrudgingly leaving scattered refuges for bears and other wildlife stragglers. Ironically, this isolation, coupled with sparse human population, is the very reason the biological uniqueness of the Albemarle wetland is relatively unknown. Without doubt, this region has the richest faunistic history in colonial America, a world explored in this and following chapters.

Alligator: Relict of an Ice-Age Warm Coastal Strip

Since before the last ice age a warm coastal strip extended as far north as northeastern North Carolina, barely getting into Virginia.[2] No fossil crocodilians are known from the Pleistocene (ice age) in Virginia or Maryland. However, a Pleistocene alligator fossil was discovered near the Neuse River at Arapahoe, Pamlico County, along with a fossil mammoth (*Mammuthus imperator*).[3] This juxtaposition of a warm-adapted reptile with a cold-adapted mammal gives insight into a food-rich period when early man lived here.

Today, the American alligator (*Alligator mississippiensis*) reaches its northern limit of distribution along the Alligator River in the Albemarle peninsula (once appropriately known as the Great Alligator Swamp). In fact, this ancient reptile has lived in the Albemarle region continuously since early prehistory, and the indigenous people ate them here at a subsistence level.[4] The archaeological record confirms that distribution of this species has been restricted to the coastal plain since at least the Late Woodland period (AD 800–1600).

John White, artist of the Roanoke Colony (1585), painted an unidentified crocodilian (labeled "Allagatto"), but it is unclear whether this was a local animal, since White had previously been in the West Indies. The earliest unequivocal historical account of an alligator in the Albemarle-Pamlico watershed was in April 1711. One of Baron von Graffenried's Swiss settlers in New Bern observed in a letter back home, "I have seen crocodiles [alligators] by the water, but they soon fled." In 1731 the Edenton-based naturalist John Brickell encountered them in a creek near Bath Town "where these animals are very plenty."[5]

Alligator found in the Tar River, Greenville, North Carolina, by James Keel (pictured) and friends, June 1960. (Daily Reflector Negative Collection [#741], Special Collections Department, J. Y. Joyner Library, East Carolina University, Greenville, NC)

In March 1864 a juvenile alligator was collected in Bachelor's Creek, site of an infamous Civil War battle, and was shipped north. In the 1880s and 1890s alligators were reported from the lower Tar and Neuse river basins, as well as from the southern part of Hyde County, around Rose Bay. In recent times a few stragglers rarely turn up in this general region.[6]

To the northeast, in the Alligator River, alligators are more common and have been documented as living here for more than two hundred years, as a visiting Englishman observed in 1798: "This large river was named 'Alligator River,' from the quantity of those dangerous animals found there, on its being first explored. When I was there in the year 1798, a young one was caught, which I had an opportunity of examining. . . . I am informed that it was sold, and exhibited in different parts, to the great emolument of the purchaser."[7]

In the Alligator River, alligators reach their greatest population on the east side of the river, where individuals in excess of twelve feet have been reported (Brickell claimed in the 1730s that they exceeded eighteen feet). In early May 1935 some lumber estimators commissioned by the Richmond Cedar Works noted that they had "found 13 alligators in the Alligator River. They averaged only about two feet. However, some have been seen and estimated to be 12 or 14 feet long. One alligator was captured alive and carried to Columbia. Captain L. L. Creef of the *Mary Steele* reported shooting and killing one. This dead alligator was carried to Buffalo City where it attracted much attention."[8] Forty years later an exceptionally large alligator (reportedly twelve feet, six inches) became intertwined in a fisherman's net. Its carcass was left to rot for some time at Grapevine Landing, Gum Neck, by which time biologists had taken samples of its teeth and bones. Similarly, in 1980 a specimen measuring just over twelve feet was killed in southern Hyde County.

Aggregates of small individuals in the waters bordering the Alligator River verify the alligator's capability of successful breeding here, especially on the east side of the river (e.g., Whipping Creek). The presence of such juveniles has been observed for many years. For example, in the 1920s an eyewitness reported that her brother caught a clutch of about a dozen small individuals near Mill Tail Creek. He brought them back to his home at Gum Neck, where he kept them in a wash tub. He "contacted someone about taking them but found no takers, so he released them."[9]

Alligators are also encountered from time to time on the west side of the Alligator River, especially in the lower half around Gum Neck. In the

1940s a four-foot-long alligator was observed sunning itself on a canal bank at Gum Neck Landing. In fact, the various landings in this area (Gum Neck, Cherry Ridge, and Grapevine) have been the most consistent places for sightings, along with the mouths of Pole Cat Creek, Tatem Canal, and Frying Pan Creek and along the narrow headwaters of the river near Kilkenny. Since the drainage dike was constructed around Gum Neck in the 1960s alligators are occasionally spotted sunning themselves on the banks of the perimeter canal, and several have been removed in recent years from the vicinity of houses within the dike. Around 1971 a large individual became trapped and died at the pumping station at Frying Pan. Although alligators are uncommon in the north and west portions of the Albemarle peninsula, a large individual was reportedly found some years ago in the Scuppernong River in the vicinity of Jaegers Fish Market in Columbia.

Sustained breeding populations of alligators are unknown north of the Albemarle Sound. As one recent observer has noted, "A popular misconception is that American alligators occurred historically in the [Great] Dismal Swamp. This belief was dispelled by N. D. Richmond (1963) based on the lack of fossil or subfossil evidence."[10] In recent years, however, alligators have been sighted in waters north of the Albemarle Sound, most notably at Merchants Millpond in Gates County. Around 1980 a large specimen was "lurking at the end of a boat pier" in the Chowan River near the Virginia border at Riddicksville, Hertford County, North Carolina.[11] Whether these released or escaped individuals can sustain a breeding population is historically improbable.

Alligators have never been known to attack humans anywhere in the Albemarle region. However, dogs may not have been so fortunate. In the 1940s, at the mouth of Gum Neck Creek, a hunting dog jumped from a boat and was swimming ashore when it suddenly disappeared in a great swirl of water, presumably from an alligator. Brickell was undoubtedly correct, in 1731, when he observed that alligators in North Carolina "frequently ate swimming dogs and swine going to drink." He was also astute when he implied that a favorite natural food of alligators is water snakes (always in abundance on the Albemarle peninsula): he saw two killed, and in their bellies "were found several sorts of snakes."[12]

The alligators in the Alligator River are of unique biological significance in that this ancient, relict population constitutes the northernmost wild breeding population of any crocodilian species in the world, including the endangered Chinese alligator (*Alligator sinensis*) of coastal China.[13] Special conservation efforts are required to preserve this genetic strain in view of recent past history. For example, in July 1959 a conservationist employed by the Soil Conservation Service was working on a rural dirt road about three miles east of Mattamuskeet Lake. He and a dragline operator had started driving down the road when he saw the "gator emerge from a roadside drainage ditch and start across the road. . . . The gator ran under the car and struck the underside, stunning the reptile. [The conservationist] then stopped the car and hit the alligator over the head with a shovel, killing the big creature. . . . [He will have the five-and-a-half-foot] animal stuffed and place his 'big catch' in his home."[14]

Waterfowl: Key to Earliest Human Habitation

The ecohistory of the Albemarle wetland has been disproportionately influenced by its rich waterfowl. During the ice age this warm coastal strip was refuge to waterfowl as well as to humans, who settled here remarkably early. Countless generations of native peoples over more than ten thousand years depended on returning waterfowl for winter food. Fittingly, the Virginian Algonquins "considered their year to begin with the return of the migratory geese in the early winter." Their name for winter was "cohonk," after the sound made by wild geese.[15]

Then, in less than two hundred years European settlers inexorably decimated waterfowl habitats for short-term gain. Ironically, however, it was the waterfowl that spurred the establishment of the first wildlife refuges in this region in the 1930s. More recently, in 2008, waterfowl were key in ultimately stopping the U.S. Navy's ecologically disastrous plan for a night-flying landing field next to the waterfowl's traditional overwintering grounds.

The first historical record of the rich overwintering waterfowl in the Albemarle region was at the time of the Roanoke Colony (1585): "In winter [there is a] great store of swannes & geese. . . . [The native inhabitants] frequent the riuers to kill with their bowes, and catche wilde ducks, swannes, and other fowles." Contemporary illustrations by John White depicted the indigenous people using bows and arrows from dugout canoes to hunt waterfowl representing several distinct species.[16]

Subsequent early naturalists, such as W. Strachey and John Lawson, recorded that in winter great numbers of waterfowl descended into these vast marshlands: "In wynter there are great plenty of swanns, geese, brants, duck, widgion, dottrell, oxeyes, mallard, teale, sheldrakes, and divers dyving fowles, and of all these sorts that aboundaunce as I dare avowe yt, no country in the world may haue more."[17] "They come here in the winter, and remain with us 'till February, in such great flocks, that I never saw more of any waterfowl in all my travels than of them, for at that season, they are in such vast numbers on each side of the fresh water rivers and creeks, that at a distance it seems to be land covered with snow."[18]

These observers consistently described three recognizable species of geese and two species of swan, which generally came and went together. The geese have been identified subsequently as the Canada goose (*Branta canadensis*), greater snow goose (*Chen caerulescens atlanticus*), and Atlantic brant (*Branta bernicla hrota*), and the swans were the tundra swan (whistling swan, *Cygnus columbianus*) and trumpeter swan (*Cygnus buccinator*). As a general rule, the Albemarle region is the approximate southern winter limit on the East Coast for each of these species (except the now-ubiquitous Canada goose). Historically, all these species migrated to Canada to breed, mostly in the tundra (today, however, many Canada geese are now resident species).

These several species of geese and swan still thrive today in large numbers in northeastern North Carolina, with the notable exception of the trumpeter swan, whose "quills and feathers [were] in great request amongst the planters."[19] Based on colonial accounts, this species was apparently common in the Albemarle region at that time but faced near extinction throughout the lower forty-eight states by 1900. For this reason, remarkably little historical information is known about the breeding and wintering ranges of the trumpeter swan. Although a controversy exists, there is general consensus that the Albemarle wetland was the southern limit of the historical wintering range of this species. Encouragingly, the first North Carolina record of the trumpeter swan accepted by the Carolina Bird Club was in late February 2004. It was banded on 25 February 2004 at the Pungo Unit of the Pocosin Lakes National Wildlife Refuge.[20]

One observer has noted that around 1910 on Pamlico Sound, "many geese and ducks came every winter to [Portsmouth Island]. . . . Redhead ducks would light on the water; so many they would look like an island. Geese would fly over in big flocks and light close by. . . . My father would shoot them sometimes for market. He shipped geese, ducks and brant by the 'sugar barel' full, and sold them to a man up north. At that time they made decorations for women's hat out of their plumage. I remember well the song that came out about that time, 'The Bird on Nellie's Hat.'"[21]

Another observer noted, "Since [Lake Mattamuskeet] was drained in 1930, the birds come into the fields during the days and then fly to the nearby Pamlico Sound for the night and return to the fields again early in the morning. . . . Canada geese migrated to the lake by the tens of thousands between 1940 and 1960. Lake Mattamuskeet was the favorite wintering spot in the Atlantic Flyway for Canada geese in those years. Since then, shifts in migratory patterns have reduced the number of Canada geese at Mattamuskeet."[22]

Over the past two hundred years the numbers and kinds of waterfowl have fluctuated in the Albemarle wetlands. Overhunting and loss of habitat were not the only reasons for this decline. Natural forces, particularly hurricanes, have variously benefited, as well as decimated, respective waterfowl species by altering water salinity and, thereby, availability of submerged grasses and other food sources.

At the time of the Roanoke Colony there were several ocean inlets along the northern stretch of the Outer Banks, allowing salt intrusion into Currituck Sound and eastern Albemarle Sound. In 1828 a powerful storm closed the last of these inlets, with the effect that these sounds changed from brackish to basically freshwater. Closing the inlet into Currituck Sound that year greatly increased waterfowl population because of growth of freshwater grasses. An observer noted that "three or more different kinds of fresh-water grasses, soon began to grow on the bottom of all the shallower waters,"[23] and "there were such changes in vegetation as brought countless thousands of ducks of species that had been only occasional before."[24] By 1850 "Currituck County began to become famous as the greatest wild-fowl-shooting territory on the Atlantic Coast."[25] The beginning of exploitation of waterfowl here following the Civil War was aided by the Albemarle and Chesapeake Canal, which brought hunters from the north.

Another observer recorded in 1868,

There are ducks of various kinds, of which the canvas-back is the most esteemed; geese and swans, which congregate in numbers exceeding all conception of any person who has not been informed. They are often so numerous as entirely to cover acres of the surface of the water, so that observers from the beach would only see ducks and no water between them. These great collections are termed "rafts." The shooting season commences in autumn and continues through the winter. . . . The following particular facts I learned from the personal knowledge of a highly respectable gentleman and proprietor on Currituck Sound. The shooting, as a business, on his shores, is done only by gunners hired by himself and for his own profit, and who are paid a fixed price for every fowl delivered to him, according to its kind, from the smallest or least-prized species of ducks to the rare and highly-valued swan. He has employed thirty gunners through a winter. . . . For his own gunners and his own premises only, in one winter he used more than a ton of gunpowder, and shot in proportion, and forty-six thousand percussion caps. From this expenditure along the shore of one large farm only, there may be formed a conception of the immensity of the operations.[26]

Hurricanes have affected waterfowl populations more recently. The best documented incidents were during the hurricanes of 1954 and 1955. Sudden salt intrusion decimated much of the aquatic vegetation of southern Hyde County and mainland Dare County, thereby greatly reducing food for waterfowl for several years. As contemporary accounts noted, on 12 August 1955 "Connie drove salt ocean water into the fresh water sounds and her sister hurricane [Diane, five days later] poured more on to that," as "Diane's slow movement to the northwest caused prolonged winds to push salt water out of Pamlico Sound and into the farms and fields of the east" and "much farm land in Hyde County was worthless for years."[27]

Newspaper headlines throughout the state reported on the effects of the storms—"Hyde County Hardest Hit by Connie"—and the accounts highlighted the extent of the devastation: "Farmers were still reeling from the 1954 hurricanes when Connie and then Diane struck. Hazel put 3,500 acres of crop land under salt water. . . . Connie raised the salt soaked land to 8,000 acres," and "what is worse [for waterfowl], the bottom grass that had provided cover and food for fish and feed for ducks was killed. The bottom was bare."[28]

Although high salinity will kill freshwater plants, the ecology of the Pamlico Sound is complex in that eelgrass (*Zostera marina*), the favorite food of brant geese in particular, prefers high salinity. Eelgrass is at its southern limit in these waters. Thus, a hurricane that adversely affects one species of waterfowl in these wetlands may favor another, in nature's dynamic balancing act.

Until the 1930s the eelgrass beds around Beaufort were not only food for brant geese, but they also constituted rich nursery grounds for many invertebrates and larval fish species. In the early 1930s the eelgrass here, as elsewhere, suffered a "wasting disease" that nearly destroyed these beds altogether. It took many years to recover, but in the 1980s a similar disease reappeared here. The causative agent is thought to be the fungus-like pathogen *Labyrinthula*, perhaps aggravated by environmental stress. The 1930s outbreak was a worldwide phenomenon, sometimes linked to global warming in that decade.[29]

In recent years Canada geese have "gone lazy." Not only do some individuals not migrate like their ancestors did, but they also eat grain from local fields (a relatively recent learned behavior, also displayed by snow geese feeding on winter wheat). This behavior is atypical in that most waterfowl in the Albemarle peninsula only spend the winter here, in large numbers, and then migrate thousands of miles to northern Canada, a most extraordinary feat of navigation. For example, one individual tundra swan (swan number 28579) was tagged locally and tracked by satellite through two annual migrations to the same nesting area near the Arctic Circle at Barbour Bay, Northwest Territories. Another tagged individual (swan number 7112) migrated even farther north and west, well above the Arctic Circle to near the Alaska border. Both individual swans returned to southern Alligator River (Gum Neck) in winter, like annual clockwork.[30]

In the mid-1990s British ornithologist Adam Kelly spent more than a year living on the east side of the Alligator River at the U.S. Air Force bombing range on mainland Dare County. He and his colleagues tracked movements of birds by means of radar and documented that most migratory birds moved primarily at night. Furthermore, they fly mainly at heights between 200 and 2,000 feet, particularly hazardous for low-level flying as practiced here by the air force. In 1994 the busiest night of the year for tundra swans was November 22; as a story in the *Virginian-Pilot* noted, "Nobody would ever have imagined that all these birds were out there. We had no idea ourselves. When we told the pilots they were horrified."[31]

Frequent low-level aircraft movements at the very terminus of one of the busiest bird flyways on the Atlantic coast is asking for trouble; again, the *Virginian-Pilot* reported that "in 1993, pilots hit 96 birds. Nine of those accidents cost the military more than $460,000."[32] In this context, the proposed U.S. Navy outlying landing field (OLF) in the Albemarle peninsula (Washington/Beaufort counties) was remarkably ill-considered. Not only is it ecologically unsound for the thousands of migrating waterfowl, but bird-induced accidents seem inevitable, avoidably expensive to the taxpayer and unsafe for local inhabitants. After years of bitter opposition the navy recently abandoned its plans for the landing field on the Albemarle peninsula. As discussed in the context of airplane-caused forest fires (chapter 10), this environmental struggle continues in the northern parts of the Albemarle watershed in North Carolina and neighboring parts of Virginia.[33]

Wild Cattle and Forest Bison: Ancient Niche Refilled

One of the most enigmatic episodes in the biological history of the Albemarle swamps was the existence of herds of wild horned cattle (*Bos taurus*). In fact, the Albemarle peninsula and the Great Dismal Swamp contained the largest herds of wild cattle in North America.

As early as 1587 explorers noted traces of wild cattle along the coast of this region, presumed to be vestiges of the ill-fated Roanoke Colony. Feral cattle herds were well established in southeastern Virginia by the 1690s and in northeastern North Carolina by 1730. As late as 1885 in mainland Dare County, "between three thousand and four thousand wild cattle roam[ed] through the woods." In the Great Dismal Swamp numbers were estimated in 1890 at five hundred in herds of twenty to fifty animals, and wild cattle reportedly still lived there as late of the 1930s.[34]

These cattle were very alert and reactive and acquired a reputation for being among the most dangerous animals in the swamps. Described as small, dark, extremely wild, and feisty, they reportedly had ferocious encounters with bears, sometimes fatal to either the cow/bull or the bear or both. Ultimately the herds were removed through human intervention, but even then they were notoriously difficult to hunt.

How was it that feral cattle thrived so improbably in these swamps, and had this niche been filled by similar animals in prehistory? The obvious candidate was the elusive eastern bison (*Bison bison*), which, interestingly, can interbreed with domestic cattle. Indeterminate numbers of bison were roaming woodlands in Virginia and North Carolina when the English settlers first arrived, much as the forest bison (*Bison bonasus*) of European preserves do today.

The Roanoke colonists themselves documented that bison hides were being traded in the Albemarle region in 1584. Later accounts detail their presence unequivocally in eastern North Carolina woods as late as 1728 (North Carolina–Virginia border) and 1730 (Neuse River): "We pursued our journey through uneven and perplexed woods, and in the thickest of them had the fortune to knock down [shoot] a young buffalo, two years old."[35]

Wild Boar and Peccary: Another Ancient Niche Refilled

Hogs (*Sus scrofa*) were accidentally introduced into the wild in the Albemarle region very early by English colonists. At that time no similar omnivorous species lived in these forests and swamps, an empty niche to which they quickly adapted and multiplied. However, coastal North Carolina once supported herds of a native peccary species (*Platygonus*), a close relative of hogs that went extinct here in the indeterminate past.

Hogs are intelligent animals and remarkably adept at escaping. Documents record various routes to the wild, including shipwrecks (on board as live food), hurricanes (regularly damaging pens and fencing), and farming practices (open ranges, factory farms). At least one intentional introduction is recorded, in the mountains of North Carolina. In 1912 European wild boar were introduced onto private land in Gratham County. Their descendants are now established in the wild there and in neighboring counties, including part of Nantahala National Forest and all of Great Smoky Mountains National Park.[36]

As early as 1585 the Roanoke colonists observed wild boar living in an uninhabited stretch of Hispaniola. More remarkably, in 1609 English sailors, shipwrecked on their way to relieve Jamestown, found herds of hogs already living on the uninhabited island of Bermuda, the nearest land to which was Cape Hatteras (570 miles). That shipwrecked hogs could not only survive but thrive under such insular conditions is credible from the observation that feral hogs were known to scavenge on dead animals on beaches of the Outer Banks.[37]

Numerous feral hogs were noted along the lower James River, Virginia, as early as 1627. To the south, in the Albemarle region, the first record was in 1665 on Collington Island at the eastern end of the Albemarle Sound, and wild boar were living on the Albemarle peninsula itself at least by 1733. The Edward Moseley map of that date clearly identified "Wild Boar Creek," just south of Stumpy Point Lake near Roanoke Island. Today, owing to "subsidence," this creek has disappeared, and the lake is a broad bay, but some modern maps still refer to "Wild Boar Point" at this location.

In 1790 wild boar hunting was a favorite sport around Lake Phelps. A Fourth of July Tournament that year had "many games including a wild boar hunt, the boars having been corralled from the adjoining swamps. The merriment was great, until a terrible accident occurred in which one of the contestants, Jonathan Hunter of Tarboro, was gored by a boar and killed."[38]

Feral hogs were living in these same swamps in the 1960s. A local hog farmer at New Lands, just east of Lake Phelps, shot wild hogs on three separate occasions. Described as having crooked back legs, being thinner than domestic hogs, and having long tusks, they were "boars" and definitely not recently escaped domestic pigs.

Today, feral hogs are considered an invasive pest in several national wildlife refuges in the Albemarle area, including Pocosin Lakes NWR at Lake Phelps. Both sexes have tusks with which they root the earth in search of nuts, roots, and other food, leaving bottomland disturbances unnatural to these swamps. A local wildlife manager observed, "Anything they can find on the ground and they can get to, they'll eat."[39] To control their numbers an annual hunt is allowed currently on some of these refuges. In 2006 hunters in Back Bay NWR and adjacent False Cape State Park took 136 of the animals.[40]

Colonial Swamp Wolf

Some sort of canine species lived wild in the Albemarle swamps until the first half of the nineteenth century, when they went extinct here. Labeled as "wolves" by the early settlers, they were so detrimental to colonial livestock, especially to sheep, that bounties were levied on them, leading eventually to its extirpation.

Ironically, in spite of the undisputed abundance of these animals in this region during the colonial period, no pelts or specimens were ever preserved to ascertain which species of canine actually lived in coastal North Carolina at that time. One thing is certain, however: the size, description, and behavior of the colonial wolf of the coastal swamps was biologically distinct from the larger, more ferocious gray wolf (*Canis lupus*) of the far north in North America and Eurasia. The gray wolf was the same species that was still surviving in the wild in Britain and Ireland at the beginning of the colonial period.

Because of the early extinction of wolves that once lived in the Albemarle swamps, its identification has been problematical. Some of the early historical accounts seem to indicate a feral-type dog or American dingo (*Canis lupus familiaris*) living primarily around settlements, whereas other accounts suggest a coyote-type wolf, probably the red wolf (*Canis rufus*).

Feral Dog or American Dingo

The earliest record of a canine species in the Albemarle watershed dates to the Paleo-Indian period in the Clovis culture along the Nottoway River (about ten thousand years ago). By means of immunological techniques several projectile points tested positive for bovine, dog, and deer antigens, which have been interpreted as bison, wolf, and deer, respectively.[41]

Much later archaeological records in North Carolina do not distinguish the wild wolf species living here from early domesticated dogs. In fact, in most prehistoric sites of the Woodland period in northeastern North Carolina, domesticated dogs played a surprisingly prominent role, usually in the context of dog burials. At one site on the Roanoke River (Gaston), for example, dog bones (nine individuals) were second only to deer bones (thirty-seven individuals); as VanDerwarker noted, "Aside from deer, domestic dog was the only other mammal that contributed significantly to the [faunal] assemblage. Most of the dog remains, however, derive from burial contexts and thus did not contribute significantly to the diet of the site's residents." Dog burials were also commonly practiced by the Virginia Algonquins.[42]

Recent genetic studies demonstrate a similarity between the DNA of New World dogs buried in the pre-Columbian period and domesticated dogs of ancient Old World origin (i.e., both were domesticated subspecies of the gray wolf, *Canis lupus*).[43]

The earliest historical record of a "wolf" in British America was in the Albemarle region by Thomas Hariot, naturalist of the Roanoke Colony (1585), but he may have been referring to the Indians' domesticated dog rather than to a wild wolf species, if such a distinction can be made.

Unlike his descriptive account of bears, Hariot made only a very brief reference to "their wolues or woluish dogges, which I haue not set downe for good meat."[44]

The artist of the colony, John White, illustrated one of these "wolf-dogs," the first picture of a native dog in the New World drawn by a European, in a village (Pomeiooc) near Lake Mattamuskeet. It was depicted as a reddish, medium-sized, short-haired dog with an upturned tail, upright ears, elongated snout, spindly legs, and nonbushy tail. Thus, at first contact the native Algonquins of the Albemarle region indisputably had domesticated a wolflike dog of unknown origin. Interestingly, Columbus may have described a similar dog domesticated by Indians on Cuba and Hispaniola in the 1490s.[45]

The historical record cannot discount the possibility that the wild canine species living around settlements in the Albemarle region was in fact a feral breed of dog, a kind of American dingo. In this context, in the 1970s a wild type of dog fitting early colonial descriptions was discovered living in packs in swamps of South Carolina. The Carolina Dog is now recognized as a primitive breed, and speculation continues that it may represent an unchanged descendant of a dog domesticated thousands of years ago by native peoples.[46]

The earliest accounts are remarkably consistent in describing a small-ish, dingolike animal that ran in packs. Captain John Smith of Jamestown stated, "The dogges of that country are like their wolues, and cannot barke but howle, and their wolues are not much bigger then our English foxes." A missionary traveling in the north Albemarle area in 1691 described how wolves would "roar about the houses" at night. William Byrd described a similar animal in the Great Dismal Swamp: the wolves are "not so large and fierce as they are in other countries more northerly. He will not attack a man in the keenest of his hunger, but run away from him. The foxes are much bolder. . . . The inhabitants hereabouts take the trouble to dig abundance of wolfpits, so deep and perpendicular that when a wolf is once tempted into them he can no more scramble out again."[47]

In 1709 the early explorer John Lawson gives the most insightful early account of the swamp wolf of colonial North Carolina: "The wolf is the Dog of the Woods. The Indians had no other curs before the Christians came amongst them. . . . When wild, they are neither so large, or fierce, as the European wolf. They are not man-slayers. . . . They go in great droves in the night, to hunt deer, which they do as well as the best pack of hounds. . . . When they hunt in the night, that there is a great many together, they make the most hideous and frightful noise, that ever was heard."[48] At this time around New Bern local wolves preyed on sheep to such an extent that the sheep needed protection at night.

The Edenton-based naturalist Brickell hinted that this swamp wolf might have had a commensal relationship with the Indians, displaying behavior not unlike feral dogs; as Brickell observed, "They go in great companies together in the evenings and at night (especially in the winter time) and will hunt down a deer in full cry. . . . [They] will follow the Indians in great droves through the woods, who only kill the deer and other beasts for their skins and generally leave most parts of the dead carcass behind them, on which the wolves feed. . . . They are but small, many being no bigger than midling dogs; not attack foals or calves, but very destructive of sheep."[49]

Red Wolf

That the Albemarle swamps may have harbored a true wolf quite distinct from the numerous small dingoes, a nuisance wild dog, is suggested by the observation of Baron von Graffenried, founder of New Bern. In 1711 he and naturalist John Lawson were captured in an Indian uprising not far from New Bern. While captive, the survivor (Graffenried) observed that wolves had spiritual significance. The conjurer/priest held a ceremony in which he placed a wolf skin at their feet and danced. In another ceremony he "hung up three wolf hides, representing as many protectors or gods," around which the Indians danced.[50]

For a brief period prior to 1731 a bounty was offered for killing wolves in the Albemarle region; as Brickell observed, "Formerly there was a reward (in this province) for all those that killed them, which made the Indians so active, that they brought in such vast quantities of their heads, that in a short time it became too burthensome to the country, so that it is now laid quite aside . . . ; great numbers killed in great pits . . . but the dogs also were attracted by the scent."[51]

A generation later, from 1748 to about 1788, the colonial government at New Bern again enacted a bounty of ten shillings for every wolf killed. The Albemarle peninsula was consistently named as one of the areas "much infested with wolves," and this indeed was the case. In a six-month period beginning in September 1767 a total of twenty wolf scalps were brought before magistrates at the Tyrrell County Court House, where bounty payment was approved. A document dated 1763 appears to be the last mention of a wolf pit in Tyrrell County. The last documented wolf in Tyrrell County appears to be a record of 1777, on the land of Isaac Alexander Sr., "by the side of the bridge where Oliver killed a wolf."[52]

In 1782 a slave named Peter earned his freedom by killing wolves. In Perquimans County a petition was made to guarantee freedom to Peter (mother Indian, father African), earlier freed by his Quaker owner on the basis of "meritorious actions in destroying vermin such as bear, wolves."[53]

In all probability a few wolves of the Albemarle peninsula survived into the nineteenth century. In any case, the last wolf killed in the Great Dismal Swamp was about 1830, when a solitary male appeared, after an absence of many years, and ravaged sheep for about a year before finally being shot. In 1997 a radio-collared red wolf reached the Great Dismal Swamp from the Alligator River National Wildlife Refuge, where it had been introduced; it was captured and returned.[54]

The swamp wolf of the Albemarle region during colonial times may have been a coyotelike species that once ranged throughout the southeast from Texas up into eastern Canada. Although extinct today in most of its original range, it survived along the Gulf coast of Texas and Louisiana, where it was known as the red wolf (*Canis rufus*). Recent genetic data indicate that it has also survived in the northern part of its former range in eastern Canada, where it is known as the eastern Canadian wolf (*Canis lycaon*). This species (*Canis rufus/lycaon*) is closely allied with the coyote (*Canis latrans*), with which it can hybridize. Both species *Canis rufus/lycaon* and *C. latrans* evolved in North America independently of the wild form of the gray wolf (*Canis lupus*), which later spread to North America from Eurasia.[55]

In 1987 the Alligator River National Wildlife Refuge was chosen for the successful reintroduction of the endangered red wolf (*Canis rufus*) back into the wild. The four pairs of introduced wolves came from a captive breeding program originating from a few remaining individuals still living in the wild along the Gulf coast of Texas and Louisiana. Several red wolves had also been part of an experimental release program in the Great Smoky Mountains National Park. When this reintroduction program was terminated in 1998 the wolves were transferred to the Alligator River NWR.[56]

Today, more than one hundred red wolves in about twenty packs live in 1.7 million acres of swampland in the Albemarle peninsula. The region is the home of the world's only wild population of red wolves, which are a source of much interest to conservationists throughout the world. According to the *Charlotte Observer*, during Hurricane Isabel in September 2003 "the storm killed one endangered red wolf when a tree fell on its captive breeding pen at Alligator River NWR. Two other wolves escaped but were recaptured."[57]

In the 1990s local residents were unhappy about wolves being introduced literally in their backyards. Elected officials in Dare and Hyde counties actively opposed the reintroduction program. One prominent commissioner even proposed that the U.S. Fish and Wildlife Service "install a fence around its 141,000 acre Alligator River NWR to prevent free-roaming red wolves from bothering mainland residents." It did not help that in the first year a male wolf was found roaming in the town of Manns Harbor. Local residents argued that the project "curtailed their traditions and freedoms," asserting that "we don't want them around here. . . . I don't know anybody over here who wants them" and "they've killed lots of pets." In 1994 a farmer in Hyde County was fined for killing a red wolf, "fearing attack on his cattle." Such was local feeling that a law was raised in the state legislature that year to allow killing red wolves on private property. However, in June 2000 the federal appeals court ruled that red wolves remained protected even on private land.[58]

More recently, most residents have reconciled living with red wolves and take pride in occasionally spotting one of these elusive creatures in a nearby field or roadside. Furthermore, there is consensus with regard to the wolves' ecotourism potential. For example, the Red Wolf Coalition, a citizen-support organization, conducts weekly howling safaris that have become popular evening attractions, particularly the annual "Howlo-ween" event (www.redwolves.com).

In retrospect, the term *wolf* conjured up a ferocious image of the gray wolf, but with experience local residents have found the red wolf reticent and benign, basically a scavenger benefiting from increased deer populations of recent years. Today, the danger for the red wolf is not so much from humans but from interbreeding with the closely allied coyote, which has recently reached the Albemarle region. The coyote is less reticent around human habitations and contributes disproportionately to conflicts with farmers. For further detail, the reader is referred to the Red Wolf Recovery Program (www.fws.gov/redwolf).[59]

Black Bear: Survivor of Coastal Swamp Refuges

The black bear (*Ursus americanus*) is the best example of how the Albemarle swamps served as the major natural refuge along the mid-Atlantic coastal plain. This large species was originally distributed throughout most of the United States. By the middle of the nineteenth century, however, it had disappeared from nearly all its former range along the coastal plain from Georgia to Maine (but it still survived in the mountains). The notable exception was the splintered bear populations that survived in the Albemarle region, long cut off from the nearest bear populations in the Appalachian Mountains.[60]

The black bear has lived continuously in these coastal swamps since prehistory, when they were eaten by native peoples. Bear bones are commonly found at prehistoric settlements (AD 800–1600) in the coastal plain, as elsewhere throughout the state.[61]

The earliest description of the black bear in the United States by English explorers was in the Albemarle peninsula. In 1588, Thomas Hariot, naturalist for the Roanoke Colony, at a time when bears still lived in England, observed "beares which are all of blacke colour. The beares of this countrey are good meat; the inhabitants in time of winter do vse to take & eate manie, so also sometime did wee. They are taken commonlie in this sort. . . . Furthermore, the Beares of the countrey are commonly very fatte, and in some places there are many: their fatness because it is so liquid, may well be termed oyle, and hath many speciall vses." Hariot went on to describe how the native Algonquins here chased the bears into trees and shot them with arrows.[62]

Bears have been hunted and eaten by settlers in the Albemarle region for more than three hundred years, somehow without depleting the population. As various accounts noted, "It is known to most persons that bears still inhabit the Dismal Swamp, though long ago driven from every other part of lower and middle Virginia. . . . They were so numerous, that there were but few men who resided near the margin of the swamp who had not killed one or more. A young gentleman of our party had shot several dozen of these beasts." Farther south in the Albemarle peninsula, "the bears are so numerous and destructive to both hogs and cattle. . . . One man in this neighborhood, (of course a great bear hunter), killed sixteen in one season, the fall of 1838."[63]

In the second half of the nineteenth century hunters from the north

Bear hunting in Craven County, North Carolina, in the early 1920s. Unidentified man and boy standing next to a killed bear lying on the running board of a 1923 Model T Ford during a hunting trip of the Camp Bryan Hunting and Fishing Club in what is now Croatan National Forest, North Carolina. (Fred I. Sutton Papers [#706], Special Collections Department, J. Y. Joyner Library, East Carolina University, Greenville, NC)

would come some distance to hunt bears in these swamps. They needed guides, one of whom was Robert Cartwright of East Lake, who was listed as a professional bear hunter in the 1880 census. In 1885 a syndicate from New York purchased an enormous tract of land on the Alligator River, consisting of most of mainland Dare County and much of Tyrrell County. This land was described as virgin wilderness, ideal for hunting bears and other wildlife.

Today, bear hunting continues to be popular in the Albemarle peninsula, but this practice is now under state wildlife management, requiring a license. In spite of this hunting, bears are more common along the Alligator River today than they were fifty years ago. Outside the hunting season, it is not unusual to spot a bear along a road in early evening. Bear paw prints, sometimes very large, and seed-rich scat are disconcertingly commonplace. Indeed, some of these bears attain a weight of more than five hundred pounds, with a few reportedly over eight hundred pounds. The biology of swamp bears here and in the Great Dismal Swamp has been the subject of recent research using radio-tracking and other field techniques.[64]

Before bear hunting came under effective state control, a killed mother sometimes left one or two cub orphans, which would be reared in captivity. For example, in 1852 a Kehuky Baptist preacher, Washington Carawan (c. 1800–1853) of Hyde County, "kept two tame bears in a stout cage in his yard."[65]

More recently, bear cubs were occasionally reared as pets along the Alligator River (Tyrrell County). In the early 1930s such a cub was kept by a farmer in Riders Creek. In the mid-1950s two bear cubs were found in the hollow of a tree by local loggers in Gum Neck. One eventually escaped after some weeks, and the other was kept at a general store near Columbia and was trained to drink cola from the upturned bottle to the amusement of customers.

The key to survival of black bears in these swamps is their dietary flexibility. Unlike wolves and panthers, they are omnivorous but exist primarily on various seasonal plants. In the autumn bears are particularly attracted to "gumberries" of the black gum (*Nyassa sylvatica* var *biflora*), a tupelo tree characteristic of these swamps. Along the Alligator River a common method of hunting bears in the 1920s was for hunters to row a skiff quietly along the shoreline until they came upon a bear up a gum tree eating gumberries. Bears exhibit similar behavior in the Great Dismal Swamp: "In October the berries of the gums ripen and then it is that one has the best opportunity to see the bears, as they climb the trees and pull in the branches with outstretched paws to eat the blue-black berries. I once saw four bears in the trees at once, all busily eating berries."[66]

Although natural food is abundant in the Albemarle peninsula, humans have inadvertently enhanced the diversity and availability of food. In this way, bears sometimes come into conflict with humans, most commonly in a field of ripe corn. More rarely, especially in winter, a hungry bear will attack pigs and other livestock. An early account occurred in the autumn of 1858 along the Alligator River (Gum Neck): "One day, while father was away on a trip to Elizabeth City and the overseer and the men were gathering corn, a black bear came out of the woods, and took a nice hog from the fattening pen, the women folks made such a racket that the bear loosed the hog and took to the woods."[67] Eighty years later, in 1937, in the same community, a bear took and killed a pig from the tenant farm belonging to my grandfather. During a three-year period he shot three bears that were menacing his corn fields. In the 1950s bears commonly knocked over beehives in this community. One owner regularly set bear traps around his hives, but on one occasion the animal severely clawed the man's hand, giving him a scar for life.

Then there was the bear that came into a house to get peanut butter, but there are just too many bear anecdotes in these swamps to relate here. To the people of the Albemarle peninsula and the Great Dismal Swamp bears have always been lurking in the leafy shadows. The point here is that, though bears were still quite common in the Albemarle swamps, they had long disappeared, for perhaps 150 years, from most of the Atlantic coastal plain.

Carolina Swamp Panther: Current Status Reassessed

The cougar (*Puma concolor*) was once the most widely distributed mammal in the Western Hemisphere. Known confusingly in different parts of North and South America as "panther," "cougar," "mountain lion," "catamount," or "puma," it is all the same species. Upon questioning the owner of a very rural general store along the Alligator River about the local presence of cougars, I was met with the following revealing response: "No cougars live here, but we have panters."

Throughout the Albemarle region the name "panther" ("painter"/ "panter") is used colloquially to label this large cat. Indeed, in these swamps it has been known only by this name for over three hundred years. Rumors have persisted for decades that *black* panthers live, or once lived, in the Albemarle swamps, but no proof of a black form has been forthcoming. Melanistic forms of *Puma concolor* are indeed known from South America but have never been proven anywhere in North America.[68]

The cougar recolonized North America from South America relatively recently, after the last ice age some ten thousand years ago. By the end of the nineteenth century it was extirpated from most of the eastern half of the United States to the point that the very existence of the eastern cougar has become a contentious issue. If the eastern cougar has survived in the coastal plain anywhere outside the Everglades, it would be in the little-studied, massive swamps of the Albemarle ecosystem. Biologists take note that these very swamps were the only place in the coastal plain where the much more vulnerable black bear survived comfortably. The cougar is infinitely more secretive than bears, a canniness that seems to defy best efforts to detect it. The first documented cougar in Illinois for one hundred years (a 110-pound male) was not discovered by wildlife biologists but was hit by a train in 2000.[69]

In prehistoric and colonial times the panther was undisputed "king" of the Albemarle swamps. This elusive cat attained lengths up to ten feet from nose to tail and was the only dangerous animal here capable of stalking man. In fact, the swamp panther was the biggest competitor of the native people in that both went to great lengths for the same prize: white-tailed deer. It is no accident that the panther and the deer have precisely the same coloration. Indeed, the name *cougar* comes from a Guarani Indian word meaning "false deer."

Thus, both the cougar and the Indian adopted the disguise of the deer, getting close enough for the kill; according to John Smith, "One savage hunting alone, vseth the skinne of a deare slit on the one side, and so put on his arme, through the neck . . . and every part as arteficially counterfeited as they can devise. Thus shrowding his body in the skinne by stalking he approacheth the deare, creeping on the ground from one tree to another. . . . So watching his best aduantage to approach, hauving shot him, hee chaseth him by his blood."[70]

Panther bones have been found in Late Woodland Indian settlements (AD 1250–1450) in the Albemarle region. We know the Algonquin Indians who lived here respected the panther to the point of reverence. For example, remains of a panther mask, dated at AD 1410, was found in a burial site in Currituck County. Nearly two hundred years after this mask was made (1585) the Roanoke colonists observed Algonquin elders wearing ceremonial garbs with distinctive long panther tails. The naturalist of that colony, Thomas Hariot, made one additional observation: "The inhabitants sometime kill the Lyon, and eat him."[71]

European settlers were bothered by these large, dangerous carnivores from the outset: "panther, nearly as large as a tyger, skin of a reddish or whitish colour . . . climb trees with agility. . . . [Their] tails are exceeding long. . . . They are very destructive to the planters, being a swift beast of prey, devouring swine, deer, or any other creature they can master." For this reason a bounty reward for panthers was implemented as early as 1727.[72]

Killing panthers for money commenced from the earliest days of the colony, first for their skins, then for bounty. However, to judge from the few kills, this canny, often nocturnal animal was remarkably elusive even then. Skins of a diversity of animals—namely, deer, fox, bobcat, otter, beaver, and raccoon—constituted valuable exports from the early colony. Only rarely was a panther skin included among the numerous shipments of furs to England. A noteworthy case in point was a bill of lading dated 26 April 1694, which listed thirteen deer skins and one "panters" skin.

In the old Albemarle County, which included a large area on both sides of the Albemarle Sound, a total of fifteen panthers were killed under a bounty program between 1678 and 1737, one every four years. A similarly small number was killed in the 1760s, especially when compared to the numbers of wolves and bobcats ("wildcats") killed under the same bounty scheme. In Tyrrell County, for example, only one panther was claimed, in February 1769: "Two tickets for a panter & a woolf scalp was allowed to Joseph Spruill by order." That panthers lurked in the Albemarle peninsula, however, is revealed in local place names, for example, "Panther Swamp" (1743) and "Panters Creek" (1777). As recently as the 1940s children of the lower Alligator River (Gum Neck) were cautioned not to go alone down Jo Reek Road because "painters live there."[73]

The panther was not only a mysterious animal to settlers in the eastern swamps of North Carolina, but it was virtually unknown as a live animal in England. The first live panther from America was sent to King George III by Governor William Tryon of New Bern (18 March 1767):

> As the panther of this continent I am told has never been imported into Europe, and as it is the King of the American forests, I presume to send a male panther under your Lordships patronage to be presented for his Majesty's acceptance. He is six months old. I have had him four months, by constantly handling he is become perfectly tame & familiar. . . . Panthers have been killed (for it is very uncommon to catch them alive) 10 feet in length from nose to the end of the tail. I am very solicitous for his safe arrival, as I am ambitious that he may be permitted to add to his Majesty's collection of wild beasts.[74]

This first live panther to make its way to England was given 160 years after Jamestown was settled, another testament to the inherent elusiveness of the swamp panther.

The most remarkable firsthand account of a panther in the Albemarle peninsula was from a naive visiting Englishman in 1798:

> In North Carolina there are a number of swamps of this description. . . . I crossed one in Alligator county, called the Little Dismal. It was about five

miles across, which saved fifteen in going the high road; but this differ-ence of distance was not so much my object, as a desire to penetrate into the interior of this desart [*sic*]. I was on horseback, and had for my guide a negro man on foot, belonging to a planter of my acquaintance, who went before me, guided by notches cut in the trees. My horse had frequently gone the road, and appeared conscious of the difficulty, recognising the marshy places; and trusting to his judgement, he avoided many broken pieces of ground with a sagacity inherent in that well-trained animal. I carried my gun in my hand, loaded with slugs, and more ammunition slung across my shoulders. About midway, and about two hundred yards before me, I saw a large quadruped nimbly climb a tree. The negro, looking in a contrary direction, did not perceive the motion, and, eager to fire, I did not inform him. We went a foot's pace, and when within gun-shot, I discovered the beast through the foliage of the wood, and imme-diately fired. The shot took effect, and my astonishment was great to see a monster, of the species of the tiger, suspended by his fore feet from the branch of a tree, growling in tones of dreadful discord. The negro was greatly terrified; and my horse, unused to the report of a gun fired from his back, plunged, and was entangled in mire. Losing the reins, I was precipitated into the morass, while the negro vociferated "Massa, Massa, we are lost!" Recovering, I beheld the ferocious brute on the ground, feebly advancing toward us. By an involuntary act I presented my empty gun, at sight of which, conscious, no doubt, that the same motion had inflicted the smart he felt, the creature made a stand, gave a hideous roar, and turned into the thickest part of the swamp, while, in haste and great agitation, I reloaded my piece. The poor slave, whose life to him was as dear as mine could be to me, held up his hands, and thanked the God he worshipped for his deliverance. I was unconscious of the danger I had courted till he told me that the beast I encountered was a panther, larger than any he had ever seen despoiling his master's flocks and herds, and that when pursued by man, those animals rally with great ferocity. Had I been apprised of this, I should have sought my safety in flight, rather than have begun an attack; but I conjectured the creature to be of no larger dimensions than a wild cat, when I fired.[75]

Preferred Food of Panthers: White-Tailed Deer

To understand the panther is to understand its primary food source, the white-tailed deer (*Odocoileus virginianus*). A precipitous decline in deer populations in North Carolina and Virginia from around 1900 has been linked to supposed extirpation of panthers. The presumption was that if there were no deer, there could be no panthers in that they depended on deer for food. Indeed, it was the case that deer were severely depleted throughout most of North Carolina at this time, and in Virginia deer reached their lowest population in 1925.

However, few people are aware that one of the refuges for deer populations was the swamps of the Albemarle region. As observed in an assessment of mammals in eastern North Carolina, "Deer are now widely distributed throughout the Coastal Plain, although from the turn of the century through the 1930s they were reduced to a few remnant herds confined to the pocosin areas of the Albemarle peninsula and to the Green Swamp area."[76] In corroboration, deer were being successfully hunted in Tyrrell County in 1933. Some deer also survived in Virginia in the Great Dismal Swamp.

Indeed, even the director of the North Carolina Museum of Natural History, H. H. Brimley, in 1939 tried to clear up this popular misconception regarding an untraveled part of the state: "The White-tail Deer is a long way from becoming extinct in many sections of the eastern part of this state. It occurs in some numbers in forty or more counties in the coastal plain area, and in possibly two thirds of these counties it may be regarded as more or less plentiful."[77]

Thus, it cannot be argued that panthers disappeared from the Albemarle region and, in particular, from the Albemarle peninsula and the Great Dismal Swamp due to loss of white-tailed deer, their preferred food.[78]

Do Panthers Still Live in the Albemarle Swamps?

At the Museum of Natural History in Raleigh the public exhibit of *Puma concolor* is captioned at this writing, "These large cats . . . were known from North Carolina until the late 1800s. . . . Biologists believe panthers may now be extinct in North Carolina."[79] This view reveals an unfamiliarity with the remote, abysmally unstudied swamps in the northeastern part of the state, much of which is still inaccessible even to biologists.

There can be no doubt that panthers survived in the Albemarle swamps significantly beyond the "late 1800s." In fact, the panther lived in the Albemarle peninsula well into the twentieth century, probably at least into the 1950s. The following sightings of panthers in the Albemarle peninsula, several of which were based on killed specimens, are selected among many others to make a point, that the panther was indeed lurking in these swamps in the period from 1930 to 1960.

Ironically, the North Carolina Museum of Natural History itself has the following record of a panther in the Albemarle peninsula dated 1930: "Washington County, Lake Phelps, panther 'skin seen by biologists.'"[80]

The following year my mother had a close encounter with a panther in the lower Alligator River (Gum Neck). She recounted the following story to me on a number of occasions, and years after her death, this incident was independently verified by Gertrude Sawyer, the only other witness. When my mother and Gertrude were "about ten years old" (i.e., 1931) the little school at the foot of Grapevine Road had let out about 3 PM as normal. The two girls were walking the long trek home to the last inhabited house on Grapevine Road. The dirt road at that time was mainly used by horse and cart and was narrower than it is now. The two girls had just passed the deep bend just beyond Stephen's Ridge when they heard a high-pitched squall behind them. This noise made them turn around, and they saw a panther that was facing them on the road where they had just passed. It was not black but rather a "browny-tan" color. It started walking toward them, gathering momentum until it was in a trot. As it ran the tail slanted out downward, not touching the ground. The two girls instinctively grabbed hands and ran as fast as they could, glancing behind from time to time. At one point the big cat suddenly jumped into the bushes, but the girls continued running all the way home. They told Gertrude's parents and thirteen-year-old brother about the incident. Together, they went back to the site, where they clearly saw big cat tracks in the dirt road. The dubious brother did not believe their story at all until he saw the tracks himself.

Five years later my maternal grandfather, Doss Weatherly, was tenant farming on the Old Columbia Road near the swampy Sea Going Woods of the Alligator River (Gum Neck), and in winter months he trapped fur animals on the side. In the winter of 1936–37 my grandfather trapped a mature long-tailed panther not once but on two different occasions. My uncle, who was about eight years old at the time, vividly remembers his father's carrying a panther by its long tail such that its head was dragging on the ground. On both occasions he witnessed his father putting the skin onto a stretcher, in preparation for sale like other furs. By his eyewitness account both of these panthers were described as "not black." Rather, the coat of each animal was "more brown than tan." These two individual cats were definitely not the smaller, short-tailed bobcat (*Felis rufus*), which were much more common and well-known to trappers.[81]

In August 1950 there was a creditable sighting of a panther swimming in the Scuppernong River after a flood: "The only report that sounded like it may have had some validity from Tyrrell Co (report 257 in my files) is from Aug. 1950. It was on the Scuppernong River near Columbia. Two observers, during the day. It was after a flood and the cat was seen at point blank range, estimated to be 100 lbs., long tail, color of a deer. It was seen swimming. Observer name I have is Guy Abell."[82]

One spring near Fairfield, Hyde County, when a local girl was "about ten years old" (i.e., 1953), some animal had been killing "cats, chickens and geese around the house." Then, a small calf was killed at the back of the field. A farmer, Stockton Sawyer, tracked the culprit and waited at the edge of the field until late in the afternoon, when he managed to kill it. The culprit was a panther, described by the eyewitness girl as being a gray color with a reddish back and having some white. It distinctly "had a long tail." Stockton skinned this particular panther, as he regularly did his more mundane fur animals. Both the girl and Stockton were well familiar with bobcats, which this was not.[83]

On the evening of 16 March 1987 a local Tyrrell County man shot and killed an eighty-eight-pound female panther at the back of the fields in Kilkenny, Tyrrell County, near the headwaters of the Alligator River. The very next evening another local man shot and killed a second (111-pound male) panther at the public dumpster, also in Kilkenny. The two men were each fined heavily for killing an endangered species (which was supposed to be extinct in North Carolina, an irony not lost on local people). The two panther carcasses were confiscated for necropsy by the state, which declared that they were obviously escapees or released pets. This may be the case for the male, but it was an unscientific presumption for the female, which had "abundant fat deposits" and whose stomach contained "flesh of medium sized mammal,"[84] demonstrating that it was well adapted to living in the wild. Since this female panther came from middle of the largest swamp refuge between Florida and Canada it is particularly unfortunate that no DNA analysis was conducted as matter of routine before both carcasses were incinerated. Fortunately, both pelts exist at North Carolina State University and prove that two cougars were living in the swamps of Kilkenny, Alligator River, in 1987. Such solid evidence, which had been accompanied by photographs, merits conservation research, especially in view of further sightings in this area.

In 1991–92 a tan-colored, long-tailed panther was spotted in Tyrrell County on several occasions at the public dumpster at Highway 94, at the beginning of Frying Pan Road. Furthermore, during this same period, two panther kittens were observed about a quarter mile from the dumpster: "Thick fat kittens . . . with long tails, like a lion's tail," rolling together in the middle of the main road. When disturbed they ran in opposite directions, one on each side of the road.[85]

More recently, there have been further encounters with panthers along the Alligator River. Frankly, little is now said to outsiders about these sightings because the previous hefty fines for killing the panthers have driven such information underground, and local cooperation is understandably minimal.

After many interviews and much correspondence I am amazed at how many panther sightings have been made in these swamps during the past twenty-five years or more, by state officials, hunters, trappers, farmers, and other creditable locals. In addition to the killed specimens and sightings in Tyrrell County that I have mentioned, another hot spot for panther sightings over this period has been in the vicinity of Lake Phelps, Washington County.

The foregoing suggests that there is a good possibility that panthers are living in the Albemarle peninsula today. Furthermore, there is evidence that they are breeding successfully. A remaining question is to what extent, if any, these animals represent a relict population of the original Carolina swamp panther, as opposed to a recolonization, benefiting from steadily increasing numbers of their preferred food, white-tailed deer.

It is preeminently reasonable that some genetic semblance of the original Carolina swamp panther may have survived in this natural swamp refuge, as did the bear and alligator. Intensive research, similar to studies of the Florida panther in the Everglades, is urgently needed before Carolina swamp panthers do indeed become extinct. Molecular genetics applied to these swamp cats is a fundamental way to shed light on the contentious status of the eastern cougar in these swamps.[86]

3 Water's Environmental Facets

For thousands of years the Albemarle region has experienced a multiplicity of significant environmental events, including storms, droughts, floods, and freezes. Over the past 450 years of recorded history some long-term patterns are detectable. Foremost is awareness that these environmental phenomena recur with regularity over the long term. Such themes are undetectable over short periods such as twenty or even fifty years.

A closer examination reveals that water in its various forms is most fundamental in understanding the ecohistory of this region. Water (or lack thereof) takes disparate forms and time frames, such as rising water from melting glacial ice, annual storms, floods, droughts (often resulting in forest fires), and frozen rivers.

About five thousand years ago the rising sea level slowed significantly to roughly its current level, so by then the Albemarle wetland looked much like what the early settlers found, a land of shallow open water, expansive marshes, and swamps. This lushness was due not only to the low elevation of the land but also to a plentiful annual rainfall, especially from passing storms that in normal years replenish this thirsty region.

Naturally, some years were drier than others, and sometimes several dry years came in succession, leading to drought conditions. Over geological time severe droughts have been a recurring theme in the tidewater wetland. We know this because studies of growth rings of ancient bald cypresses have documented with precision when droughts have occurred in North Carolina, as far back as AD 372. Periods of drought, succeeded by periods of wetness, have occurred continually for over sixteen hundred years to the present.

Severe droughts would have had significant consequences for human culture in this region, primarily because of acute shortages of maize and other food. Especially noteworthy for Indian prehistory were two exceptionally prolonged droughts, approximately in AD 560–625 and, even more severely, in AD 950–1040. In historic times, the Roanoke colonists "disappeared during the most extreme drought in 800 years" (1587–1589), and similarly the struggling Jamestown settlement "occurred during the driest 7-year episode in 770 years" (1606–1612). In May to July 1668 the fledgling Albemarle settlements endured a three-month drought that decimated that year's crops of corn and tobacco. Such periodic droughts continue in this region; the most recent one, in 2007, had a severe impact on all major crops.[1]

On very rare occasions the Albemarle Sound and adjacent waterways freeze over. During these infrequent periods lasting a week or more this region temporarily resembles the prevailing conditions experienced immediately north of the Albemarle region during the last ice age. In historic times such events have occurred here about once or twice every hundred years. The early explorer John Lawson recounted that local Indians had a system of marks on reeds whereby dates of important past events were recorded. By way of example, they explained to him that 105 years earlier (i.e., 1596) the sounds had frozen so badly that the wild geese resorted to eating acorns in the woods. The Albemarle Sound also froze in 1703, January 1780, 1816–17 (1816 was the year without summer when crops failed as a result of the volcanic eruption of Mount Tambora in Indonesia the previous year), January 1857, December 1892–February 1893 (during which the steamer *Neuse* stuck in ice for two weeks), and December 1917–January 1918 (when great numbers of porpoises suffocated under ice). The latter was the coldest period in the twentieth century in the Albemarle region.[2]

In the late Pleistocene, sometime between 24,000 and 50,000 years ago, a huge submarine landslide (Currituck slide) occurred in the vicinity of the paleo-Roanoke River and paleo-James River (i.e., located today offshore approximately from today's North Carolina–Virginia border). Apparently triggered by an earthquake, it probably generated a tsunami in the Albemarle region at a time when the sea level was much lower than it is today. The potential remains today for another such landside-caused tsunami in this region, such as the one that hit Newfoundland as recently as 1929.[3]

In recorded history the strongest earthquake originating in the Albemarle region occurred on 8 March 1735 in the Bath area, and it may have been less than 5.0 on the intensity scale. That earthquake is anomalous in that the Albemarle region does not appear to lie over bedrock of much earthquake activity. However, some peculiar seismic phenomena (abrupt subsidence, sonic booms, offshore landslides) have been recorded here from earthquakes originating great distances away. For example, by far the greatest seismic event in American history occurred in the winter of 1811–12 as a series of monumental quakes in the middle Mississippi Valley (centered at New Madrid, Missouri). These tremors were strongly felt in the North Carolina and Virginia wetland, in Edenton, New Bern, Suffolk, and Norfolk. At Georgetown, South Carolina, a coastal strip of land abruptly "settled from one to two inches below its former level."[4]

A major earthquake hit Charleston, South Carolina, on 31 August 1886, the most destructive earthquake, in human terms, in the United States until the San Francisco quake of 1906. Few people are aware that the Charleston earthquake was strongly felt in the Albemarle region, especially at Cape Hatteras Lighthouse ("sway backward and forward like a tree shaken by the wind"), Portsmouth Island ("houses were destroyed"), and Nags Head ("many houses were down"). Most amazingly, the southern part of Hyde County, at Waupopin Creek and Oyster Creek, reportedly sank "12 to 18 inches overnight." Witnesses at the time of the 1886 quake consistently described a loud "rumbling noise," and similar noises are occasionally heard today over Pamlico Sound (as they are in Seneca Guns). In prehistory a major earthquake centered in Charleston also occurred in AD 929 and again in AD 1404, with probable effects on the Albemarle region.[5]

These infrequent, abrupt episodes of land settlement in the southeastern Albemarle region, if confirmed, may explain why Roanoke Island was once connected to the mainland by a marsh in the 1580s but is now divided by a navigable channel (Croatan Sound), as well as why Stumpy Point has changed from being a lake as recently as 1860 to a broad bay today. The entire Albemarle region lies over one of the greatest alluvial deposits in North America and may be very susceptible to incremental settling, quite apart from a gradually rising sea level.

Thousands of years before the arrival of European settlers, storms and floods scoured the lakes, unclogged creeks, and most importantly, replenished the water table; severe freezes eliminated northward encroachment of plants and animals; lightning-caused forest fires encouraged those plant species preadapted to such fires; droughts allowed natural reseeding of water-loving trees such as cypress and gum/tupelo; salt bursts from prolonged droughts, storm surges, or ever-changing inlets on the Outer Banks maintained the delicate balance of the flora and fauna of the estuaries. As recently as 2007 the Albemarle region experienced a severe drought that resulted in crop failure, with the soybean yield being the lowest since 1983.

These events are natural phenomena, essential to the tidewater region over the long term. They occur with infrequent but inexorable regularity, a kind of natural periodicity without which this wetland would have disappeared long ago. We will see in the following pages that man's modification of this watery environment, over only a few hundred years, has significantly exacerbated their impact. This is most demonstrable with recent forest fires to an extent unparalleled in the South.

In this context, a seemingly small incident encapsulates an environmentally significant story of far-reaching consequences. In 1702 Thomas Blount, a member of the North Carolina House of Burgesses, built a mill on Kendrick's Creek near what is now Roper, on the north shore of the Albemarle peninsula. Shortly thereafter Thomas Lee constructed a dam there, making Lee's Mill "the oldest developed waterpower in North Carolina." From the outset this obstruction caused periodic flooding in adjacent fields, a chronic problem persisting for generations. Finally, in 1921, a year of particularly heavy flooding on Kendrick's Creek, outraged local farmers intentionally blew up the dam, ending 215 years of obstruction.[6]

Dominion of Hurricanes

Of all the natural forces affecting the Albemarle region none has had more impact than the tropical storms that sweep this "hurricane alley" nearly every summer or autumn. Such storms usually pass over benignly, bringing with them bountiful rainfall soaked up by pocosin swamps. Every few years a named storm, such as Hazel (1954), Connie (1955), Diane (1955), Donna (1960), and Isabel (2003), caused enough damage to linger in popular memory, but meteorologically they were relatively minor storms.

Far more importantly, two or three times every century an extremely intense storm (category 3, 4, or 5) reimposes its dominion over this wetland. Such megastorms occurred in the Albemarle region on 13 June

1587, 27 August 1667, 23 September 1761, 7 September 1769, 6 September 1846, 18 August 1879, 17–18 August 1899, 15–16 September 1933, 14 September 1944, 7 March 1962 (northeaster), and 16 September 1999 (Floyd). Each of these storms was accompanied by sometimes incredible instances of death and destruction. For example, in the hurricane of 22 August 1899 many lives were lost, including fourteen fisherman drowned at Swan Island, and a number of ships were sunk. With locals fearing that Portsmouth Island was gone, this hurricane was described at the time as "the worst ever known in Pamlico Sound."[7]

The environmental significance of these infrequent but superpowerful hurricanes and northeasters in shaping the Albemarle wetland over geological time can hardly be overstated. Over the past four hundred years these intense foci of tropical energy have altered local geography, especially on the ever-changing Outer Banks. They have sculptured the shape of lakes, changed salinity in the great sounds, temporarily reversed the flow of rivers, changed feeding patterns of overwintering waterfowl, altered fish migration routes, and caused prolonged famine and sickness throughout the entire region. Indeed, an unrecorded storm of this magnitude in the late 1580s could easily explain the failure of the vulnerable colony on Roanoke Island. In a perverse irony, in September 1960 Hurricane Donna demolished "The Lost Colony," or rather the Waterside Theatre, home of the annual outside pageant of that name on Roanoke Island.[8]

Formation of Pocosin Lakes

In terms of size, shape, and orientation the pocosin lakes so characteristic of the Albemarle region greatly resemble the equally mysterious Carolina bays unique to the mid-Atlantic coastal plain from southern New Jersey to northern Florida. However, Carolina bays are more inland, not typically water filled, and surrounded by dry land. They give the appearance of being geologically "frozen," well removed from the conditions that formed them. The pocosin lakes, on the other hand, are water filled and surrounded by peat swamps (pocosins), very much in the present.

It is reasonable to view pocosin lakes as Carolina bays in the making, in this sense constituting a unique biogeological laboratory found nowhere else in America. A corollary of such a view is that wherever Carolina bays are found, there once existed conditions not unlike those existing today in the Albemarle tidewater. In this context, an "extinct" lake lies north of the Albemarle Sound between Edenton and the Chowan River. Rockyhock Bay is described in the literature as a Carolina bay that formed about 30,000 years ago. Today it is filled with sediment and peat and forested with "pocosin shrub."

The geological origin of Carolina bays remains contentious, with theories ranging from extraterrestrial meteorite impacts to artesian wells. An attractive explanation, and one compatible with the pocosin lakes being incipient bays, is that they were formed by circulating water currents. Such currents could have been generated, for example, by exceptionally powerful hurricanes under certain conditions. A hollowed depression forms in the wetlands, for example, when a long-smoldering fire burns away a thick layer of peat, and this hollow eventually fills with water to form a pond or lake.[9]

When a major hurricane directly hits the Albemarle region, it typically approaches from the south, with strong northeast winds on approach followed by southwest winds as it passes. These winds generate strong currents, circulating water first to the west and then to the east. These currents reshape the lake into an ellipse (long dimension at right angles to the storm's trajectory). Wave energy deposits sand at the area of lowest velocity, forming a raised rim characteristic of both Carolina bays and pocosin lakes. It may be thirty years or more before another direct hit will continue the scouring process, but in "hurricane alley" it will inevitably come.

Evidence that powerful circulating currents can occur in pocosin lakes during storms has been observed at the causeway across the middle of Lake Mattamuskeet (NC 94), according to one account:

When the wind comes out of the east for any appreciable length of time, it pushes all the water in the two sections of the lake up against their western edges, leaving the eastern edges, not dry, but with no noticeable water. At the causeway, this means the water level drops on the eastern side and is raised on the western side. . . . A few hours later, as the storm system moves north, the situation is reversed, with the water piled up on the western side rushing to find its way east through the culverts. . . . And all the water rushing through the culverts creates more problems, because the continuing scouring effect digs massive holes at both ends of the culverts, creating a dangerous anomaly in the average depth of the water in the lake.[10]

This man-made causeway impedes full circulation of water during a storm, of course, but its presence has revealed an infrequent phenomenon that has the energy to reshape the lake into an elliptical form.

Changing Salinity of Albemarle Sound

The Albemarle wetland lies in remarkably close proximity to the Atlantic Ocean. Over geological time fresh water and salt water have competed for supremacy. Today, the Albemarle Sound is basically freshwater with increasing brackishness toward the east, whereas the Pamlico Sound is basically brackish, with increasing saltiness toward the south and east. These gradations in salinity dictate the numbers and kinds of various species of fish and shellfish.

Within recorded history a series of great storms altered salinity of the Albemarle Sound from brackish to fresh water. In the 1580s the Albemarle Sound was saltier than it is today, owing to several navigable inlets (actually outlets) along the northern stretch of the Outer Banks. The significant ones were Old Currituck Inlet, Roanoke Inlet, and New Currituck Inlet, which closed in the hurricanes of 1731, 1811, and 1828, respectively.

In any case, by 1828 the Albemarle Sound had no connection directly to the ocean, and incoming river and rain water soon freshened this sound and adjacent waters. The dramatic effect on Currituck Sound and its wildfowl populations was discussed in the preceding chapter. In due course the Albemarle Sound scoured a new channel (Croatan Sound) southward into Pamlico Sound. The remarkable hurricane of 6 September 1846 created two new navigable outlets from Pamlico Sound, namely, Oregon "Inlet," just south of Roanoke Island, and Hatteras "Inlet," both of which are still in existence.[11]

Quite apart from this long-term historical change in salinity, lesser hurricanes from time to time also impose short-term, sudden increases in salinity that can distress local fish populations. Perhaps the best example is the salt kill associated with the back-to-back hurricanes of 1954 (Hazel) and, especially, 1955 (Connie and Diane). Reinforcing each other, these storms dumped massive amounts of ocean water into the sounds. The sudden onslaught of salt water killed many freshwater fish in the Albemarle basin, and "many thousands of them floated dead on the water." So unusual was this particular fish kill that in May 1956 the *New York Times* announced nationally, "Bass Are Back in Carolina Fresh Waters Salted by Hurricanes in 1955."[12]

Inland storms periodically cause significant floods that dump enormous quantities of fresh water into the sounds, flushing out salt encroachment. An early account of such a major flood in the tidewater region occurred on the Roanoke River during 22–28 May 1771: "We were greatly alarmed with an amazing quantity of trees and rubbish coming out of the mouth of Roanoke. . . . The whole bay and sound opposite to Edenton were soon covered with loggs fence rails scantling and parts of broken houses with corn stalks and a variety of other trash so that it was with difficulty boats could pass. . . . A most terrible inundation in Roanoke River exceeding any thing in the memory of the oldest man in the country." Most recently was the flood on the Tar-Pamlico River associated with Hurricane Floyd in September 1999. In one area of study, the Pamlico estuary, the floodwaters changed the estuary from markedly brackish to essentially fresh water.[13]

Conversely, prolonged droughts can increase salinity in the sounds. A case in point was the drought of 1930. According to a story in the *Daily Advance*, "The long drought . . . left swamps dry and dusty, accompanied by a northeast wind which has not changed for two weeks" and by early October "on account of the extremely dry summer the Albemarle Sound is so brackish that blue fish, mullet and other salt water fish can be caught in its waters." "Not in memory of Plymouth's oldest inhabitants have crabs and menhaden been seen in large quantities in Roanoke River, or has the river been known to be brackish or salty."[14]

These long-term and short-term changes in salinity are natural events and an integral part of this basically freshwater ecosystem. Only in recent decades, however, has humanity tipped the balance in favor of salt encroachment, primarily via canals linked ultimately to the ocean, as discussed in chapter 10. Nothing will kill freshwater ecosystems like chronic exposure to salt.

Unique Meteorological Phenomenon

About every thirty to fifty years the Albemarle region experiences a meteorological phenomenon unique to these lagoons (sounds). Under certain conditions of intense storm wind the shallow water of the eastern part of the sounds is driven with such force that it exposes the bottom of the sound for a considerable distance.

At the same time, on the other side of the sound, the water is funneled into the pocosin rivers of the Albemarle peninsula and causes extreme flooding. Furthermore, this sudden thrust of water up the pocosin rivers clears headwater channels of silt and debris in a direction opposite from virtually all other rivers of the world. Speculatively, reverse deposition could help explain why none of the rivers of the Albemarle peninsula has a natural connection with its respective pocosin lake.

This phenomenon of exposure of the sound bed accompanied with reverse-flow flooding of the pocosin rivers was recorded in 1899, 1933, and 1944 and presumably occurred periodically well into prehistory. The Great Hurricane ("San Ciriaco") of 17–18 August 1899, one eyewitness said, "left the Pasquotank [River], ordinarily a fifth of a mile wide at the foot of Main Street, a mere ribbon of water hardly more than 75 feet in width. I walked out on the bed of the river 40 or 50 feet from Flora's wharf at the time . . . [and] three men in hip boots walked across the river at Woodley's Wharf, where much of the local shipping usually docks." The hurricane of 15–16 September 1933, which caused the greatest flood in the Alligator River in the twentieth century, produced a similar effect in eastern Albemarle Sound: "At the height of the storm the sound tide [at the Manteo Bridge near Whalebone] was at the lowest mark [one local man] had ever seen it. When the tide turned as the wind abated, the water came back with a rush, rising two feet in an hour."[15]

This phenomenon was observed again eleven years later, virtually to the day, during the Great Atlantic Hurricane of 14 September 1944: "During the storm's approach, strong southeast winds had filled the sounds with ocean water, backing up all the rivers, creeks, and marshes on the mainland side. Some on Hatteras Island reported that the winds had blown the waters so far west that the sound was left dry for nearly a mile. But as the eye passed and the winds turned around, the waters of Pamlico and Albemarle Sounds rushed back toward the banks, flooding villages from Hatteras to Nags Head."[16]

Northeasters (Coastal Winter Storms): Ash Wednesday Storm

Northeasters ("nor'easters") are coastal, winter storms peculiar to the northeastern United States and adjacent maritime Canada. Owing to the intrusion of northeastern North Carolina into the Atlantic, and aided by the warm Gulf Stream, classical northeasters start here when meteorological depressions move eastward over the ocean and gain sudden strength from the warm Gulf water. As one observer put it, "The warm Gulf Stream turns deadly when it meets Arctic cold to form the Northeast's worst winter storms."[17] Thus, it is no accident that the Albemarle region represents the southern limit of this type of storm, which contributes disproportionately to the infamous Hatteras coast being called the "Graveyard of the Atlantic." By way of perspective, the Albemarle can expect several strong northeasters each year, but they usually pass with minimal damage.

Northeasters differ from hurricanes in a number of respects. Northeasters are energized by the temperature difference when cold continental air from the north contacts warm ocean air from the south. This counterclockwise collision can occur with amazing speed and with little predictability. The winds are typically only thirty to forty miles per hour, but the area of damage is much larger than that of a hurricane. Most significantly, northeasters move slowly, sometimes taking days rather than hours to pass. The devastation caused by northeasters is primarily coastal flooding. The winds, coming as they do from the northeast, push coastal water relentlessly inland. Water from a high tide cannot ebb due to incoming wind-driven water, compounding the flooding with each successive high tide. This wind-driven water has great consequences throughout the tidewater region. Just as the worst hurricanes are associated with the September equinox (autumnal high tides), the worst northeasters strike near the March equinox (spring high tides).

The most destructive of all northeasters to strike the Albemarle tidewater in modern times occurred without warning on 7 March 1962. The speed and scale of this winter storm caught nearly everyone by surprise. It hit not only during the highest tides of the year (spring tides) but also when the moon was closest to the earth (perigee). Furthermore, this storm did not move for three days because it was blocked by a high-pressure center to the north. The consequence was a unique juxtaposition of meteorological events that created a monstrous northeaster, the notorious Ash Wednesday Storm. (It was also called the "Five High" Storm because it lasted through five successive high tides, over three days.) The U.S. Geological Survey called it one of the most destructive storms to hit the mid-Atlantic region. It ranks as one of the ten worst storms to hit the United States in the twentieth Century.[18]

Starting on the night of 6 March, freezing temperatures, snow, and strong winds hit an unprepared Elizabeth City. By the next morning residents were virtually isolated, without electricity and telephone, compounded by snarled road communications. Far worse was what was happening on Nags Head and adjacent communities of the Outer Banks. David Stick's *The Ash Wednesday Storm* is a firsthand and moving account of how these storm-hardened people woke up to the sea rising impossibly quickly, in many cases already inside their homes. Unprecedented ocean waves destroyed in excess of sixty houses and businesses and severely damaged thirteen hundred others. Destruction slowly passed from Virginia to New York, killing over forty people.[19]

In many communities along the eastern Albemarle region flooding from the Ash Wednesday Storm was of an order of magnitude not seen for thirty years, surpassed only by the disastrous hurricane of September 1933. In fact, it resulted in the first major introduction of ocean salt into Currituck Sound since the '33 storm.[20]

On the Alligator River (Gum Neck) fields were deeply inundated over a great area, with isolated farmhouses standing as islands in a massive, choppy lake. As a direct consequence of this particularly destructive storm, farmers in this community sought a permanent solution to repeated flooding losses. Thus, from 1964 until 1968 they embarked on an ambitious project of building a dike system around this low-lying community, financed by a levy on landowners located within the dike. At times of storm or heavy rain a central pumping station now pumps water from within the dike into the Alligator River.

This Gum Neck dike is of historical significance because it was the first of its kind to counteract flooding in areas identified as especially vulnerable to rising sea level along the East Coast of the United States.[21] Since then a number of other dikes have been built in the "sinking" Albemarle peninsula with benefit to landowners. However, potential negative impacts of these dikes to the health of the inhabitants—for example, through pesticides accumulating in stagnant water—as well as to the environment (erosion, oxidation), have never been critically evaluated.

The first dike system in the Albemarle-Pamlico region was built around a low-lying community on the Alligator River (Gum Neck) to protect farmland from chronic flooding in response to the Ash Wednesday Storm of March 1962. Shown is the Gum Neck pumping station, which lowers the water level within the dike as storms approach. (Author's photograph)

Other powerful northeasters have hit northeastern North Carolina over the centuries. The "Great Blizzard of 1888" formed off Hatteras on 11–14 March 1888 and was featured in the first issue of *National Geographic.* The following year, on 12 April 1889, a newspaper account noted that the "recent storm on Albemarle Sound" sank four named ships and took many lives: "The schooners *Caroline, Susannah, Parrot* and *Susan* foundered in the sound, and their entire crews perished. . . . The farmers along the banks of the sound sustained heavy losses. Houses were washed away and cattle drowned. It is estimated that a dozen fishing craft were wrecked on the sound."[22]

4 Period of European Colonization

Hunter-gatherers roamed the Albemarle-Pamlico region thousands of years before agriculture eventually supported semipermanent settlements there, from about 1000 BC. The moist, rich soil was especially conducive to the growing of corn (maize). These more sedentary, "modern" Indians cleared land for planting corn and other crops, utilized a surprising amount of underbrush to fuel cooking, intentionally (and also, no doubt, accidentally) set local forest fires, and organized group hunting and fishing expeditions using traps and nets. Finally, the most recent Indians to live in the Albemarle wetland, the Carolina Algonquins, were the first Native Americans to come in intimate contact with the English, with the arrival of the colony at Roanoke Island in the 1580s.

The first Europeans to reach the vicinity of this region were probably Spanish. The Waldseemuller map of 1507 indicates that ships had passed offshore by this date. However, the Gulf Stream initially limited the extent of exploration. Although vessels could easily negotiate the Gulf Stream northward, there was an initial reluctance to do so because it was virtually impossible to return against these strong currents. However, by 1519 the Gulf Stream was well known, and ships regularly returned to Europe via this route, departing the mainland at Cape Hatteras.[1]

Thereafter, explorers periodically ventured along the North Carolina and Virginia coasts, including Verrazano (1524, Pamlico Sound), Ayllon (1526, Bald Head Island), and de Segura (Mission at Ajacan, Chesapeake Bay, 1560, 1566, 1570). In other words, for two or three generations before the English colony at Roanoke Island a number of Spanish and French explorers had visited this area and interacted with local Indians.

England's first, but unsuccessful, colony in the New World was established on Roanoke Island in 1585. Using the island as a base, these colonists thoroughly explored the Albemarle and Pamlico sounds and adjacent rivers. John White and Thomas Hariot described the natural history of this area firsthand, accompanied by contemporary drawings, maps, and narratives. As a result, a remarkable number of new animals and plants were described for the first time. Indeed, the now extinct Carolina parakeet, and even the turkey, were first recorded from these swamps. In addition, White and Hariot described in great detail the nature and habits of the Carolina Algonquin Indians, who dominated this area. This was the first real account of any Native Americans to reach England.[2]

In 1607 the first permanent English colony was established at Jamestown on the James River in the Virginia tidewater. This land was home to the Virginia Algonquins (Powhatans), who were closely allied to Indians previously encountered in the Albemarle tidewater. A major transportation link existed between the two regions: the Chowan-Blackwater River comes within five miles of the James River itself. Almost right away colonists resumed exploration of the Albemarle-Pamlico region, this time from the base at Jamestown. Around 1650, planters started coming to this area, at first to settle along the north shore of the Albemarle Sound. Taking the long view, the early history of the Albemarle and Virginia colonies constitutes one continuing story of English settlement.

The settlers who returned to the Albemarle frontier in the 1650s began a new chapter of environmental change, already begun by the Indians who had lived here for countless generations. Using slave labor, then steam power, these irrepressible immigrants changed the entire ecosystem. They drained most of the swampland by digging countless miles of ditches and canals, cut thousands of acres of virgin forests, dammed rivers, and tried to drain entire lakes.

Settlement from Virginia

Settlement of the Albemarle region dates from about 1653, when English settlers started emigrating overland from Virginia. Many of these emigrants were Quakers and other dissenters seeking religious freedom offered by the Lords Proprietors to entice people to "Carolina." Remarkably, the founder of the Quakers, the Englishman George Fox, made a personal journey to the Albemarle region in 1672. He and his designates described in detail what was probably an ancient Indian route from tidewater Virginia to the Albemarle. This particular route was from the Nansemond River via land (Somerton) to the Chowan River, and as one account noted: "Our way to Carolina grew worse, being much of it plashy, and pretty full of great bogs and swamps, so we were commonly wet to the knees. . . . And it was perilous traveling, for the Indians were not yet subdued, but did mischief and murdered several. They haunted much in the wilderness between Virginia and Carolina, so scarce any durst travel that way unarmed."[3]

This period of settlement was one of great religious, political, and social upheaval both in England and in the colonies. But most immigrants, whatever their reason for coming to the Albemarle region at this time, were basically farmers needing to earn a living. They came to a land that had been occupied for centuries only by a native culture based on small semipermanent villages dotted along rivers and creeks. The planters soon overwhelmed the Indians, who were for the most part displaced. By 1710 some of them were Christianized and adopted English dress and agriculture, particularly the rearing of cattle and pigs.[4]

The planters adopted Indian agriculture as well, in particular the cultivation of maize, but they also brought with them crops new to the region, notably rice, wheat, and tobacco, along with hogs, cattle, and other types of livestock. As increasing numbers of settlers cleared and drained ever more land, a flourishing agrarian society became established along the north shore of the Albemarle Sound. The history of agriculture in this region is discussed in detail in the next chapter.

The Albemarle colony had little formal currency, so crops and naval stores—in particular corn, hogs, pitch, and tar—were used alternatively. According to the *Colonial and State Records of North Carolina*, "In this province, there is no money, every one buys and pays with their commodities," whose "prices are fixed by law." It was commonplace for local courts to assign fines or settle debts in terms of salted pork or corn, as in the following examples from colonial records: "against the said estate for 7s 3d in porke & 1/2 of a bore [boar] barrow" (1693); "We the jury find for the plaintife three pounds seven shillings & one penny in porke" (1694); "Debt for four pounds seventeen shillings & six pence half pork &

half corne"; "Debt for two pounds nyne shillings & eight pence payable in corne or pork" (1704); "ordered to pay as much porke as will fill a barrell" (1705).[5]

In this early period North Carolina was synonymous with the Albemarle region ("Ye Countie of Albemarle in Carolina"), especially north of the Albemarle Sound. A commercial and political center grew up at Edenton, a major customs port ("Port of Roanoke") and the first colonial capital of North Carolina. Prior to 1750 Edenton was the major destination for vessels entering the Albemarle-Pamlico region via the "bar" (Ocracoke Inlet). Edenton was also strategically located at the beginning of another overland route to Virginia (an ancient beach or ridge called the Suffolk scarp).

The region south of the Albemarle Sound at this time was effectively Indian country. During the period between 1640 and 1670, for example, there was an established Indian settlement, Amity Site, at the heart of the Albemarle peninsula, to the southeast of Lake Mattamuskeet. Settlement of the south shore of the Albemarle Sound was initially discouraged so as not to interfere with Indian trade in skins. Governor Peter Carteret, who left his position in 1763, failed the Lords Proprietors by "discouraging the planting on the south side of the river Albemarle. The latter was extreamly the interest of the Proprietors, but crost allwayes by the Governors and some of the cheife of the country, who had ingrosit the Indian trade to themselves and feared that it would be intercepted by those that should plant farther amongst them."[6]

Inevitably, this south shore region opened up to settlement, at Kendricks Creek (1668), Scuppernong River (1680), and the mouth of Alligator River (1694). About this time settlers also gravitated further south to the Pamlico Sound region. With increasing population came establishment of the ports of Bath (1705) on the Tar-Pamlico River and New Bern (1710) on the Neuse River. By the second half of the eighteenth century New Bern overtook Edenton as the main commercial and political center of the Albemarle-Pamlico region. Most ports at this time were rated by their distance to "the bar." By this criterion New Bern easily won over Edenton.

Settlers also went up the several large rivers, in particular the Roanoke, which enters the Albemarle Sound. Already by this time the Roanoke's fertile flood plain, most of which lies in Virginia, constituted an integral part of the economy of the Albemarle ecosystem. In 1765 a traveler observed, "there comes a considerable quantity of wheat and corn down this river, and about 3000 hhds tobacco which is shiped at Edenton; the soil along the sides of this river is rekoned fertile and rich, which is owing to its yearly overflow." Noting the similarity in this respect to the Nile River, he further observed that the floods on the Roanoke River can be very high, "sometimes rises 40 feet perpendicular," and that the river carries "everything on its way before it." Such floods usually occurred at the end of September and beginning of October.[7]

Settlement on the Alligator River (Gum Neck)

Representative of farming communities sprouting up in the Albemarle region in the eighteenth century was one located on the Alligator River at the heart of the Albemarle peninsula. During the colonial period it assumed several names on various documents and maps: Camp Branch (1723), Isaac Meekins Landing (1755–78), Great Alligator (1757), and finally its current name of Gum Neck (1757). For most of its history Gum Neck was the largest community on the Alligator River, and by virtue of its location and history it serves in later chapters as a microcosmic community for the entire Albemarle tidewater.

In fact, Gum Neck is one the oldest documented continuously inhabited communities in the United States. It was first depicted as the Algonquin village of Tramaskecook on a map by Roanoke colonists in the 1580s. White settlers moved here safely only after 1713, when local Indians were removed to a reservation at nearby Lake Mattamuskeet (following a surprise massacre of early settlers on the Alligator River). For the most part the first land grants here went to absentee landlords living along the established north shore of the Albemarle Sound. It was a generation later, from the mid-1740s, that owner-occupiers came to stay, and their descendants still live here more than 250 years later. By 1755 Gum Neck (Meekins Landing) was recognized as an integral part of the tidewater economy in that it was designated as an official customs inspection station for rice, indigo, pork, beef, and the like—a position it held for at least fifteen years.[8]

As an official customs port whose taxes were ultimately for the benefit of King George, Gum Neck would have been caught up in the increasingly serious taxation disputes with England in the mid-1770s. During these latter days of British rule, taxes and other issues reached a crisis point at Edenton. There, on 25 October 1774, a group of determined ladies of the town staged the little-known Edenton Tea Party.

In July 1798, a few years after the War of American Independence, a visiting Englishman captured a rare glimpse of commercial life on the Alligator River:

> On the great Alligator River . . . the country appears congenial to the bee. The natives derive great profit from their labour; every family having a number of hives in their gardens. Many families even depend upon their honey and wax to barter for winter stores and clothing. . . .
>
> At this time a number of trading boats arrive from Edenton, [Nixonton], Windsor, and the adjacent places, with merchandize, tobacco, and large supplies of rum, in order to exchange their commodities for honey and wax. A scene of drunkenness and riot ensues; the traders' boats drawing the people from a distance, like a country fair. They are here, as in most parts of the southern states, dissipated and lazy; great cheats and horrible blasphemers.[9]

It is noteworthy that the visitor remarked particularly on honey and beeswax as being a specialty of this area. Like rice and wheat, the honeybee was another European import, being first introduced into Virginia in 1622. Indeed, the Algonquin Indians had no words for honey or honeybee but referred to them as "white man's flies."[10]

Crop Failures, Famines, and Sickness

Well before the Europeans arrived, the semisedentary native culture of the Albemarle tidewater became increasingly dependent on cultivation of corn (maize) for survival. In so doing, however, the Indians became increasingly vulnerable to crop failures, especially due to hurricanes. We can extrapolate with confidence from the historical record that these Indians of prehistory suffered from serious hurricane-caused famines with a rough periodicity of at least once or twice a century. They were especially susceptible when crops failed two or three years in succession.

Hurricanes of 1667–70
Peter Carteret served seven years as the Lords Proprietors' agent for the incipient North Carolina settlement then called "Albemarle Countie." He

lived on and improved a plantation on Collington Island at the eastern end of the Albemarle Sound, a little to the north of Roanoke Island. During the period between 1667 and 1670 Carteret was the first to record a remarkable succession of devastating hurricanes in this region.

On 27 August 1667, the first of the storms hit Collington Island, destroying that year's corn (and tobacco) crops. This was apparently the same storm that also passed over neighboring parts of Virginia on 6 September, reportedly accompanied by twelve days of rain. In 1668 it rained heavily for most of August, following a three-month drought that had already stunted the corn. On 18 August 1669, a hurricane again spoiled most of that year's corn crop.

Still another violent hurricane hit the following year, on 6 August 1670. This one lasted twenty-four hours and felled trees, blew down houses, and even washed away one house, but, even worse, it destroyed once again both the corn and tobacco crops. About a month later a second but less violent storm passed the area, by which point Carteret was lamenting the likelihood of "a famine amongst us." Carteret wrote the Lords Proprietors, "it hath pleased God of his providence to inflict such a generall calamitie upon the inhabitans of these countreys that for severall years they have nott injoyed the fruitts of their labours which causes them generally to growne under the burtyn of poverty & many times famine."[11]

Hurricanes of 1727–28
In 1727 a hurricane destroyed nearly all of that year's crop of "Indian corn" (maize). Then, on 19 August 1728, another hurricane again decimated the corn crop, such that "little short of a famine threatened the land. . . . These mischievous winds raised the price of corn to five times the usual rate, port from 45s a barr[el] was sold for five and six pounds." These and later losses eventually led to the North Carolina Act of 1753, which forbid the exportation of grain during times of scarcity.[12]

Hurricanes of 1842
The best documented famine due to unusual hurricane activity in the Albemarle region occurred in 1842. The timing and intensity of the hurricane of 12–13 July 1842 was such that it destroyed that year's crop. Furthermore, a replacement crop was destroyed by a second storm on 24 August. These two back-to-back storms resulted in an unprecedented

famine for the people of the Albemarle peninsula that has gone virtually unrecorded.

The two storms in the summer of 1842 destroyed virtually all corn, wheat, and fodder, not only on smaller farms but also on the two big, normally productive plantations located at Lake Phelps. Furthermore, destruction was so widespread that there were no alternative sources of food in the region.

Ordinary folk, especially those on the Alligator River, suffered disproportionately, and their plight of hunger, disease, and despair reached a peak the following spring. They were saved from starvation in May 1843 by the extraordinary efforts of Ebenezer Pettigrew (Bonarva plantation) and Josiah Collins (Somerset Place plantation) of Lake Phelps. Somehow they managed to ship some old corn from Maryland directly to the starving people on the Alligator River, at no benefit to themselves.[13]

Poignant descriptions of the human effects of these storms were recorded in the correspondence of Ebenezer Pettigrew at Lake Phelps from July 1842 to December 1843. They give invaluable snapshots of life in the tidewater at that time:[14]

> I have not been to the Lake since the storm . . . as we can pass no other way than by water, but I learn today by my Jim that the field is yet under water and that the corn is nearly all dead and dying and there is no hope that I can raise one hundred barrels. . . . Seven hundred barrels is the least I can sustain my family with. . . . We have reason to expect a most desperate sickly fall, & I fear a deadly one & God knows who will be able to live. Such a storm & such destruction I never have before seen. Every thing blown to pieces & destroyed. [19 July 1842]

The second storm, at the end of August, was in its own way just as destructive as the first, especially to the neighboring Collins plantation. It was described by one resident as "the heaviest fall of water he ever knew." It destroyed the young corn planted after the first storm and decimated the remaining fodder for horses and cows. Fruit, in particular peaches and watermelon, were also in unprecedented short supply: "there never was such a year about here before for we cant get fruit that is fit to eat."

Failure of that summer's harvest was widespread, extending well into tidewater Virginia: "the prospect of corn was as bad as they can be anywhere. Hundreds of acres that will produce not a single grain. Large fields, but wretched farmers, low grounds without ditches."

The little remaining corn that survived the two storms was harvested at the end of September, but even this was being stolen from the field by desperate men trying to feed their families. Similarly, a local man was caught stealing a bag of wheat from the mill. Cash was very scarce, such that land values plummeted and land near Lake Phelps was being sold for twelve dollars per acre. "Now is the time for those who have money to make their fortunes."

By September there was already an air of desperation:

> Times are hard in Scuppernong, and the prospect is that they will be worse: I cannot think how, many will support themselves through the year. . . . We seem to be doomed to destruction in Scuppernong. . . . Grain & Flower are very low here and every where else. . . . I feel much for the poor & what will become of them I cannot think, something must be done or they will starve outright before any thing can be raised from the earth. . . . There is not corn enough to last longer than the first day December. . . . The people are literally starving. . . . If there was anything offered to the people that they could do to procure bread they would work. . . .
>
> . . . Up to this time the people who I have employed to clear ground, have behaved well, not one has intruded himself at my house yet. In truth they are distressingly humble, for they have got nothing to eat, no money & no credit. I learn that a number of those who work at Magnolia have not a mouthfull of meat. . . . Poor women are going from house to house to beg one pint of meal. But let me drop this & wish that I could die. . . . [24 February 1843]
>
> . . . The season is exceedingly backward so much so that they have not commenced to plant corn yet and the trees look like January. It does seem as if we are to have a dreadful famine; for the wheat promises badly. . . . [28 March 1843]
>
> . . . The season has been one of the most backward ever known, but vegetation has at last burst forth, & wheat has much improved, & the young corn seems to be putting forth, with considerable force. The country is now in a most wretched state of poverty, & starvation, & if they can possibly get through or keep alive to the coming crop it will be the utmost. The corn I must buy for my self & give to the starving will amount to something like twenty four hundred dollars, & nothing to sell to pay it, but the wheat crop, which looks pretty fair but, under the best circumstance will not be sufficient. . . . [30 April 1843]

Dear Sir [i.e., Ebenezer Pettigrew], We wrote you on the 12. Inst—with [invoice and bill of lading] corn &c. p^r *Elvira Jane,* and this morning have your favour of the 16th. At the time we shipped the corn to Little and Great Alligator [now known as Gum Neck], it was impossible to obtain any but that we sent—opportunities of shipping to these places seldom offer, and supposing the people were in immediate and great need of the corn, we considered it best to send it. It was old, but the quality was very good—heavy white Maryland corn, and but slightly touched with weavel [*sic*], and very good for bread—They may consider themselves fortunate indeed, if they can always get such—We have long thought that nine tenths of our charities, were improperly bestowed—tending to make those we desire to benefit, more indolent and lazy—they possess very little gratitude. . . . Very few indeed appreciate properly, the favours and charities they receive . . . [19 May 1843, Norfolk]

. . . Mr [John Baptist] Beasley informed me that the Storm last year, did more damage than ever had been known in you[r] part of the Country, and that it look more like affamon [a famine], than any thing that ever been seen in that parts—and that the poorer clase of people had nothing to buy bread with—But you, and Mr Collins, had bought a large quanty [*sic*], of Corn & Potatoes expressly to save them from suffering, (if not from starving) how grate is the reward, to him the feed the hungry & cloth the naked. [21 June 1843]

In December 1843 Ebenezer Pettigrew painted a pessimistic picture: "From the allmost entire loss of the corn crop of 1842, & but 2/3 of one this year in consequence of the drought, our country is in a very embarrassed pecuniary state, & it is my opinion will not recover from it in less than ten years."

Even in normal years the months of August, September, and October were called the "sickly season," attributable primarily to malaria ("fever and ague"). Mosquitoes thrived following heavy rains; the wetter the season, the more malaria. However, there were other reasons for the correlation of sickness and heavy rains. For example, when diseases were more accurately diagnosed, it can be seen in retrospect that typhoid epidemics, such as one that hit the Alligator River in October 1912, often resulted from family wells contaminated with surface water.

In any case, the stormy years 1841–44 were far more sickly than usual, with smallpox, cholera, whooping cough, mumps, and scarlet fever. At the beginning of this period Ebenezer Pettigrew was prescient:

"we have reason to expect a most desperate sickly fall, & I fear a deadly one." In fact, Pettigrew himself contracted cholera in April 1843: "A fortnight ago, I was taken with cholera morbus, & come very near dying. ... This country had never been more sickly, attended with a considerable number of deaths." Indeed, between 1841 and 1844 a disproportionate number of farmers with young families died prematurely of sickness along the Alligator River.

Thus, during the 1840s the Albemarle region experienced an unsettled period of extraordinary tropical storm activity. This was an excessively wet period that coincided with a local famine and unusual levels of sickness and death. On the other side of the Atlantic, Ireland experienced a horrific potato famine that resulted in massive immigration to America (1845–49). We now know that the Irish potato blight was caused by a water mold (*Phytophthora infestans*) triggered by an unusually wet period.

Another early-summer storm remarkably similar to the one in 1842 struck the Alligator River area a century later, on 25 June 1945. As in the earlier storm, there was significant damage to the corn crop in 1945, according to the *Daily Advance:* "The hurricane which struck the Albemarle section early Monday night did considerable damage to the corn and other crops in Tyrrell County. Nearly all of the corn was flattened to the ground by the strong winds."[15]

5 *Agricultural History*

In early prehistory the native peoples of the Albemarle region were hunters and gatherers, living off game and edible plants that abounded in this wetland. They tended to move about seasonally in search of food, such as waterfowl in winter and migratory fish in spring. Starting about 1000 BC a fundamental change began to occur in this region that manifested itself in artifacts associated with more permanent settlement, most notably pottery (Woodland Period). Coinciding with these changes was the rise of agriculture, particularly maize, or "Indian corn."

Maize (*Zea mays*) was the first nonnative grain to be introduced into the Albemarle region. It is a type of grass that had been domesticated as a food crop in Mexico as early as ten thousand years ago. This staple crop has thrived in the exceptionally rich, moist soil of the Albemarle region for up to three thousand years, but exactly when it first came here is contentious. Maize pollen grains dating back to about 200 BC have been found in peat of the Great Dismal Swamp, "the oldest evidence for maize in the Middle Atlantic region."[1]

Further discoveries of prehistoric maize pollen east of the Mississippi have led to the revised consensus that maize has been grown in the eastern United States from at least 1000 BC. However, data from macrobotanical remains of maize (corncobs, kernels, etc.) indicate that, as an intensive crop, it was grown in North Carolina and Virginia relatively late, after AD 800. Perhaps the earliest such record for the coastal plain of North Carolina is about AD 1000 at Camp Lejeune, Onslow County.[2]

With the advent of agriculture, small, semipermanent settlements grew up in the Albemarle region, and these villages had characteristics peculiar to this wetland. As a general rule they were located on "islands" in the swamps, accessible by dugout canoe. Early Indians learned that a creek leading into an otherwise impenetrable swamp usually leads to relatively dry land suitable for habitation. Such isolated islands in the swamp were accessible to the river by a natural process. Over millennia, surface water running off these slightly elevated ridges ever so slowly cut a channel to the river. The bigger the creek, the higher the island.

At first contact with the Roanoke colonists in the 1580s these swamp islands were occupied by Algonquin-speaking Indians whose villages were located, described, and drawn in detail by Thomas Hariot and John White. Apart from having dogs, they had no domesticated livestock, no horses, cows, pigs, or chickens. Meat was normally plentiful from hunting deer, bear, smaller mammals, turkeys, and an abundance of overwintering waterfowl, as well as ubiquitous fish and terrapins.

Although no livestock were cultivated, these Algonquin villages were heavily involved in agriculture prior to contact with Europeans. In addition to maize, they cultivated supplementary crops of beans/peas, native cucurbits (gourds, squashes, and pumpkins), sunflowers, and lesser-known plants, some of which simply grew up around human habitation.

Two other nonnative cucurbits are noteworthy here: the cucumber and watermelon originated in India and Africa, respectively, and were known to the Romans. However, they reached the New World very early in Spanish colonization. Both were being grown in the West Indies and Florida by the mid-sixteenth century and spread rapidly to other Native Americans. Thus, they may have possibly reached the Albemarle region by the time of the Roanoke Colony, especially in view of a Spanish Jesuit mission in the Chesapeake area (Ajacan) in 1570–71.

The usual practice was to plant the corn and beans/peas in the same hill, so that the corn stalks afforded support for the legumes. In this context, it is noteworthy that as late as 1839 farmers in the Albemarle region planted corn and peas together, yielding two crops before the livestock were "turned in."

An inescapable observation at this point is that the natives of the Albemarle tidewater, as no doubt in innumerable similar settlements up and down the eastern seaboard, had already altered their immediate environment. For generations, perhaps hundreds of years, they had been clearing wooded land adjacent to their settlements for firewood and to make open fields for growing maize. The parallel between maize agriculture and disturbed environments has been noted elsewhere in the southeastern United States. Evidence from shell middens indicates that, from about AD 1000, such agriculture affected water quality, resulting in the decline of freshwater mussels (*Epioblasma*) in Appalachian drainage streams.[3]

Furthermore, the very existence of intensive farming of maize had tipped the balance in favor of opportunistic species, most notably birds, which stole food directly from the fields in the form of seeds, seedlings, or mature crops. This was such a problem in the 1580s that at the edge of a cultivated field the Algonquins in this region erected a raised platform ("scaffold") that was regularly manned by a noisy watchman, the original American scarecrow.

Agriculture-based settlements were very widespread in prehistory, extending in pockets over much of eastern North America. Furthermore, such sites had been in existence for a very long time, at least a thousand years in the Albemarle region. It would be surprising if the semipermanent native cultures did *not* create some degree of ecological imbalance, at least in the vicinity of their settlements.

In this context, it could be argued that the enormous numbers of the now extinct passenger pigeon (*Ectopistes migratorius*) may have been a manifestation of such an imbalance. Early observers attested to the fact that great populations of this species were present prior to European settlement in eastern North America. For example, flocks of these migratory pigeons were observed very early in coastal Maine (July 1604: "infinite number of pigeons") and in Virginia (1612: "manie thousands in one flock"; 1615: "in winter beyond number or imagination").[4]

Great flocks continued for a while after the English settlers arrived. In 1640 and again in 1675 in Virginia were seen "flights of pigeons in breadth nigh a quarter of the mid-hemisphere, and of their length was no visible end; whose weights brake down the limbs of large trees whereon these rested at nights, of which the fowlers shot abundance and eat them."[5]

John Lawson wrote about the pigeons in North Carolina in January 1702 (NS):

We went to shoot pigeons, which were so numerous in these parts that you might see many millions in a flock; they sometimes split off the limbs of stout oaks, and other trees, upon which they roost o' nights. You may find several Indian towns, of not above 17 houses, that have more than 100 gallons of pigeon oil, or fat; they using it with pulse, or bread, as we do butter. . . . The Indians take a light, and go among them in the night, and bring away some thousands, killing them with long poles, as they roost in the trees. At this time of year, the flocks as they pass by, in great measure, obstruct the light of the day.[6]

The passenger pigeon was a migratory species that spent its winters in Virginia and North Carolina (and southward), and Lawson particularly noted their presence during the hard winter of 1707. Each spring they flew north to breed, and literally billions of individuals migrated at this time. Interestingly, in 1848 a single exhausted specimen was captured alive in Ireland, presumably blown off course by a hurricane.

The preferred natural food for passenger pigeons was mast (acorns and nuts), but the last known wild passenger pigeon in the world was shot "eating grains of corn in a barnyard" in March 1900 in Pike County, Ohio.[7]

English Settlers Adopt "Indian Corn"

From the outset white planters in the Albemarle region quickly adopted "Indian corn" as their own, and it has continued to be a major staple crop for settlers in this area for over 350 years. From the beginning they found a further use for corn in that its leaves, as well as the grain, served as fodder for their horses, cattle, and pigs, all animals unknown to the Indians.

Thus, corn has been an integral part of the annual cycle of life in the Albemarle region for well over two thousand years. Like annual clockwork, the planter sowed this grain in mid- to late April and hoped against a dry spell or, worse, a severe drought, which hits this region periodically. In the eighteenth and nineteenth centuries the ears were allowed to mature on withering stalks well into autumn, and harvest was quite late, often into November or even early December. Such late harvests made a standing crop of otherwise fine corn especially vulnerable to autumnal hurricanes, which blew stalks onto the ground. Today, mechanized harvesting of corn takes place much earlier, in late summer.

Farmers of the low-lying Albemarle region faced challenges in grinding maize and other grains because of the virtual absence of water power. One innovative solution was to use windmills, as they did in Holland. Such windmills were known in most of the tidewater counties.[8]

As settlers expanded acreage for corn cultivation they magnified the

Windmill in Carteret County, North Carolina, c. 1900. Note that a wheel device allowed it to be turned into the wind. (Frank C. Salisbury Collection [#99], Special Collections Department, J. Y. Joyner Library, East Carolina University, Greenville, NC)

problem of "vermin" associated with this crop and other grains introduced later. Such was this (man-made) problem across the colony that from the 1740s laws were enacted that rewarded destruction of "black birds, crows and squirrels." In fact, the roosting of "blackbirds" in these eastern swamps can be phenomenal, even today. In recent times, for example, one roost in the Great Dismal Swamp contained thirty million blackbirds, a mixture of species undoubtedly including the red-winged blackbird *Agelaius phoeniceus*.[9]

In early summer of 1803, Charles Pettigrew wrote at his plantation at Lake Phelps that birds were attacking his corn so badly that he had to employ almost all his workers to keep them out, as well as to replant new corn. His son Ebenezer Pettigrew later (1817) resorted to poisoning the birds with "Nux Vomica" (strychnine), with mixed results.[10]

Considering that corn had been cultivated in the Albemarle region continuously for many hundreds of years, it is noteworthy that the first corn pest was not noted until 1824. The little chinch bug (*Blissus leu-*

copterus) appeared that year at Lake Phelps, as Ebenezer Pettigrew bemoaned: "I planted last spring 100 acres of ground in corn, it was in fine order and the season was good, but the chince bug (an enemy I never saw before) attacked it and instead of 1200 barrils I gathered but 600." Fifteen years later chinch bugs were still a problem, at nearby Somerset Place, being responsible for a poor corn harvest in 1839.[11]

Wheat

Wheat was the first grain to be introduced successfully into the Albemarle region from European sources. During the interval between the Roanoke Colony (1587) and Jamestown (1607), the English made several little-known excursions to "Virginia," in some cases ostensibly to find out what happened to the "lost colony." These were really exploratory missions to assess further attempts to colonize the region. Toward that end it was useful to know what English crops could be grown in the region. Two small ships financed by the merchants of Bristol left Wales (Milford Haven) in April 1603 and eventually landed in an imprecise part of "Virginia," and one account noted that "while they were there, they digged up the earth with shovels, and sowed wheat, barley, oats, peas, and sundry sorts of garden seeds, which in about seven weeks came up very well, giving certain testimonial of the goodness of the climate and the soil." Thus, wheat, along with barley and oats, both of which later proved to be of secondary importance here, was grown successfully somewhere in "Virginia" in the summer of 1603 and no doubt accompanied the Jamestown colonists four years later.[12]

The first mention of "English wheat" (*Triticum* sp.) specifically in the Albemarle region was by an anonymous English visitor to the area in 1649. By 1709 Lawson observed that wheat was a major crop, second only to corn, and that both were export crops by this time: "great quantities of wheat and Indian corn, in which this country is very fruitful."[13]

Known also as "winter wheat," this crop was planted normally in November each year and harvested from mid- to late June. What was unusual, if not unique, about the Albemarle region was that cold-dependent wheat was a winter crop in the same locality that warm-dependent rice was a summer crop.

By 1728 wheat in North Carolina was being attacked by "wheat fly" (this was probably the Hessian fly *Mayetiola destructor*). In 1768 the prestigious American Philosophical Society reported, "the injury of wheat from flies began in North Carolina, about 40 years past . . . that these mischievous flies have extended gradually from Carolina into Virginia, Maryland, and the lower counties, on Delaware; to the last of which places they did not arrive until seven years ago, and have not yet penetrated into Pennsylvania." This is perhaps the first account of an insect pest to crops in North Carolina, as well as one of the earliest scientific assessments of such a pest in the United States.[14]

The earliest definite record of wheat in the Albemarle peninsula itself was by 1751, in Hyde County.[15] Throughout the nineteenth century winter wheat here was second only to corn as an export crop. In 1818 Ebenezer Pettigrew shipped 1,250 bushels to New York, where he realized a price of $1.84 per bushel. Whereas Pettigrew grew wheat in some quantity, the nearby plantation, Somerset Place, was having difficulty with this crop. By November 1839 Josiah Collins had recently abandoned wheat except for a small scale for his home consumption: "One important cause of failure is the great growth of partridge pea [*Chamaecrista fasciculata*]. Another plant which grows with remarkable vigor is chick-weed [*Stellaria media*], which I have not seen abundant anywhere else." By this date, Somerset Place cultivated corn almost exclusively.[16]

These problems notwithstanding, wheat has continued to be a major crop in the Albemarle region, even today. For example, in 2004 Tyrrell County was the sixth-largest producer of wheat in North Carolina, at 923,000 bushels.[17]

Rice: An Albemarle First

The Albemarle region was possibly the first place in the English colonies of America to cultivate rice successfully. This highly profitable crop was particularly suited to the nearly saturated, muddy soils of this wetland, in a sense working with nature like no other crop. For example, planting in April reputedly coincided with phases of the moon to anticipate spring tidal flooding of the rice seedlings. Furthermore, fields could be submerged periodically to remove insects. Harvesting was by hand in September and October, a labor-intensive process dependent on slavery.

The first mention of rice in the context of the Albemarle region was by an anonymous English visitor to this region in 1649, in anticipation of settlement of "Albemarle Countie." In 1709 John Lawson made the general observation regarding Carolina rice, "There are several sorts of rice, some bearded, others not, besides the red and white; but the white rice is the best . . . the rice of Carolina being esteem'd the best that comes to that quarter of the world [i.e., Europe]," and he further observed that it "thrives best in wild land, that has never been broken up before." Rice was being grown along the lower Neuse River (New Bern) prior to 1711.[18]

The story of rice in the Albemarle region became an integral part of the trade disputes between the American colonies and Britain. For example, prior to 1767, the British applied an import duty on Carolina rice of about six shillings and four pence per hundredweight. This discouraged the growing of rice. After that year, however, Carolina rice was admitted into England without duty. Perhaps this was the incentive that increased rice cultivation in this region in the years just prior to the American Revolution.[19]

Rice was grown about this time in the Great Dismal Swamp of Virginia using slave labor. In 1774 John Washington, "kinsman" of George Washington, reportedly grew seven tons of rice in these partially drained swamps. He was unable to find a market for his rice in Virginia, so he shipped fifty-five casks to Antigua. Perhaps revealing an inferiority complex, this crop was compared very favorably to rice from South Carolina. Rice continued to be grown in the Dismal Swamp area well into the 1790s, but the rice crop of 1787 was lost because of a severe drought that summer.[20]

Robert Williams established the first recorded rice plantation in Carteret County early in 1776. The Williams plantation consisted of 2,000 acres with a dammed pond of 300 to 400 acres. Thirty acres had been cleared and planted in rice, but as many as 80 acres could be flooded by raising water at the dam by 10 to 12 inches. In addition, Williams had built a two-story rice barn on navigable water. When war broke out Williams neglected his rice crop, claiming a loss of £80, to make salt for the war effort, but he returned to his rice at harvest time in mid-September. Interestingly, he sold his rice plantation after only two crops, claiming his advanced age as the reason.[21]

An ecological footnote is that rice cultivation in the Albemarle region in the 1700s and beyond served inadvertently as food for the voracious rice bird, or bobolink (*Dolichonyx oryzivorous*), a type of migratory "blackbird." Most damage occurred in autumn, when large numbers in their annual southward migration would descend on fields of mature rice. Slaves were used to keep them away at Lake Phelps.[22]

Rice was grown on the Albemarle peninsula (Alligator River) by at least 1730, and the Indians themselves were growing rice along the shore of Lake Mattamuskeet prior to 1746. In August 1732 William Ludford (c. 1674–1733) of Tyrrell County wrote a will that is the first mention of rice as a local cash crop in the Albemarle peninsula. In this document he instructed his wife to "take all ye rice into her keeping and have it all made fit for sale . . . to be laid out for to buy a negro man to work for her." By inference, Ludford had planted a small-scale field of rice without slave labor but wanted to sell the rice to buy a slave man to work for his soon-to-be-widowed wife.[23]

In the first few decades after the Revolutionary War, rice was grown as a highly profitable crop at Lake Phelps, benefiting from irrigation afforded by the lake itself. Charles Pettigrew shipped quantities of his rice as far away as the West Indies (Jamaica, St. Bartholomew) and Lisbon, Portugal. Quantities shipped from this plantation increased steadily: 7,825 hundredweight (cwt) in 1793, 10,119 cwt in 1795, 20,529 cwt in 1807, and 19,443 cwt in 1809. In 1795 a market price of $7.00 per hundredweight was mentioned, but by 1809 a shipment went unsold at $3.50. In June 1809 Ebenezer Pettigrew's agent wrote from New York, "We have closed the sales of your wheat and done every thing in our power to sell the rice but find it impossable without sacrafising. . . . We are in hopes the Continent will be soon opened to our trade."[24]

Rice culture on such a commercial scale was labor intensive. Thus, Charles Pettigrew was also one of the largest slave owners on the Albemarle peninsula. He wrote on 1 October 1795, "When I arrived I found the negroes had been cutting rice almost all the week—we finished reaping yesterday, & there is a good deal down which I must see put up in stacks before I leave them."[25]

By April 1817 rice cultivation was terminated at the Pettigrew plantation, Bonarva: "Our wheat is very promising. I am now preparing the rice fields for corn. Rice we discontinued altogether." On the adjacent plantation, Somerset Place, rice cultivation was abandoned because it caused too much sickness (probably malaria) among the slaves. In any case, decline of large-scale rice farming in the Albemarle peninsula at this time was for economic reasons, rather than a result of horticultural problems associated with growing rice so far north.[26]

Nonetheless, rice continued to be grown in this region into the twentieth century, with a revival following the Civil War. At what was left of Somerset Place at Lake Phelps some rice was still being grown in 1885, according to one account: "Harvesting the rice was especially interesting to me. Many hundreds of bushels of grain were gleaned from the huge piles of straw by a machine called a rice thrasher, drawn and operated by a large horizontal steam engine."[27]

About this same time rice was also being grown in neighboring Hyde County. For example, in 1884 Hyde County produced over 300,000 pounds of rice, and in 1896 Tyrrell County produced about 500,000 pounds of rice, "to which the drained swamp land is well adapted." As late as 1903 one of the largest rice farmers in North Carolina was D. H. Carter (1855–1944) of Fairfield; one observer reported that "he has modern machinery for flooding his rice lands and for the cultivation of this product."[28]

A century later (2005) rice reappeared in the Albemarle peninsula in a new, controversial guise. A variety of rice genetically engineered to produce commercial quantities of proteins found in human milk and saliva (lactoferrin and lysozyme) was being grown in an experimental farm near Plymouth, in Washington County.[29]

Soybeans

The soybean (*Glycine max*), the most recent of the great crops in the United States, owes much to the Albemarle tidewater. This region was first in the United States to grow soybeans commercially on a large scale and the first in the nation to crush domestically grown soybeans to produce soy oil, a forerunner of today's biofuel industry. The first soy oil extraction was carried out in 1915 at the cottonseed mill of Elizabeth City Oil and Fertilizer Company. However, for much of the history of the soybean ("stock pea") in this region the main use was to feed livestock, as hay and forage, rather than for human consumption of the bean itself.

In North Carolina soybean seeds reportedly first came from the Far East to Hyde County in the 1870s. From there they flourished and spread to neighboring counties along the coast. As late as 1927 it was said that Hyde County "for many years has been the leading soybean producing county in the country."[30] Furthermore, North Carolina was the primary state producer of soybeans by acreage until 1924.

Unlike the other great crops, soybeans first appeared here after agriculture became a science (and after the abolition of slavery). Analysis of its disease history has been most illuminating and is probably relevant to crop diseases generally. Studies have shown that the various microbial diseases of soybeans in North Carolina were introduced on the seeds imported from the Far East, the original homeland of the soybean.[31]

Today, the Albemarle region of North Carolina continues to be a major producer of soybeans. About 50 percent of the crop grown in this region is genetically engineered to be resistant to the controversial herbicide Roundup.[32]

Hogs and Agricultural Pollution

The early settlers to the Albemarle region brought with them horses, cattle, hogs, goats, sheep, chickens, and other livestock, none of which was known to local Indians. One remarkable feature of rearing livestock, by today's standards, was that some of these, most notably cattle and pigs, were allowed to roam freely in the woods, especially in winter, when foraging was problematic for the farmer. Each livestock owner kept track of his animals by cutting the ears with a unique owner's mark that was duly registered at the county court house.

Another aspect of letting these animals roam freely is that they sometimes went feral and on occasion formed quite large herds. The "Banker" ponies on the Outer Banks are a well-known example. Less known is that the largest herds of wild cattle in North America were once found in the Albemarle swamps, as discussed in chapter 2. The wild cattle are now gone, but the legacy of hogs in the Albemarle tidewater is an enduring story that significantly affects this entire region today.

Swine were first brought to the New World by Christopher Columbus in 1493. The first to reach the mainland United States were brought in 1539 by Hernando de Soto, who landed with about six hundred men and a herd of hogs at Tampa Bay, Florida. The presence of hogs on this expedition was confirmed by the archaeological finding of a pig jawbone at a site near Tallahassee, used by de Soto in the winter of 1539–40.

These animals are claimed to be the source of the "razorbacks" found wild in the Gulf region even today. De Soto's men drove these hogs overland as a source of fresh meat during his expedition inland, including up the Catawba River into North Carolina. Thus, the first hogs entered this state in 1540, nearly 470 years ago.[33]

Forty-five years later, in 1585, the English brought hogs to Roanoke Island. The colonists acquired these on Puerto Rico and Hispaniola before sailing north that year to Roanoke. Acquisitions of hogs, cattle, and horses, specifically for use by the colonists, are confirmed in contemporary documents. They knew in advance that these livestock were not endemic to the Albemarle region. Unfortunately, the records are silent with regard to what happened to their newly introduced livestock, but mention was made by another explorer of finding "traces of cattle and a stray dark-brown mule" in 1587.[34]

The Algonquin Indians in the Albemarle region did not domesticate animals, with the exception of the pre-Columbian dog (discussed in chapter 2). Furthermore, they were initially unreceptive to raising cattle, horses, and other livestock introduced by early settlers at Jamestown. The exception was the hog, which was the first and, for a while, the only farm animal to be accepted by the native people in this general region.[35]

Hogs quickly became a mainstay of small farmers throughout the Albemarle region, where these animals were allowed to roam wild in nearby woods. A contemporary account noted that "in order that they may not become entirely wild, they are, every ten days, gotten into the habit of coming to the house by the blowing of a horn, and then a little Indian corn is thrown down before them. Now when they hear the horn blow they run straight for home."[36]

Hog farming has been big business in northeastern North Carolina from the earliest settlement of this region. In 1665, almost immediately after King Charles II granted Carolina to eight Lords Proprietors, one of them, John Colleton, arranged to import 100 breeding sows and 10 boars to establish a hog farm on Collington Island and nearby Powells Point at the eastern end of the Albemarle Sound. These corn-fed swine were housed in a large, partitioned hog house 20 by 80 feet within a fenced enclosure. This enterprise optimistically anticipated soon being able to export quantities of salt-preserved hog meat to Barbados, the profit from which would be used to purchase slaves.[37]

By 1737 hog farming was firmly established in the Albemarle-Pamlico region on a large scale:

> The swine are more numerous here than in any of the English Provinces, and the pork exceeds any in Europe for goodness. The plenty of acorns, nuts, and other fruits, which the woods naturally afford, makes their flesh of an excellent taste, and produces great quantities of them; some planters produce several hundreds, and vast numbers are to be met with in the woods, which are every persons property that can kill them, for no one claims them as his own, except they bear his own mark or

brand, and it is so with horses and cows, that are wild in the woods. The planters export vast quantities of pork to the islands in the West Indies (such as Barbados and Antigua).[38]

Hogs were also a form of currency in the 1750s during the French and Indian Wars, when hogs (and cattle) were driven up north from North Carolina to pay the province's soldiers in lieu of its paper money.[39]

By 1765 hogs were well established in the western portion of the Albemarle peninsula, as witnessed by a contemporary visitor traveling between Bath and Plymouth:

> Set out from bath, Crossed through forests and uncultivated lands. . . . The soil seems beter gradually as I come to the norwd, and a greater mixture of oak trees than hitherto. . . . Great troops or flocks of swine which run wild in the woods and feed on the pine seeds and acorns, which is their only food. It is not surprising that their pork is not so firm or good in any sheap [shape] as to the norwd where they feed them with corn etc. . . . Bacon is the chief suport of all the inhabitants, when fishing is out of season. It is a dainty dish here tho ever so fat or rare.[40]

Four years later a hurricane revealed the social significance of hogs to the coastal region, as one observer concluded that "the country will I fear be greatly distressed this winter . . . for the people will not only be short of corn, but the hogs which are the support of many families will lose the Acrons [sic] and nuts in the woods which used to fat them for market, the wind having stripped every acron from the trees before they were ripe."[41]

By this time virtually every farm in northeastern North Carolina kept hogs for its own use, a farming tradition that continued here for another two hundred years, to about the 1950s. For generations, "hog killing" was an important social event in the annual calendar. This invariably occurred in late autumn or early winter because "hogs killed in summer and not bled properly went off quickly."[42]

Environmental Impact of Hog Farming

From these auspicious colonial beginnings, hog farming in North Carolina has expanded into an industry of about ten million hogs worth more than one billion dollars annually. With more hogs than people, North Carolina is the second-largest hog-producing state in the country, behind Iowa. Since the early 1980s a few large, mainly out-of-state corporations have replaced the numerous family-owned hog farms. This trend has had a significant social impact in that the number of family hog farms in North Carolina has decreased precipitously in recent years, from 23,400 in 1983 to 3,582 in 1997 and 2,542 in 2002. The sheer size of the factory hog operations, coupled with the smells and enormous amounts of raw sewage, is also having a significant environmental impact. An investigative exposé of the social, environmental, and political problems associated with hog farming on this scale in eastern North Carolina was awarded the national Pulitzer Prize for Public Service in 1996.[43]

Hog farming in North Carolina generated 4.4 billion gallons of wastes and 220 million pounds of nitrogen in 1997 alone, making hog waste the largest contributor of animal waste pollution in the state. Unlike human waste, hog urine and feces are untreated, apart from being contained in large dirt-lined ponds called "lagoons." There is evidence that this waste can spill into adjacent waterways.

Most hog farms in North Carolina lie in the Albemarle-Pamlico drainage basin, where the environmental effects of these and other agricultural pollutants are seriously detrimental to the wetlands ecosystem. According to the North Carolina Riverkeepers and Waterkeepers Alliance, the Roanoke, Chowan, Neuse, and Tar rivers, for example, "carry more than 13,000 tons of nitrogen, and 1,100 tons of phosphorus to the Albemarle-Pamlico sounds each year."[44] This nutrient enrichment can result in "algal blooms," sometimes associated with fish kills.

The single largest hog farm on the Albemarle peninsula raised 70,000 hogs, which produced 32 million gallons of hog urine/feces, including 1.6 million pounds of nitrogen and 550,000 pounds of phosphorus—just in 1997. Other hog farms on the peninsula are smaller, but the cumulative total impact of hog farming on adjacent wetlands cannot be ignored, especially since these lowlands lie in the most hurricane-prone region of the state.[45]

Hurricane Floyd hit eastern North Carolina in September 1999, causing some of the greatest known floods in this region. Such high floods are infrequent but natural over the long term. However, this was the first major flood here since modern farming practices. Accordingly, it exposed a problem of agricultural pollution unprecedented in the United States; the *New York Times* reported that the "September flood picked up huge amounts of organic matter in the form of decomposing vegetation, topsoil, farm and lawn fertilizer, raw sewage, hog waste from containment ponds maintained by the state corporate farms . . . [and] surged directly into the [Albemarle-Pamlico] estuary. . . . 'It's like flushing the toilet' into the estuary."[46]

In addition to drowning "2.5 million chickens, 500,000 turkeys and 100,000 hogs," the floodwaters overwhelmed some of the "lagoons" containing significant quantities of hog urine and feces, which entered the Albemarle-Pamlico drainage basin. Concomitant increases in nitrogen levels have been monitored in some detail in the Neuse River estuary.[47]

In 2007 the Neuse River was identified by the American Rivers Foundation as the eighth most endangered river in the United States, specifically citing "massive hog operations" in its watershed as a primary cause. Earlier, in 1991 a major fish kill occurred in the Neuse estuary. The causative agent was identified, for the first time anywhere, as the dinoflagellate *Pfiesteria piscicida*, which has also been linked, contentiously, to fish kills in other estuaries. The interrelationship between hog waste and other agricultural pollution (nutrient enrichment), harmful algal blooms, *Pfiesteria* fish kills, and even human disease is an important unfolding environmental story of national significance. Interestingly, a fish-kill outbreak in the Neuse estuary in July 1998 was terminated by a severe storm, which eliminated toxic conditions. More recently, kills of over 100,000 fish at Merchants Millpond State Park were associated in 2003 with Hurricane Isabel and in 2008 attributed to oxygen depletion from rotting parrotfeather (*Myriophyllum aquaticum*), an invasive aquatic plant.[48]

By historical caveat, however, fish kills in the Albemarle-Pamlico basin are not just a modern problem linked simply to the recent rise in hog waste. The earliest known fish kill in the region was observed in New Bern in 1765 at the confluence of the Neuse and Trent rivers, long before the rise of modern agriculture: "The stagnating waters of these great rivers where there is no tide or current but what is occasioned by the winds, on hot calm days youl see a thick scum on the water, which occasions a disagreable stensh. At this time the fishes ly dead on the water."[49]

The Europeans who settled in the Albemarle region found exceptionally rich, organic soil on which they built a thriving agrarian society. At the same, however, they embarked on a pernicious process of land reclamation involving wholesale drainage of vulnerable wetlands. The environ-

mental impact of this network of myriad drainage canals has been perva-
sive throughout the subsequent history of this region, including the
effect on fisheries (see chapter 6), reduction of the great pocosin lakes (see
chapter 7), use of slave labor (see chapter 8), encouragement of salt penetration (see chapter 10), increase in the number and severity of forest
fires (see chapter 12), and irreversible oxidation of organic soils (see
chapter 13).

6 Sturgeon, Herring, and Other Fisheries

The Albemarle region once constituted the richest resource of nonmarine fish in the United States. Since early prehistory the native peoples relied on food from these waterways to make a significant annual contribution toward their very survival. A wide range of residential, year-round fish (e.g., crappie, perch, sunfish, bluegill and other panfish, black bass, bowfin, garfish), shellfish, and turtles formed a major portion of a subsistence diet.

Then, like celestial clockwork, each spring these waterways became alive with unimaginable numbers of anadromous fish migrating from the sea to freshwater breeding grounds. For the indigenous people of the region, the crucial significance of these spring migrations was that plentiful fish arrive at the very leanest time of year, that is, after winter stores are used up and before ripening of the corn in July. As one scholar phrased it somewhat poetically, "The moon of the peak migration was known as the Spearfish Moon—the Algonquin April Moon."[1]

Integral to these vast natural fisheries are the great sounds, which grade from a few salty inlets into the Pamlico Sound, through its expansive brackish marshes to lazy, dark creeks and water-saturated swamps of the Albemarle Sound. In turn, both the Albemarle and Pamlico sounds receive great rivers whose tributaries lead to breeding grounds for sturgeon, river herring, shad, striped bass, and other anadromous species.

With regard to river herring and shad, none equals the Chowan River, which flows southward into the Albemarle Sound. Near the Virginia border, it branches into the Meherrin, Nottoway, and aptly named Black-water rivers (the Chowan-Meherrin is approximately 130 miles long).

When English settlers first came to this region in the 1580s the entire sound region was controlled by Algonquin-speaking native people who prospered here at the southernmost periphery of Powhatan's "Empire" of Virginia Algonquins. The fish-rich Chowan River at the western end of the Albemarle Sound was the home of a tribe of Carolina Algonquins (Chowanocs) contiguous with the Virginia Algonquins (Nansemonds) to the north. Further inland, away from the sounds, the rivers at this time were largely controlled by Iroquois-speaking Indians (Tuscarora, Notto-ways, and Meherrins) (and, reportedly, some Sioux-speaking Indians who were retreating southward in the face of a relatively recent intrusion of Iroquois from the north).[2]

During the Late Woodland Period (AD 1250–1650) fish constituted a significantly greater portion of the diet of natives living in the lower Roanoke River than those living further upstream in the piedmont. Spe-cifically, in Jordan's Landing, an Indian village on the Roanoke River about thirty miles from the Albemarle Sound, fish were "accounting for 70% of the faunal remains." Furthermore, fish constituted three of the five most consumed foods (bowfin, gar, Atlantic croaker, in that order); herrings (family Clupeidae) were also widely consumed.[3]

After the English settled the Albemarle region from the mid-1600s, the sounds and their heavily trafficked rivers contributed disproportion-ately to the economy of colonial North Carolina, and commercial fish-eries played an important role throughout. The foremost authority on North Carolina fish observed in 1907, "At one time more American shad and striped bass were caught in North Carolina than any other state."[4]

Thus, a number of commercial species abounded in the waters of the Albemarle-Pamlico ecosystem, including sturgeon, river herring, shad, and striped bass, not to mention whales, porpoises, diamondback terra-pins, oysters, shrimp, and blue crabs, each of which was fished commer-cially at one time or other.

Sturgeon: Jurassic Survivor

The Atlantic sturgeon (*Acipenser oxyrhynchus*) is a veritable living fossil, a Jurassic survivor literally from the days of dinosaurs. Sturgeons were once common throughout the Albemarle-Pamlico region and up the Roanoke River into Virginia. In bygone days it must have been a sight to witness 10- to 14-foot, 1,000-pound sturgeons literally jumping out of the Roanoke River, as they do today in the similar Suwannee River at headwaters of the Okefenokee Swamp of Georgia and northern Florida.

A zoo-archaeological study of Late Woodland native villages along the Roanoke River documented that sturgeons served as food sources in this river beyond the Virginia border. The village in question was occupied AD 1000–1400, but today its site lies beneath Lake Gaston, the hydroelectric reservoir for the Virginia Power and Light Company.[5]

In 1588 Thomas Hariot, natural historian for the Roanoke Colony, observed in the Albemarle Sound, "For foure monethes of the yeere, February, March, Aprill and May, there are plentie of Sturgeons."[6] During much of the 1600s and 1700s the sturgeon in the Albemarle were considered to be a royal fish requiring a license to catch, plus 10 percent of the value of the fish to be paid to the Lords Proprietors.

In the 1880s and 1890s sturgeon were regularly caught in the Tar River, and on at least one occasion a passenger steamboat hit one. The first sturgeon fishery in North Carolina was reportedly founded in 1889 at Avoca at the western end of the Albemarle Sound. In the same year a sturgeon fishery also started on the ocean side of the Outer Banks, using gill nets along the beaches. A decline in sturgeon numbers was noted only four years later. This decline also coincided with construction of dams, notably on the Roanoke River.[7]

Today, the Atlantic sturgeon in this region is at historical lows and is classified as a species of "special concern." Individual records of sizeable specimens have been so rare since 1900 as to be noteworthy. In May 1908 a sturgeon 8 feet, 8 inches long was captured on the Roanoke River at the dam at Weldon. In 1919 a 10-foot sturgeon weighing 340 pounds was caught in a seine in the Meherrin River. In the 1920s a large sturgeon, whose roe was sold for $90, was netted in the Alligator River. So rare was this catch that this professional fisherman never caught another in his career. Two large sturgeons were caught in the 1930s, one 7 feet long with 25 pounds of roe in early September 1933 in the Albemarle Sound, and one 8 feet, 6 inches long and weighing 400 pounds in April 1935 in the Pamlico Sound.

Interestingly, the few river sturgeons netted in recent years have been encountered in the very early hours in April and May, suggesting a possible link to the annual herring migrations discussed in the following section: 4 AM, 8 May 1959, 6 feet, 2 inches, 80.5 pounds, Tar River; 5:15 AM, 28 May 1964, 45 inches, 18.5 pounds, Tar River; "morning," 15 April 1977, 7 feet, 1 inch, 180 pounds, Chowan River. In late summer 1997, as part of a scientific study, the two largest specimens netted in the Albemarle Sound were 4 feet, 7 inches and 4 feet, 5 inches in length.[8]

In addition to the Atlantic sturgeon, the shortnose sturgeon (*Acipenser brevirostrum*) is also native to the Albemarle-Pamlico region. The shortnose sturgeon is so endangered that it is the only seagoing fish federally protected by the Endangered Species Act. One account of this sturgeon noted, "There are numerous reports of shortnose sturgeon taken in North Carolina in early 1800s, but its status and distribution here has never been well known. In fact no shortnose sturgeon had been reported in our waters since 1881, and it was thought to be extinct here. . . . In 1987, however, a fisherman caught a shortnose sturgeon in the Brunswick River. Since then several shortnose have been caught in the Brunswick and Cape Fear Rivers by commercial fishermen." In April 1998 a single shortnose sturgeon was captured in Batchelor Bay, near the mouth of the Roanoke River at the western end of the Albemarle Sound.[9]

Herring and Shad

Of all the commercial fish in the Albemarle region, by far the most important for the region's ecohistory were the American shad (*Alosa sapidissima*) and river herring. The latter actually consisted of two closely related species, alewife (*Alosa pseudoharengus*) and blueback herring (*Alosa aestivalis*). These three species represent a group of fish (Clupeidae) of very similar lifestyle and appearance. All spend their adult lives offshore, typically in the Gulf of Maine, but all three enter freshwater in the spring to spawn (anadromous).

The Albemarle Sound constituted one of the most important breeding grounds for river herring along the Atlantic coast. As the North Carolina Division of Marine Fisheries explained, "Historically the Albemarle Sound area was the center of river herring (alewife and blueback herring) harvest since colonial times. There were also substantial runs in other river systems of the state, notably the Neuse and Tar/Pamlico rivers, but these fisheries never compared to the ones in the Albemarle Sound area. As an example, from 1889 to 1994, the Albemarle Sound area accounted for 66 to 100 percent of the state's total river herring landings, with the contiguous Chowan River pound net fishery accounting for 43 to 97 percent of the state's total river herring landings from 1962 to 1994."[10]

River herring can be considered a "bellwether species" in that these fish constitute a sensitive indicator of the environmental health of this wetland. The alewife is especially interesting because the southern limit of this species is North Carolina, particularly the Albemarle Sound and its tributaries. The blueback herring also abounds in the Albemarle Sound, spawning two to three weeks later, but its range extends southward to northern Florida (as does that of the shad).[11]

Adult alewife migrate into the Albemarle Sound to spawn when the water reaches about 10.5°C (51°F), typically in March or April. As a general rule they return to the same stream where they hatched two to four years earlier. They migrate in schools of immense numbers, serving as food for striped bass and bluefish. The eggs are laid in a variety of opportunistic sites, from the midriver to shallow, sluggish creeks and ponds. Adults return to the sea soon after spawning. Juveniles on the other hand remain in their freshwater or slightly brackish nursery grounds throughout the summer, where they feed primarily on freshwater plankton, such as cladocerans and copepods.

In this context, it cannot be overemphasized that freshwater plankton constitute the primary food source in the aquatic food chain of the Albemarle ecosystem. Such plankton in these rivers and streams proliferate in the organic richness of adjacent, *undrained* swamps. From this food source herring (and other oily fish) accumulate energy-rich fats in anticipation of the long migration to the Gulf of Maine. Interestingly, it is plankton that manufacture fat-soluble vitamin D in response to sunlight. Contrary to popular belief, oily fish cannot manufacture their own vitamin D, emphasizing the fundamental importance of plankton.[12]

Completing the cycle, juvenile alewives (and other river herring) of the Albemarle migrate to the Atlantic Ocean (Gulf of Maine) in autumn, triggered by heavy rains and/or a sudden drop in water temperature, such as associated with annual tropical storms.

River herring have been migrating into their natal spawning grounds in the Albemarle region since time immemorial. During the four hundred years of recorded history, some interesting environmental changes have occurred in this region, the biological significance of which is noteworthy here. Some of these changes have been natural, whereas others were caused by man, but in either case resilience of river herring to these changes has been remarkable.

Today, river herring migrate southward from the northwest Atlantic and enter the Albemarle Sound from the Pamlico Sound, primarily via Oregon Inlet, located to the south of Roanoke Island.

At the time of the Roanoke Colony (1585), however, river herring were able to enter the Albemarle Sound from the ocean directly via several inlets that existed at that time. Then, as a result of various storms, the northern inlets along the Outer Banks closed successively. With the storm of 1828 came closure of (New) Currituck Inlet (1713–1828), the last inlet connecting directly into the Albemarle Sound. Thereafter, schools of migrating river herring had to enter from Pamlico Sound via inlets to the south of Roanoke Island,.such as Oregon Inlet (1585–1770, 1846–) and, at one time, New Inlet (1708–1922, 1932–45).[13]

Indeed, there is tantalizing historical evidence that four hundred years ago the migration route for river herring may have been reverse that of today, that is, they may have entered first the Albemarle Sound and from there into Pamlico Sound. In 1585 John White clearly depicts the native fishermen strategically positioning a large reed weir toward the middle of the narrow Roanoke Sound to the east of Roanoke Island. This weir is positioned to catch fish coming *from the north,* if the accuracy of his drawing is to be believed.[14]

Before the settlers came, none of the large pocosin lakes that characterize the Albemarle peninsula was linked directly to adjacent rivers or sounds. As discussed in chapter 7, one by one each of these lakes was connected by transportation and drainage canals to outside waters. For example, major canals were dug from Lake Mattamuskeet directly to Pamlico Sound in 1800, 1838, and again during the infamous 1914–32 period. Similarly, canals from Lake Phelps to the Scuppernong River were dug in 1788 (Collins Canal) and in 1843 (Pettigrew Canal). By the twentieth century each lake was associated with three or four canals.

Historically, then, river herring did not migrate into these pocosin lakes at all until man linked them via canals approximately 150 to 200 years ago. River herring soon found these new canals, and even the lakes, and migrated into them in numbers, belying their instinct to return to natal waters.

In this context, Lake Mattamuskeet is particularly interesting. Alewives migrating into this lake were studied in the three-year period from 1969 to 1971. Peak runs occurred on 5 and 6 April 1970 and 2 and 3 April 1971 (water temperatures 12.9°C and 13.1°C, respectively). At that time four canals connected the lake to the Pamlico Sound, but only one of these canals carried 97 percent of the alewives into the lake. Subsequent gate changes in 1989 have greatly restricted these herring runs into the lake.[15]

River herring never flourished in Lake Phelps. For one thing the lake is higher and much less accessible by direct canal continuity. However, in the past Bee Tree Canal was known locally for containing large numbers of migrating herring. When the water controls from the lake were opened to this canal from time to time, herring reportedly entered the lake. To judge from the presence of juvenile herring, some of these were able to spawn in the lake. A more recent study was not able to duplicate spawning in the lake: "In 1984 an experimental fish ladder was installed by [North Carolina Wildlife] from Bee Tree Canal in an attempt to enhance herring migration into Lake Phelps. Although water levels were sufficient to operate the fish ladders in 1984 and part of 1985, use of the fish ladder by river herring was not apparent, and adult river herring were not collected in Lake Phelps in those years."[16]

Prehistoric, Colonial, and Antebellum Fisheries

Long before Europeans arrived here, the Carolina Algonquins had a sophisticated herring fishery in the Albemarle Sound, where they had developed a system of fencelike reed weirs for catching quantities of migrating fish in the shallows. Each weir led to a series of compartments of decreasing size that trapped the fish, not unlike today's efficient "pound nets." The Roanoke colonists of 1585 were genuinely impressed: "They also make weares, with setting opp reedes or twigges in the water, whiche they soe plant one within a nother, that they growe still narrower, and narrower. . . . Ther was neuer seene amonge vs soe cunninge a way to take fish withall."[17]

Herring fishing in the Albemarle Sound was revived on a much larger scale by the early colonists, especially in the Chowan River, which was unusually rich in river herring. The Chowan has been a major center for commercial fishing since the 1740s, an early industry attributed to John Campbell and his son-in-law Richard Brownrigg. In April 1765 an anonymous French visitor to the area observed, "there is great quantitys of fish catched in this river, especially herin and others." One evening, he personally watched his host, Richard Brownrigg, fish for herring on the east side of the river. In about an hour the Frenchman claimed they had caught about a hundred barrels of fish, including many striped bass, white perch, and several other sorts. (Shortly before, while in the New Bern area, this Frenchman had already observed the catching and salting of herring and shad, for shipment to the West Indies.)[18]

Richard Brownrigg was an Irish immigrant whose fishery at the mouth of Indian Creek on the Chowan River was operational at least as early as 1769. Here, his renown plantation, Wingfield, developed into a busy commercial complex, including a sizeable wharf with storehouses, a lumber mill, and a water-generated grain mill. With the aid of a brother who lived in the West Indies, he conducted profitable trade with that region.[19]

From that beginning other commercial fisheries sprang up and flourished along the Chowan, Roanoke, and other waterways of the Albemarle Sound area. Merchants in Edenton, such as William Littlejohn, dominated these regional fisheries at the time.

River herring became so important to the local economy that, in at least one instance, they even became a currency for the sale of slaves. This was indicated in a letter written during the 1787 herring run on the Chowan River to John Gray Blount (1752–1833), an eminent merchant at "Little Washington" on the Tar-Pamlico River: "I have inquired about fish and have tryed to sell your Negroes for fish but they seam to hold their fish as high as from 25/ to 30/ p. barrell tho I am sure that I could get you £100 a piece for them and 1/4 in hard money or the exhainge at 12/ to the doller."[20]

During the colonial period the main method of catching river herring was by placing long nets along the river channel in the path of the migrating herring. Already by 1769 there was disquiet about the impact of putting seines completely across narrow stretches of the Chowan River and its tributaries. That year a law was proposed to regulate such seine fishing on the Meherrin River. This act to "prevent the unreasonable destruction of fish" was rejected by Governor William Tryon on the grounds that it was not in North Carolina's commercial interest (while blatantly disregarding the fishermen upstream in Virginia):

I rejected, esteeming it prejudicial to the General Interest of the Country, and destructive of that spirit of industry and commerce so much wanted to be encouraged in this Colony. If the inhabitants up Meherrin River who are getting into a considerable trade by the Herring Fishery to the West India markets, were prevented from joining many seines together at the proper season, when the herrings are in shoals, the Fishery would be destroyed; as the success of one seine would be very inconsiderable on account of the width of the Meherrin River, even above where it forks with the Nottoway. It is remarkable the Virginians do not complain of a want of herrings in the Meherrin River at the proper season. Upon these principles I rejected the Bill herein inclosed.[21]

One hundred thirty years later this problem arose again, this time at the other end of the Albemarle Sound, at the entry point of the river herring into the sound:

After entering the inlets [Oregon and New] the fish reached Albemarle Sound by way of Croatan Sound [narrow bottleneck at the western edge of Roanoke Island], and this water body . . . was lined with so many pound nets, particularly on the western shore, that the fish had to run a veritable gauntlet before the Albemarle fishermen could have a chance at them. This situation resulted in the Vann Law of 1905, which provided that an open channel be maintained from the inlets to the spawning grounds. . . . Albemarle fishermen reported that the Vann Law gave them immediate relief from the formerly oppressive situation.[22]

The last viable herring fisheries, notably in the Chowan River waterways, struggled against declining catches until relatively recent times. Most notable was the Perry-Wynns Fish Company at Colerain on the Chowan River. For several decades this was the largest freshwater herring fishery in the world. In September 2003 Hurricane Isabel destroyed nine of its eleven buildings.

The last haul seine fishery in North Carolina (2006) was Williams Fishery on the Meherrin River, two miles east of Murfreesboro in Hertford County. In 2007 the North Carolina Marine Fisheries Commission imposed a ban on herring fishing in North Carolina, and its future is uncertain. The rich tradition of herring fishing in the Chowan and Meherrin rivers is exquisitely illustrated in a series of recent publications by Frank Stephenson.[23]

Herring Fishing on the Alligator River

Of special interest in the context of herring fishing is the Alligator River, one of the most pristine but least known waterways in the Albemarle-Pamlico ecosystem. The herring fishing here, especially at Frying Pan, was known for its "immense number of fish" since at least the early 1800s.[24]

The first known attempt to establish a commercial fishery on this river was in 1817 by the ever enterprising Ebenezer Pettigrew, owner of Bonarva plantation at Lake Phelps. He formed a partnership to acquire a property at "Alligator" and installed a local man, Lemuel Basnight, as manager. Here they proposed to construct a fifty-foot shelter and a salt house for preparing and preserving 750 barrels of fish. They went so far as to commission a boat captain as well as a cooper to build barrels (twenty-five cents each). However, the project was half-hearted, and the several investors dissolved their relationship in 1822.[25]

In December 1868 an established herring fishery at Frying Pan was sold by John and Mary Wilson to Edward Wood of Hayes plantation for the remarkable sum of three thousand dollars. In the years immediately prior to the Civil War, Wood had owned a number of fisheries along the north shore of the Albemarle Sound, with his main operation at the Greenfield Fishery near Edenton. Wood's heirs still owned six acres at the Frying Pan Fishery as late as 1891. Commercial fishing continued here until the 1930s.[26]

The following account of a particularly notable fish camp on the west side of the Alligator River at Frying Pan in the 1910s and 1920s is a microcosm of bygone days throughout much of the greater Albemarle region.[27]

When river herring were running on the river each year, in April and May, fish camps sprang up temporarily along the river. They came in varying sizes, but they were all built on wood pilings at the water's edge for processing fish near where they were freshly caught. On spring evenings lantern lights could be seen all along the river shore, giving the false impression of a large population. Today, in sharp contrast, the Alligator River by night is pitch black along virtually its entire length.

For the most part the Frying Pan fishery is a story of seasonal jobs for small farmers during that brief period in the farm year between crop planting and harvest. One could always tell, however, who were the few "professional" fishermen in local communities because in the off-season their yards were strewn with nets that were in the process of being made or mended (i.e., "tied" with a hand-carved, wooden spindle or "netting needle") and then waterproofed with tar.

In the 1920s and earlier the largest fish camp in the area was at the mouth of Frying Pan Lake. This camp is long gone, but the pilings are still there, preserved by the tea-colored water. During the fishing season men from nearby Gum Neck would live at this camp from Monday to Friday. On Monday mornings the men would make the half-hour trip in their "shad boats," powered by "Gray Marine" engines. The men worked all week at the camp, sleeping and cooking in the same place. The boats were so sluggish that when the men returned home late on Fridays, they only went as far as Grapevine landing, still several miles by a dirt lane to their respective homes. Grapevine was the smallest of the three river landings that served the sprawling community of Gum Neck, but it was the nearest to the fish camp.

The Frying Pan fish camp was a large wooden structure built right over the water. It had to be large enough to hang fishing nets over log joists. On the back of the structure was the camp itself, which consisted of two rooms—one where the men cooked and ate and the other where the men slept in barrack style. At the end of the building was an important ice room for cooling the striped bass, white perch, red fin, and other freshwater fish caught in the main river (but not the river herring, which was normally salted). In those days a freight/passenger boat called the *Alma* plied the river between Fairfield and Elizabeth City two or three times a week. It would dock at the fish camp, bringing large cakes of ice, each reportedly weighing three to four hundred pounds. These crystalline blocks were kept from melting in the ice room by means of insulating sacks of sawdust.

The fishermen here used two main types of nets in the river. One was the fight (fyke) net, which was characterized by round loops. By local account these were used in winter for fish species other than herring. Spring herring were caught in pound nets, whose series of narrow openings impounded the fish in large numbers. From shallow-bottomed shad boats men used dip nets to get the trapped herring until the shad boat was loaded.

The freshly caught herring were then taken directly to the fish camp, where they were processed immediately. First they went to the "cutting bench," which had slats over the water. A special herring knife was used in such a way that both the heads and attached entrails fell overboard through the slats. In this way the men did not have to handle the entrails at all. However, a few of the professional fishermen used to plow fish heads and entrails into their corn fields as fertilizer, a practice claimed locally to be of Indian origin.

Parenthetically, today the area of the old Frying Pan fish camp harbors a local population of alligators, possibly for the same reason that, in the 1950s and 1960s, alligators lurked in the Scuppernong River around Jaeger's Fish Market, within the town limits of Columbia. As late as the 1980s a large alligator became entangled in a local fisherman's net on the Alligator River, probably attracted by trapped fish. The dead alligator lay rotting at Grapevine Landing for several weeks.

A great deal of roe also went overboard when the herring were being dressed. This part of the fish was not commercially attractive, but some roe was brined for local consumption. In any case, the dressed fish were thrown into a barrel of water positioned by each person. These were emptied into a push cart with slats allowing the water to escape. The fish were then scaled by hand, after which they were put into a salting tray, a process that involved striking with a stick, presumably to remove excess salt. The lightly salted fish were placed finally into a big container (fish tank), where more salt was put over them periodically by shovel. The men developed a rapid way of counting as they sorted by holding five in each hand, using both hands at the same time.

Periodically the freight boats would take the fish to Elizabeth City, from which they made their way to fish markets in Norfolk, Baltimore, and even New York City. Some of these big-city wholesalers included Fass Brothers and Fulton Fish Market. In due course, payment for the exported fish would arrive by check in the mail. The price of the fish varied depending on the season and other factors. "Not a lot of money was paid. . . . They only made a living."

Naturally the men took some fish home for their families, so that brined herring (and brined roe) were not uncommon at breakfast and other meals. For some local families, however, herring was considered primarily for emergency, one of several important food sources that had failed them in the Civil War, as discussed in chapter 9.

By one local account, white perch (*Morone americana*) was considered the most flavorful of the fish species caught on the river. Ironically, this species is a predator of herring. It cannot be concluded, however, that such predation led to the later decline of herring, because the two species had coexisted here successfully for many decades. For example, on the morning of 1 April 1869, the catch at Frying Pan consisted of "350 herrings and 500 perch," which led one local man to say, "I think we will have plenty of herrings for the spring."[28]

Smaller fish camps, employing only two or three men, were located closer to Gum Neck. For example, at the sharp bend of the river was (aptly named) Deep Point, immediately across from which was Bear Wharf (Buck Ridge landing). The former camp was indeed deep enough for freight boats to dock, but the latter was too shallow. Thus, one or two men had to go out in their small boat to intercept the freighters once or twice a week. This led to a fatal accident during the herring season of 1917. On 13 April, a thirty-four-year-old local farmer and part-time fisherman went out to intercept when the *Alma* accidentally capsized his boat. He could not swim, and his body was found in the river a day or two later. Fishing throughout the Albemarle region was periodically punctuated by such tragedies.

Spring runs of river herring on the Alligator River declined markedly in the 1930s, according to local accounts. Some old-timers blamed this on the opening of the Alligator-Pungo portion of the intracoastal waterway canal. "The Alligator River used to be entirely freshwater before that," one local man claimed with confidence.[29] In the early 1940s a small fishery was located at Cherry Ridge landing, which was accessible by road, unlike the bygone fish camp at Frying Pan. Even at that time some herring were still being cut and salted, and other fish were iced. In either case the processed fish were now being taken to market by truck.

By the 1940s commercial fishing focused mainly on salt- and brackishwater fish and shellfish in the sounds: menhaden, mullet, bluefish, oysters, and increasingly, shrimp and crabs. The nearest center for such fishing was in the vicinity of Roanoke Island at Mann's Harbor and Wanchese, to which some fishermen from the Alligator River moved permanently.

In this context, in the 1920s oyster boats would come down the Alligator River to Gum Neck from Mann's Harbor with bushels of fresh oysters, which were sold or traded for bushels of peas/beans or corn. In the 1930s, after the inland waterway opened, oyster boats then came up the Alligator-Pungo canal from Swan Quarter and Engelhard.

Decline of River Herring: Human Impact

Since early prehistory river herring constituted a major fishery in the Albemarle region, but today these once mighty fish have been declared officially "depleted" throughout North Carolina. The sharp decline of river herring in recent years has been variously attributed to many factors: depletion of zoo-plankton in nursery grounds, salt penetration, eutrophication (oxygen depletion), drainage and channelization of adjacent wetlands, dams blocking migration routes, pollution, overfishing, and predation. Although the origins of most of these factors can be traced to some degree to the colonial and antebellum periods, the scale and severity of these disturbances accelerated with economic growth.

A full treatment of the factors contributing to the precipitous decline of river herring and other fish in this region lies outside the scope of this book. However, for more information, the North Carolina Division of Marine Fisheries has published an excellent, detailed account of the plight of river herring in the Albemarle Sound basin.[30]

Of ecohistorical interest is the observation that techniques for catching river herring in this region became increasingly efficient, resulting in overfishing. Such techniques evolved over decades, a social history that reflected availability of seasonal labor (slavery), advancements in engine power (first steam, followed by internal combustion), and improved design of nets (the more efficient pound net came to this region in 1869 or 1870). Prior to the Civil War, fish were taken in large haul seines set manually along the shore of the Albemarle Sound, reportedly labored to a great extent by free colored men. After the Civil War, fishermen gradually exploited steam technology to minimize dependence on labor. For example, in 1869 a steam winch was used to haul in heavy nets containing innumerable fish, and in 1879 small steamboats allowed them to lay out very long nets.[31]

These advances in the efficiency of fishing in the Albemarle and Pamlico Sounds resulted in some remarkable fish stories: "As many as two hundred thousand herring have been brought to shore at one haul in a seine twenty-five hundred yards long," and use of "a mile-long seine powered from shore to catch fish, mainly shad (enough to fill a boat)." Whatever the truth in these claims, fishing for river herring and shad was big business in the engine-powered years following the Civil War.[32]

More recent has been the insidious effect of disturbing organic soils, specifically by land drainage and peat mining. Peat has peculiar chemical properties the biological significance of which is only beginning to be appreciated. The complex humic substances that compose peat bind to a number of inorganic chemicals and lock them away for thousands of years. These chemicals include nitrogen, phosphorous, lead, arsenic, cadmium, and mercury, many of which can be detrimental in an aquatic ecosystem. Two environmentalists have noted that "in North Carolina run-off from drained peatland had three times the nitrogen and twenty-eight times the phosphorus concentration found in run-off from un-drained peatland." Such runoff is associated with eutrophication (oxygen depletion).[33]

One of the most toxic of the chemicals found in peat is mercury, which becomes sequestered in peat from rainfall accumulating over eons. When peat is disturbed, such as when it was mined here in the 1970s and 1980s, mercury can be released into the waterways. Once in the ecosystem mercury concentrates in body tissues as it ascends the food chain. This biohazard has been studied in the Florida Everglades, whose peatlands have been severely disturbed. There, the livers of local alligators had extremely high concentrations of mercury.

According to Bear Pocosin.org, "A lawsuit in Hyde County in the [nineteen-] eighties won national attention when First Colony Farms sought to mine the peat from the pocosin. The environmental degradation was clearly demonstrated when mercury levels started rising in these waters." High levels of mercury were reported at one time in predatory fish near the top of the aquatic food chain, such as largemouth bass (1.3 ppm) from Lake Phelps and Lake Mattamuskeet, and even higher in chain pickerel (4.3 ppm) in Lake Drummond, Great Dismal Swamp.[34]

On a positive note, there is evidence that restoring normal hydrology of pocosins, simply by stopping land drainage and resubmerging the peat, may reverse mercury elevations. As part of an Atlantic white cedar restoration project near Pungo Lake in 1994–98, "indications are that mercury levels were reduced in conjunction with the restoration."[35]

Shellfish

Shellfish have played an important role in the ecohistory of the Albemarle region for thousands of years. Some species, like oysters, scallops, and conchs, were consumed from antiquity, as indicated by numerous prehistoric middens. Furthermore, some shell products such as "wampum," beads, and pearls were used as currency and decoration by local natives.

With the exception of freshwater mussels, most useful shellfish in this region are brackish and saltwater species and therefore fall outside the scope of this book. However, ancient oyster beds, such as those found at the mouth of the Alligator River, reflect the changing salinity history of the Albemarle Sound. The oyster industry in Currituck Sound, for example, effectively terminated when the last inlet closed in 1828, "God's vengeance some said." The brackish Pamlico Sound has been the center of an oyster fishery in this region since the earliest colonial days. In 1711, for example, a Swiss settler in the new colony of New Bern observed a little old Englishman selling oysters in the town.[36]

In the mid-1880s oysters in the Chesapeake Bay declined, leading to "an invasion" of Virginia oyster fishermen into the Pamlico Sound. About this time the state of North Carolina granted segments of the Pamlico oyster beds to private individuals who proceeded to farm them. Prior to that time oyster beds here were common land and open to all, but the new system of licensing led to disputes. For example, in 1891 three poachers were "found dead with bullet wounds in their heads." The problem of poaching became so great that the governor threatened to send state militia to the area.[37]

Over the years the Pamlico shellfish have had good periods and bad, attributed anecdotally to storm shifting of bottom sands. However, in recent years shellfish beds have suffered increasingly from pollution from adjacent waterways and encroaching human habitation, especially from the intensely populated Outer Banks.

At forty-four thousand acres, Open Grounds Farm in Carteret County is one of the largest farms in eastern North Carolina. From 1927 to 1936 it had been owned by the University of Chicago, which modified the land for cultivation by digging drainage ditches and canals. In the winter of 1974–75 the Corps of Engineers ordered Open Grounds, by then owned by an Italian firm, to close the gates on its drainage canal and stop water discharge that was threatening shellfish in the South River, a tributary of the Neuse estuary. In 1992 the state closed most of the South River area to shell fishing because of bacterial pollution. Today, on the north side of the Pamlico Sound, commercial oystermen have amassed huge piles of oyster shells around Rose Bay, Engelhard, and other ports along southern Hyde County.

Blue crabs were always abundant here, but there was no commercial market for them prior to 1880. At that time they were reportedly eaten mainly by African Americans as a means of supplementing their diet. The crab fishery here grew rapidly from the 1890s, and by 1955 "crabbing was the healthiest fishery on Roanoke Island."[38]

Shrimping is another relatively new local industry, being nonexistent in 1880. In the lower Neuse estuary (South River) shrimping did not begin until the 1930s. By 1948 shrimping was a significant business around Engelhard. Interestingly, the Pamlico Sound is the most northern body of water in the United States where shrimp are caught commercially.

A Word about Turtles

The word *terrapin* came from the Algonquin language, reflecting the fact that fresh- and brackish-water turtles (commonly called terrapins) were a common subsistence food for these people. In fact, terrapins constituted an important subsistence food in this region thousands of years before the Algonquins arrived. At the Cactus Hill archaeological site on the Nottoway River, a tributary of the Albemarle Sound, bones of several species date from at least the Early Archaic Period (10,000 BP). Interestingly, terrapins may even have been associated with some spiritual significance. In Carteret County a grave dated AD 445 "contained two semi-flexed individuals, multiple turtle shells and ceramic vessels."[39]

The most commonly consumed species of turtle in the Albemarle region was the box turtle (*Terrapene carolina*). This terrestrial species was consistently one of the five main food sources for each of the prehistoric villages studied along the Roanoke River (AD 1250–1450), from the coastal plain to the piedmont. The aquatic snapping turtle (*Chelydra serpentina*) was a major food source for villages in the coastal plain, but it featured increasingly less so in villages into the piedmont. This species was the fourth most abundant food source at the Jordan's Landing village, some thirty miles up the Roanoke River from the Albemarle Sound.[40]

In 1585 Thomas Hariot of the Roanoke Colony observed, "There are many Tortoyses both of land and sea kinde. . . . They are very good meate, as also their eggs." The colonists particularly prized the box turtle ("A land Tort which the Sauages esteeme aboue all other Torts"). In fact, the box turtle was prized by the Carolina and Virginia Algonquins not only for meat but, smoothed inside, as ladles, as found in archaeological digs at Jamestown.[41]

Two hundred years later (1798), terrapins were still a source of food in the Albemarle peninsula (Alligator River):

> The swamps produce a variety of what may be denominated land turtles. The natives call them loggerheads, tarapins, snappers, and hawsbills. In the summer, the slaves catch them in abundance, and bring them to market. On this account they are but little valued by their masters; but I pronounced them the greatest luxury of the dog-days in this burning climate. When well cooked, they are a tolerable substitute for the sea turtle. . . . They make an excellent dish; and, in fact, reflecting at this moment, I think that I could scarce have found a substitute for fresh meat in the scarcity of summer, had it not been for loggerheads and tarapins. I have purchased them from ten to fifteen pounds weight, for an English shilling a piece; and the females would frequently yield a score or more eggs, several larger than the yolk of an hen's egg, and of nearly as good a flavour.[42]

The Roanoke colonists identified, and illustrated for the first time anywhere (1585), still another type of turtle that is not normally found in the Roanoke River or western parts of the Albemarle Sound. This was the brackish-water diamondback terrapin (*Malaclemys terrapin*). It is the only terrapin once commonly found in the brackish marshes of the Pamlico and Roanoke sounds. For decades they were collected here by hand in summer for local consumption.

The demise of this species started in 1845 in the marshes at the southern end of Roanoke Island. In the winter of that year William Midgett developed a device similar to an oyster dredge for catching dormant terrapins for his own use. Four years later, Captain John B. Etheridge, once keeper of the nearby Bodie Island Lighthouse and later fisherman from Manteo, made local terrapins a financially attractive commodity. In 1849 he sold 4,050 diamondback terrapins for $750 to markets in Norfolk and Baltimore, that is, 19 cents apiece.

Etheridge's business ignited local interest, and pressure on the terrapin increased markedly. Prices rose to the dizzy heights of $0.40 each. Since the "terrapin drag" worked only in winter, when terrapins were torpid, other methods were developed to collect them in warmer months, including a baited trap similar to a lobster pot. Most remarkably, dogs were trained to detect terrapin tracks on land when they left water to deposit eggs. In the Beaufort region marshes were burned in winter to drive terrapins from dormancy.

Such was the scale of the diamondback terrapin business in this area that two holding ponds were created, one on Roanoke Island (1875) and another at Sladesville in Hyde County (1877). On Roanoke Island a serious attempt was made to culture them in a tidal four-acre pond. This involved bringing undersized terrapins to marketable size, as well as encouragement of egg laying and hatching in artificial sand piles. In 1879 a total of 17,000 terrapins were collected in the Pamlico Sound, including many that were undersized. Of these, 3,000 were sold in New York, 5,000 in Philadelphia, and 2,000 in Baltimore.

By 1880, North Carolina had become the second-largest exporter of diamondback terrapins in the United States (123,000 individuals valued at $10,850), second only to Chesapeake Bay (165,600 at $18,550). By World War I the population of the diamondback terrapin was seriously depleted, from which it has not recovered in spite of a federally sponsored terrapin breeding facility at Beaufort (1902–48).[43]

Finally, large sea turtles were known to both the Carolina Algonquins and the Roanoke colonists. Of the five species found along the Outer Banks and even within the Pamlico Sound, some are quite rare, as attested by the finding in June 1935 of a leatherback turtle (*Dermochelys coriacea*), the world's largest turtle species:

> A monstrous black sea turtle caught in the nets of Recorder W. F. Baum . . . near Nags head Saturday is exciting much curiosity hereabouts. . . . The turtle is tied to the wharf near the Trent dock, and is proving an attraction for youngsters and grownups too. . . . Estimates place the weight of the turtle at 750 pounds. From the tip of the nose down the back to the tip of its tail the curiosity measures seven feet almost to the inch. From the end of one flipper to the tip of the other measures seven and one half feet. . . . Ryan Midgett, fisherman and guide, said it was a 'leatherback turtle,' a kind seldom found in shallow water. The soft black shell of the turtle does closely resemble leather. No one could be found hereabouts who had seen one before. . . . Mr Baum said the turtle was for sale if a buyer could be found. It had to be hauled to Manteo Saturday on a truck.[44]

A telegraphed offer of twenty dollars from the fish hatchery at Beaufort arrived the day after the turtle accidentally drowned in captivity.

7 *Antebellum Golden Age*

TRANSPORTATION CANALS

Dugout canoes dating back to 3095 BC have been found in the pocosin lakes at the center of the Albemarle peninsula. Nearly five thousand years later, dugouts of the same time-tested design were still being used here. When the Roanoke colonists arrived in 1584, the native Algonquins were described as exceptionally skilled watermen who routinely crossed the precarious Albemarle and Pamlico sounds in large dugouts. Thus, the record shows that for millennia the Albemarle tidewater was far better suited for travel by water than by land. This continued to be the case until only about eighty years ago, when the once bustling water highway, and a romantic way of life, came to an end.

In colonial times the English chose to settle along the Albemarle waterways precisely because they afforded an extensive network of shallow sounds and tributaries, some extending within a few miles of Jamestown. There was nothing else like it in the New World, a vast "waterland" of promise for the taking. Wind-driven, shallow-draft vessels linked a sprawling network of riverside settlements that took root in the fertile organic soil of the Albemarle basin. The previously isolated pocosin lakes of the Albemarle peninsula were soon connected to the water highway by transport canals, along with the great navigable rivers contiguous with the sounds.

One of the earliest identified commercial vessels to ply the Albemarle Sound was in fact involved in smuggling or, more accurately, tax evasion on the Alligator River. In December 1769 the incoming sloop *Lovely*

Peggy was required to dock at Edenton (Port of Roanoke) to pay import duty to the British Crown (King George III). Instead, the wind-driven vessel "illegally landed goods along the Alligator River" before proceeding to the designated port for inspection.[1]

The king's comptroller of customs at Edenton, James Iredell Sr. (1751–1799), learned of this contraband and hired a sloop to investigate, an expensive exercise that lasted nine days and cost £31 9s. 6d. After official condemnation by the admiralty judge in New Bern, the *Lovely Peggy* was sold at public auction for £27 5s. in April 1770. Smuggling was apparently not an uncommon practice, since this was one of three vessels that Iredell seized that winter, including also the *Dolphin* and *Sally* on the Scuppernong River. (Ironically, Iredell later became critical of the British Crown's abuses against the colonies, including the Stamp Act and other duties and taxation. President George Washington appointed Iredell to the first U.S. Supreme Court, on which he served for nearly a decade.)

As the eighteenth century came to a close, farming was indisputably the economic backbone of the Albemarle region. The chief agricultural products for export consisted of several grains (corn, wheat, and rice) and salt-preserved meat (pork and beef), along with honey and wax, a local speciality. Coinciding with agricultural advancement were efforts to improve water transportation to markets in Virginia and beyond. Farming communities at this time were invariably located on natural waterways, whose local landing was key to distant markets. At this time products were conveyed from these landings by wind-driven vessels to regional centers at Edenton or New Bern. From Edenton journeys were either by boat via the bar at Ocracoke or overland to Suffolk and beyond. One such overland journey from Edenton to Baltimore was recounted in detail in 1804.[2]

Dismal Swamp Canal: Commercial Access to Chesapeake Bay

In one generation life in the Albemarle region changed dramatically, ushering in a veritable golden age based on a commercial water highway unique in American history. Between 1810 and 1830 several advancements significantly improved life throughout the region. Foremost, the steam engine propelled larger and faster commercial vessels, no longer dependent on vicissitudes of the wind. Of great commercial significance was the addition of transportation canals to the water highway, most importantly the Dismal Swamp Canal (1814) and later the Albemarle and

Chesapeake Canal (1859). Although initially conceived in 1780s in part for military purposes as an escape route for Norfolk, the Dismal Swamp Canal was also seen as direct access from Albemarle Sound to lucrative markets in Norfolk, Baltimore, and New York.

In June 1814 a most significant event took place that affected generations of people in the Albemarle region. The occasion was passage through the Dismal Swamp Canal of the first boat, other than a shingle flat boat, from Albemarle Sound to Chesapeake Bay. In that month a twenty-ton vessel carrying bacon and brandy arrived at Norfolk from Scotland Neck on the Roanoke River.[3]

The Dismal Swamp Canal was an ambitious, long-awaited project to link the waters of the Pasquotank River (Elizabeth City) to that of the Elizabeth River (Norfolk). Work on the twenty-two-mile canal commenced in 1792 at both ends, using hired slaves and laborers from local planters during the off-season. The two ends met in 1805, but at that time it was "little more than a muddy ditch," with only enough draft for shingle flats. With improvements in depth and the lock system the canal was navigable in 1814, ushering in a dynamic new period of water transportation for the people of the entire Albemarle-Pamlico region.[4]

As one might expect of a project of this scale, the canal was periodically closed for improvements. In December 1828 the newly enlarged canal reopened, with stage coaches using the parallel road. A few months later the remarkable Lake Drummond Hotel opened on the canal. This 128-foot-long building straddled the state line, with four of its rooms in Virginia and four in North Carolina.[5]

Until 1814 passengers and goods from the Albemarle and Pamlico Sounds had no direct route to Virginia. Many went south via the unpredictable Ocracoke Inlet into the open Atlantic and then northward into the Chesapeake Bay. Alternatively, some boats went via a northern river route, first to Edenton and from there up the Chowan River into Virginia via its navigable tributaries, such as the Meherrin, Nottoway, and Blackwater rivers. This Chowan River route continued long after the opening of the Dismal Swamp Canal.

By 1830, thanks to the Dismal Swamp Canal, Elizabeth City had become the new undisputed center of transport from New Bern via the direct water route to Norfolk, Baltimore, and even New York. It had suddenly become cosmopolitan, with an increasing number of visitors in transit between New York and Charleston via New Bern. Yet this canal was plagued with technical problems and never lived up to its promise.

In 1856 work began on an alternative to the Dismal Swamp Canal. This was the Albemarle and Chesapeake Canal, which would connect Norfolk's Elizabeth River to the Currituck Sound. Having only one lock, instead of the Dismal Swamp's seven, it promised to be significantly quicker. Furthermore, being deeper and wider, the proposed new canal promised to handle larger commercial boats. The new canal also had the advantage of the new steam-powered technology. Under the supervision of the master canal builder Marshall Parks (1820–1900), seven steam dredges on floating platforms finished the canal by 1858. The first vessel passed through the Albemarle and Chesapeake Canal in January 1859 when the side-wheel steamer *Calypso* pulled a 75-ton barge. During the Civil War nine thousand vessels made the passage. So well known was this canal that "Ferdinand DeLesseps studied the Albemarle & Chesapeake before beginning the Suez Canal." Today the Albemarle and Chesapeake Canal is an integral part of the coastal inland waterway system from New England to Texas.[6]

Pocosin Lakes: Early Transportation Canals

The Dismal Swamp Canal and Albemarle and Chesapeake Canal were only two of the canal-building ventures during the colonial and antebellum periods. Of particular importance were the transportation canals that linked the various pocosin lakes to the Albemarle and Pamlico sounds. In fact, the ecohistory of the Albemarle region cannot be understood without an appreciation of how these canals affected these lakes and their respective farming communities. Most enduring among these was the Fairfield Canal, which linked rich farm land around Lake Mattamuskeet and the Alligator River to markets in Elizabeth City, Norfolk, Baltimore, and New York. This important water highway on the Alligator River survived until the 1930s, when roads finally reached these isolated communities.

In addition to the distinctive shape and raised rim of the four pocosin lakes—Lake Mattamuskeet, Lake Phelps, Alligator Lake (New Lake), and Pungo Lake—they have another peculiar feature in common. None of these lakes has a natural outlet to a nearby river. At the same time, each is close to the headwaters of a river, which inexplicably does not quite connect to the lake. It is for this reason that these lakes, in spite of their size, do not show up on early maps. Early settlers did not discover these lakes until after 1750, as they were not accessible by boat. The exception was Lake Mattamuskeet, to which the Roanoke colonists were taken by footpath by the native inhabitants in 1585.

Once the lakes were discovered, however, farmers were quick to settle on the characteristic raised ridge, where the ground was dry and farming productive. One major problem was the lack of direct (water) communications to the outside world, that is, no practical way to get supplies or transport crops to market. Thus, from the outset the planters connected each of these lakes to the nearest river by means of a navigable canal.

In addition, each lake and its adjacent pocosins were drained to claim rich bottom land. The primary motivation for draining these lakes was that the exposed treeless bottomland would bypass the laborious process of felling trees and removing stumps. Thus, farmers could work hundreds (and in the case of Lake Mattamuskeet thousands) of acres of exceptionally fertile land from the moment they could put their plows in the soil. In some cases the dredged soil adjacent to each drainage canal created a raised road or turnpike, but water communications reigned supreme until relatively recently.

These and other profound environmental changes depended on wholesale slavery. With only one or two notable exceptions, African slaves dug virtually all the great navigation and drainage canals in the Albemarle region prior to the Civil War. The conditions under which these slaved manually dug through miles of inhospitable swampland are unimaginable. For example, the transportation canal and turnpike in the Rose Bay area of western Lake Mattamuskeet involved a gang of about sixty slaves "whose daily work was in water, often up to the middle, and constantly knee deep." Similarly, on the twenty-five-foot-wide canal south from Pungo Lake two hundred and fifty "negroes worked all day in water and muck, generally knee deep . . . and were housed in shanties on the banks of the canals." Interestingly, these laborers who worked so intimately in the tannin-rich waters were conspicuously free of malaria.[7]

Lake Phelps: Collins Canal (1788)

The second-largest of the pocosin lakes, Lake Phelps (Scuppernong Lake), was discovered, it is commonly accepted, in 1755 by two local men, Benjamin Tarkington and Josiah Phelps. About three decades later one of the largest plantations in North Carolina was established along this lake.

This plantation (Somerset Place) comprised over one hundred thousand acres, much of which was exceptionally fertile farmland. This commercial enterprise was founded by a post–Revolutionary War syndicate

(Lake Company) dominated by English-born Josiah Collins (1735–1819), who eventually ended up owning the entire company. The Lake Company was granted permission by the North Carolina General Assembly to dig a canal to drain much of Lake Phelps to turn the lakebed into arable land.[8]

Lake Phelps was not drained, as its water was deemed better used for irrigating adjacent rice fields. However, a lengthy canal was indeed dug between 1784 and 1788, using slave labor. It was twenty feet wide and extended from the lake to the Scuppernong River, a distance of nearly six miles. Most significantly, this canal served for decades to transport crops from Somerset Place and nearby Bonarva, belonging to Charles Pettigrew, to markets as far as New York.

Over the years numerous other drainage canals and ditches crisscrossed the growing expanse of plantation fields around Lake Phelps as their use changed from rice to corn and wheat. Indeed, the Pettigrews dug another large, seven-mile canal from the lake as late as 1843.[9]

Alligator Lake: Dunbar Canal (1823)

Dark-watered Alligator Lake (also known as New Lake) is the third largest of the pocosin lakes of the Albemarle peninsula. To be so unknown to outsiders today, the lake itself is surprisingly large, 3.4 by 3 miles. Its highest rim lies on the northeast quadrant, elevation eleven feet. The lake itself is not quite reached by the Southwest Fork of the Alligator River. The history of its settlement is a microcosm of religious and agricultural events occurring elsewhere in northeastern North Carolina.

Alligator Lake was discovered prior to 1765, and the community of "New Lake" was settled shortly before 1780 on the northeast ridge by a group thought to be Mennonites.[10] Among these farmers, allied through their common religion, were James Dunbar and John Cohoon, both of whom show up in the 1782 tax list as "Menonists." In 1784 the state granted adjacent land to the same group of men. This parcel was located on the southeast rim of the lake and consisted of a strip of 320 acres, 2 miles long and 0.25 miles wide.

There was much intermarrying within this particular group at New Lake, especially within the Cohoon and Dunbar families. Consequently, by 1800 most of the lake was occupied by members of these two families. Foremost among these was Thomas Dunbar (c. 1760–1844), who had eight sons and five daughters. Thus, by midcentury New Lake became synonymous with the large and influential Dunbar family.

At some indeterminate time after 1784 a narrow canal, variously called

"Old Dunbar Ditch" or "Squyars Canal," was dug from the swampy southeast rim of the lake to a small tributary of the Alligator River (New Lake Fork). This early access to the river connected the isolated New Lake settlement by canal to the equally remote communities of Head of the River and Kilkenny.

In 1823 the Dunbar family dug a much larger canal, "Dunbar Canal," from the northeast rim to Southwest Fork of the Alligator River, a distance approaching two miles through the swamp. This substantial waterway significantly upgraded New Lake's agricultural commerce via the Alligator River. In fact, one of Thomas Dunbar's sons, Captain John Dunbar (1798–1867), became a prominent boat captain who worked closely with Ebenezer Pettigrew's huge Bonarva plantation at Lake Phelps.

For more than sixty years the community of New Lake was inaccessible by road. Then, in 1840–41 state civil engineers under the personal direction of Walter Gwynn (1802–1882), later a Confederate general, dug a canal between Alligator Lake and the Pungo River (to reduce the level of the lake), such that the embankment became the first road to this lake. More than anything else this overland route turned New Lake community toward Hyde County. For one thing, the county seat of Swan Quarter was now much more accessible than was Columbia, county seat of Tyrrell County. In the boundary settlement of April 1890 the communities of New Lake and Head of the River were formally annexed by Hyde County, thus severing their historical administrative ties to Tyrrell County and eventually their now forgotten life on the Alligator River.[11]

Pungo Lake: Canal (1840)

Pungo Lake at twenty-eight hundred acres is the smallest of the pocosin lakes, with its affinity closest to its namesake Pungo River. It is the only one of the four lakes historically not to have a thriving farming settlement linked to outside markets by a navigable canal.

Nonetheless, serious attempts were made to drain Pungo Lake in order to retrieve its potentially rich bottomland. In 1840 a state-backed organization, with the improbable name of Literary Board, drained the lake by five feet, using slave labor to dig a twenty-five-foot canal to the Pungo River. In the coming years the board tried to sell the land at Pungo Lake, with little success. Nonetheless, draining the area around Pungo Lake continued until at least the early 1850s, when it was described as "an extensive and systematic plan of drainage, by canaling and ditching."

Today, the Pungo Lake Canal still extends due south from the lake to the Pungo River, and the water table continues to be unnaturally lowered.[12]

Lake Mattamuskeet (Lake Landing Canal 1838; Outfall Canal 1914)

The largest natural lake in North Carolina, Lake Mattamuskeet, has suffered unbelievably at the hands of land developers who tried to drain it entirely. By any measure, this ambitious project was a financial and ecological disaster, and nature is still reclaiming this once larger body of water.

A navigation canal southward from Lake Mattamuskeet to Pamlico Sound via Wyesocking Creek was proposed by local inhabitants in 1773. This project was approved by the Assembly but rejected by Royal Governor Josiah Martin, on grounds of a tax principle, namely, that King George would not approve local commissioners' levying land taxes to fund the project. A canal project was resurrected again in 1789 in the early federal period, but again without implementation. About 1800, Thomas Blount used slave labor to construct a transportation canal and, more importantly, a well-used turnpike in the Rose Bay area at the western end of the lake. The Rose Bay Turnpike Company's road was owned by public shares until at least 1826.

In 1836 floods from a hurricane damaged crops in the vicinity of Mattamuskeet. As a direct consequence slaves were made to dig a lengthy canal southward to Pamlico Sound via the original Wyesocking Creek route, completing it two years later. Unlike later canals, the crooked route of a nearby natural creek was followed. This state canal (Lake Landing Canal) reduced the lake from 110,000 acres to 55,000 acres. The resultant rich farmland created antebellum prosperity in Hyde County, well known for its bountiful agriculture during the Civil War.

The final assault on the lake came from 1914 to 1932, when appropriately named New Holland Farms drained the entire lake via long, straight Outfall Canal, using the world's largest pumping station. The soil was indeed extremely productive, but for a variety of reasons the lake relentlessly refilled and the project was finally abandoned in 1932. The once bustling village of New Holland, built optimistically in the lake bed itself, became another ghost town dotted in the Albemarle peninsula. The pumping station, later a hunting lodge, still exists, perhaps as a futuristic reminder of the bizarre history of Lake Mattamuskeet and New Holland.[13]

Fairfield Canal (c. 1845)

Construction of a transport canal between Lake Mattamuskeet area and the Alligator River was first mooted around 1800 by Thomas Blount, "for the purpose of transporting lumber, with which the country abounds, to a sea-port." Later, in 1824, Dr. Hugh Jones of Hyde County proposed that his slaves dig a canal ten feet wide and two feet deep from Alligator River to his land on the north side of the lake. In 1830 a more ambitious, but never executed, canal was proposed linking Pamlico Sound to Lake Mattamuskeet, via the Rose Bay Canal, and continuing to a new canal linking the lake to the Alligator River. In any case, H. S. Tanner's map of Hyde County clearly shows a canal to the Alligator River existed prior to 1834. The latter was probably a narrow, shallow forerunner of the commercially important Fairfield Canal.[14]

Of all the transport canals dug in the Albemarle peninsula in the eighteenth and nineteenth centuries none was more enduring, and profitable, than the Fairfield Canal, which linked the agriculture-rich community of Fairfield at Lake Mattamuskeet to the Alligator River (Gum Neck), and from there to Elizabeth City, Norfolk, and beyond. More than anything else, the Fairfield Canal brought a golden age to those living on this particular water highway.

The single most important person responsible for construction and success of the Fairfield Canal was canal pioneer Marshall Parks (1820–1900), a Virginian whose father had been involved in building the Dismal Swamp Canal in 1814. Parks was later responsible for digging the more competitive Albemarle and Chesapeake (1859).

Unlike the state canal on the south side of Lake Mattamuskeet (Lake Landing Canal, 1838), the Fairfield Canal was privately funded and operated. The charter for the Fairfield Canal and Turnpike Company was granted on 29 January 1840, and Parks was its president in the mid-1850s. It was Parks who projected the exact route from the Alligator River and determined that it would be four miles long and twenty feet wide, with a turnaround "Recess" (which still exists). The actual digging was done by a dredging company from Wilmington.[15]

Astutely, Parks made the seemingly illogical decision not to extend the canal into Lake Mattamuskeet. This was because silt from the lake would "choke" the canal, as was happening with the state canal already by 1861. The water level of the Fairfield Canal was perpetually that of the reliable, silt-free Alligator River. For people living on the south part of Lake

Mattamuskeet, it became easier to bring supplies up the Alligator River, then across the lake to the south shore, rather than use the state canal from Pamlico Sound (e.g., timber for the George Israel Watson House in 1896).

Ironically, the Fairfield Canal was used against the people living around Lake Mattamuskeet during the Civil War. On one occasion the canal was the route of a successful surprise attack during a snowstorm. After the war, this canal flourished under leadership of two prominent Fairfield men who served as presidents of the Fairfield Canal Company. These were Colonel William S. Carter (1833–1902) and then Captain F. F. Spencer (1859–1931). Over the ensuing years, successive steamboat companies, such as Fairfield and Elizabeth City Transportation Company, Old Dominion Steamship Company, and Newberry Produce Company, operated reliable passenger and freight service between Fairfield and Elizabeth City.

In addition to fees set by the steamboats themselves, the Fairfield Canal Company imposed its own freight charges. For example, in 1884 to ship forty head of cattle from Fairfield to Norfolk the canal toll was $0.80 per head, and the freight charge by the boat was $4.00 per head, making a total cost of $192.00.

The economic dominance of the Fairfield Canal reigned until the early 1930s, when roads and trucks made river transport uncompetitive. Life on the Alligator River dimmed permanently when the last river boat was withdrawn (see chapter 14).[16]

Antebellum Commerce

In the period just preceding the Civil War the Albemarle-Pamlico waterways were bustling with freight and passenger steamers, ushering in a prosperous golden age. The rich organic soil yielded impressive quantities of corn, wheat, pork, and other produce, much of which was the result of slave labor. It is not too much of an exaggeration to say that the Albemarle tidewater lifestyle at this time was reminiscent of a slavery-based, rural Venice.

The sixty-ton steamer *Lady of the Lake* was designed specifically for navigating the Dismal Swamp Canal between Elizabeth City and Norfolk. It was built in the spring of 1829 in partnership between Captain John Dunbar (1798–1867) and Ebenezer Pettigrew (1783–1848) of Bonarva plantation, Lake Phelps. A letter dated 28 December 1829 revealed that the *Lady* was located on the Alligator River at that moment under the command of Captain Dunbar. In subsequent years, 1833 and 1834, the *Lady* was known to transport Pettigrew's wheat and corn to markets in New York City. The *Lady* was abandoned at sea on 15 January 1837.[17]

By perverse irony, this network of Albemarle-Pamlico waterways that brought antebellum prosperity to the region made this area exceptionally vulnerable to northern invasion during the Civil War. The Union navy soon controlled the sounds and steadily tightened its control of vital tributaries and transportation canals. For four years these once productive water highways became military corridors that blocked local commercial vessels, many of which were confiscated or destroyed (see chapter 9).

In the decades following this disastrous war, commercial traffic on the Albemarle and Pamlico sounds eventually returned, but never again with the same vitality. Steamers such as the *Neuse* and *New Bern* resumed regular trips between New Bern and Elizabeth City. The latter town was still an important water hub, linked by a new network of scheduled boats, such as the *M. E. Roberts*, to communities dotted along the Albemarle Sound and its tributaries. These smaller ports included Edenton, Plymouth, Columbia, Manteo, Nags Head, East Lake, Gum Neck, and Fairfield.

The best known of these "modern" vessels was the 112-foot *Estelle Randall*, which was built in 1898 in Baltimore for service in the Chesapeake Bay. By 1909 it belonged to the Farmers and Merchants Line of North Carolina, which overhauled it for service on the Albemarle Sound. Described as one of the grandest passenger and freight steamers in the state, the *Estelle Randall* carried mail, among other cargo, between Elizabeth City and Norfolk, as well as stopping at various port towns on the Albemarle.

On the evening of 17 January 1910, while docked on the Scuppernong River in Columbia, the *Estelle Randall* caught fire and sank. Its crew of ten escaped, except the cook, William Exley, "who returned to help others and perished." Such was the *Estelle Randall*'s historical significance that in 1992 the North Carolina Underwater Archaeology Unit recovered its steam engine and other artifacts that survived more than eighty years at the bottom of the Scuppernong River.[18]

Brief History of Scheduled Steamboat Service

The first steamboat service between New Bern and Elizabeth City took place in the spring of 1818, when the *Norfolk* commenced two round trips a week. The 132-foot *Norfolk* had been built in Norfolk in 1817 and purchased by a syndicate of gentlemen from New Bern for $53,000. The vessel arrived in New Bern on 10 April 1818, in anticipation of its maiden voyage to Elizabeth City. This event called for a local celebration, in which people thronged the wharves in New Bern. The venture was immediately acclaimed a success: "The steam boat stock holders will begin to hold up their heads, four passengers come in the stage for the steam boat which carried 7 to Elizabeth [City]. Dr. B. told it with as much pleasure as though he was principally concerned." Unfortunately, in spite of the hype, the commercial results were "disappointing at first."[19]

Later, a more advanced competitor, the steamer *Pamplico*, began operating out of Washington on the Tar River in 1827.[20] In the summer season this steamer took holiday travelers from Edenton and neighboring ports to the increasingly popular resort of Nags Head. In 1857 a vessel by this same name was still plying Pamlico Sound waters between Washington and New Bern. It was described as being 125 feet long, drew 8 feet, had a speed of 15 miles per hour, and most significantly for environmental reasons, consumed 1.3 cords of wood per hour.

In late 1857 the town of New Bern eclipsed Washington as a commercial port on the Pamlico Sound because of its link to the newly completed Atlantic and North Carolina Railroad, which connected New Bern (and Beaufort) to the inland town of Goldsboro. Prior to this time, the 133-ton steamer *Post Boy* plied between Washington and Hyde County and Beaufort. In early 1858, however, the route was extended to New Bern, with a weekly round trip from New Bern to Hyde County (stopping at Enterprise, Swan Quarter, and Wyesocking) and Washington.

In the Albemarle Sound in the late 1850s the paddlewheel steamboat *Curlew* regularly carried passengers and freight between Edenton, Hertford, Elizabeth City, and Nags Head. Josiah Collins, owner of Somerset Place on Lake Phelps, even shipped ten mules and four horses across the sound on this vessel. At the outbreak of the Civil War, the *Curlew*, like many vessels in the sound country, was taken into war service. It served in the Confederate navy before being run aground and burned at the Battle for Roanoke Island on 7 February 1862.

With construction of Nag's Head Hotel in 1838, the resort community of Nags Head was gaining popularity as a holiday destination, especially during the autumnal sickly season. At this time Nags Head was only accessible by boat from the sound, rather than the ocean. A fare between

Edenton and Nags Head on the *Curlew* was set at two dollars, and slaves were "required to have a written permit from their owners."[21]

While indispensable for the local economy, this river traffic contributed to a modern problem, namely, the spread of communicable diseases. As one account observed, "We learn from New Bern that . . . it is dreadfully sickly there with scarlet fever[,] mumps & small-pox.—Mrs Snell . . . died about a fortnight since with small-pox[;] she took it from her son who carried it there in a vessel, he recovered, but another son . . . took the disease & before he was aware of having it, spread it in different parts of the town, he has since died with it" (22 Jan. 1841).[22]

On the eve of the Civil War social changes were palpable throughout the Albemarle. On 18 August 1859 the *Armeca* sailed from the lower Alligator River (Gum Neck) amid much fanfare. The occasion was the departure of a well-respected local farmer Ludford Cohoon (1816–1881) and his young family. Ludford had been persuaded by an earlier émigré from Gum Neck that life was bustling in Elizabeth City. One factor in their quest for a new life was a sad event that occurred some time earlier. Ludford's sister had developed gangrene following the birth of her only child. To relieve her unbearable suffering she was mercy-killed by the family's house slave, named "Love," who smothered her mistress with a pillow. In keeping with commonsense justice at the time, no criminal prosecutions were raised under the circumstances.

Ludford's departure was a big event locally, and the entire farming establishment of this community showed up to see them off, as reported in the *Tar Heel:* "At the river's edge a great host of people gathered to say goodbye. This was the largest gathering of people we had seen up to that time."[23] This group of prominent citizens was a veritable who's who of local plantation owners and big farmers, all of whom had considerable land and slave holdings in this community. The world of these influential planters, magistrates, and politicians was soon turned upside down by the impending war.

After embarking from Gum Neck, the *Armeca* sailed during the night across the Albemarle Sound into a whole new (urban) life. One of Ludford's children later reminisced,

> This was our first trip on the water and from the horrible accounts we had of the Albemarle Sound, we were almost frightened to death when we were told that it was near ahead. We went below in the cabin and re-

mained there until about half way across when our father pulled us up on deck. We slept but little that night and when we neared Elizabeth City we heard someone say the town was on fire. It was the large grist mill of Griffin and White. . . . Next morning August 19 . . . we stood on the deck of the sail craft *Armeca* [and] viewed the Pasquotank [River] and the water front of Elizabeth City. . . . The harbor was full of sailing vessels, many large seagoing [luggers]. . . . The active shipbuilding yards showed much business. After breakfast we landed right at our future home. I was the first of that once large family to place my barefoot on the sands of Pasquotank shore.[24]

This barefoot boy, Frederick Franklin Cohoon, later became publisher of the influential Elizabeth City newspaper the *Tar Heel*, which published his article "Looking Backward Fifty Years" (1909). Two and a half years after they arrived, virtually to the day, Elizabeth City was occupied by Yankee soldiers.[25]

Navigable Rivers

The major rivers flowing into the Albemarle basin also became an integral part of this expanding water highway. Limited only by the rocky fall line, river boats carried commercial traffic up the Roanoke River to Weldon (Roanoke Rapids), Neuse River to Kinston and Waynesborough (Goldsboro), Tar River to Tarboro, and the Chowan and its tributaries into Virginia. Insidiously, however, a growing inland railroad system was beginning to dictate commercial viability of certain coastal ports over others. Portsmouth, Wilmington, and New Bern were on the ascendancy, whereas Edenton, Plymouth, and Washington were on the wane.

As early as 1834 passengers could take the Portsmouth and Roanoke Railway the thirty-four-mile distance from Portsmouth to the sluggish Blackwater River to board the steamer *Fox*, which took them down the Blackwater and Chowan rivers as far as Edenton. Ongoing passengers then switched to the *Bravo* to cross Albemarle Sound to Plymouth and Jamesville, a short distance up the Roanoke River. The *Bravo* burned in 1835, but the *Fox*, formerly a Manhattan Island (New York) ferry, monopolized the Blackwater-Chowan route for the next fifteen years. In 1851 a new steamer, *Schultz*, took over the Blackwater-Chowan route to Edenton.

In November 1839 the noted agriculturist Edmund Ruffin of Petersburg (Virginia) vividly described a memorable journey down the narrow, winding Blackwater and broad Chowan rivers to Edenton, presumably on the *Fox*. On a moonlit night, he crossed Albemarle Sound from Edenton into one of several mouths of the Roanoke River to reach his destination, Plymouth. Ruffin pointed out, however, that this was mainly a passenger service and recommended the Dismal Swamp Canal for commercial traffic.[26]

The newly constructed Dismal Swamp Canal greatly benefited farming communities along the Roanoke River. However, this river was only navigable for about a hundred miles inland because of the "great falls" above Weldon. To overcome this (human) obstacle the Roanoke Canal was started in 1819 and completed in 1823. This navigational canal and its locks linked commercial traffic on the piedmont portion of this long river to the coastal plain and beyond. This project was a partial economic success, but it suffered from expensive repairs due to periodic flooding and from being superseded quite early by trains. From 1841, because of Weldon's strategic location, this town became one of the nation's first railroad hubs, with connections to Wilmington, Petersburg, and Portsmouth.

The Roanoke River continues to be especially important to the overall ecohistory of the Albemarle region, contributing well over half its freshwater input. Most of its watershed of 8,900 square miles lies in Virginia, but the Roanoke is the longest river discharging in North Carolina. At 442 miles long it is by far the largest of the four major rivers flowing into the Albemarle and Pamlico sounds and harbors an impressive diversity of fish (119 species at last count). Also flowing into the Albemarle Sound is the Chowan-Meherrin system, which is approximately 130 miles long. Further south the Pamlico Sound receives the Tar and Neuse rivers, both of which extend well inland (215 and 195 miles, respectively).[27]

The Roanoke River is representative of the ecological fate of rivers draining eastward in the Carolinas, Virginia, and Georgia. Foremost, virtually all these rivers were dammed within the past century, to the detriment of migratory fish on which coastal fisheries once depended. Taking the long view, however, the Roanoke and other piedmont rivers were partially dammed hundreds of years earlier, in prehistory by the native inhabitants. In the narrower streams and rivers well above the fall line they constructed stone weirs in the shape of a V or W. The points faced downstream, at which wicker baskets trapped fish. Some of these prehistoric overtures to modern dams are still observable today in various rivers in the piedmont.[28]

The Roanoke River consists of two parts, flowing through the coastal plain and piedmont sections, respectively. The lower and upper parts of the river are demarcated abruptly by the fall line, a geological feature common to the mid-Atlantic states where a steep rise in elevation creates cascades and falls. These are natural features that present no impediment to migrating fish. Historically, the navigable portion of the Roanoke River proceeded inland in the coastal plain for about a hundred miles, but at the "great falls" above Weldon the river rises 85 feet in nine miles. In 1823 the Roanoke Canal and locks were constructed to allow boat navigation well into the piedmont, but this project did not block the main river.

By 1900, however, a dam for water power did block the Roanoke River at Weldon, without providing fish passage, apart from "fish slides" constructed to harvest striped bass (*Morone saxatilis*). In 1955 Dominion Power (former Virginia Electric and Power Company) built a 3,000-foot-wide dam at the same locality to generate electricity, to control floods, and to create the huge Roanoke Rapids Lake for recreation. Today, seven major dams exist on the Roanoke River.

Migratory fish have been unable to proceed to ancient nursery grounds beyond Roanoke Rapids for over one hundred years. Spawning is now restricted to inferior sites below the dam, to the detriment of the entire Albemarle ecosystem. Among the species severely curtailed is the Atlantic sturgeon, once common throughout the Albemarle region. The demise of this majestic fish is symptomatic of the biologically impoverished Roanoke River above the dam at Roanoke Rapids. Everyone will benefit when the sturgeon, America's largest freshwater fish, and other migratory fish return to the upper Roanoke.

Another impact of the Roanoke Rapids dam is artificial control of flooding. It is now known that periodic inundations, interspersed with droughts, are natural phenomena.[29] In fact, they are essential to maintain viability of wetlands downstream, including the Roanoke River National Wildlife Refuge. For example, bald cypress, black gum, and other bottomland vegetation need natural fluctuations in water levels to thrive; stream beds need occasional flushing to discharge unnatural sedimentation and revitalize spawning beds; and migratory fish require the natural cycle of the river to trigger successful reproduction.

Growing public awareness of the environmental impact of dams on the

Roanoke River begs an irrepressible question, whether the human benefit outweighs the environmental cost. A way forward was recently demonstrated in another part of the Albemarle-Pamlico watershed. In 1997 North Carolina Power and Light Company tore down its dam at Quaker Neck near Goldsboro, opening 75 miles of the Neuse River and more than 900 miles of its tributaries to spawning striped bass, hickory shad, and the endangered shortnose sturgeon. According to news accounts, "this was the first large dam in the United States to be removed solely for environmental reasons."[30]

Chemical pollution has had a much more insidious effect on the biology of the Roanoke River–Albemarle watershed. In 1943 a claim that river pollution was killing commercial fish reached the courts, but the challenge failed. The case of *W. R. Hampton v. North Carolina Pulp Company* went to the North Carolina Supreme Court. Hampton was the owner of a fishery on the Roanoke River near Plymouth. Migratory fish on which he depended for a living had to pass the property of North Carolina Pulp Company and allegedly were killed by the "daily discharge into that stream of poisonous and deleterious matter at a point below plaintiff's fisheries."[31] Hampton made a claim for damages of $30,000. The case was heard by Judge Isaac M. Meekins, originally from the Alligator River (Gum Neck) and well familiar with commercial fishing. He denied the claim on the basis that any award would have been for fish never caught but belonging to the general public. This landmark judgment was cited by the Exxon Corporation in relation to the disastrous oil spill by the *Exxon Valdez* in Alaska in 1989.

In 1957 North Carolina Pulp Company was merged with Weyerhaeuser, "North Carolina's largest private landowner, managing over 550,000 acres primarily to produce timber." In 2003 the Environmental Protection Agency confirmed chemical contamination in the Roanoke River in the vicinity of Weyerhaeuser near Plymouth.[32]

In the decades prior to the Civil War the people of the Albemarle enjoyed a period of prosperity. As a flourishing agrarian society they built an ingenious network of transportation canals, including the notable Dismal Swamp Canal, which for the first time allowed the inhabitants direct access to commercial markets in Norfolk and beyond. Passenger and freight steamboats linked all parts of the Albemarle-Pamlico waterways to create a veritable "rural Venice." However, much of this prosperity was built on the institution of slavery, an issue that during the Civil War came to divide local allegiances here more than in the Deep South (see chapter 8). Ironically, these very waterways made the Albemarle region particularly vulnerable to the superior Union navy (see chapter 9).

8 *African American Experience*

The first Africans in the English colonies of America arrived in the Albemarle region in June 1586. Francis Drake had taken on about a hundred "Negroes" during his skirmishes with the Spanish at Santo Domingo and Cartagena. It is said he planned to use them to strengthen the incipient English colony on Roanoke Island. However, what actually happened to these people remains a mystery, and it is unclear if they were off-loaded when Drake arrived at the ill-fated colony on Roanoke Island.[1]

After a hiatus of nearly seventy years, Africans returned to the Albemarle region. They came overland from Virginia about 1653, when the first English settlers migrated to the north shore of Albemarle Sound (where "African Americans came with at least four of the ten English settlers who obtained land prior to 1663"). As early as 1670 "Negroes," and a few Indians, were being claimed as headrights, that is, land was given to the master for each person imported into the colony, whether white (indentured), Indian, or African. Between 1670 and 1697 a total of 311 "Negroes" were so listed.[2]

The majority of slaves here came from neighboring states rather than directly from Africa. An early exception occurred in the mid-1680s when a ship delivered about ninety slaves who had been purchased along coastal Nigeria (Calabar). These were divided between Virginia and North Carolina.

During much of this early period the condition of Africans in the Albemarle region was not necessarily that of slavery. However, by the early 1690s Africans were clearly inheritable property. This is confirmed

African American laborers working in a cucumber field in the Tar River valley near Greenville, North Carolina, 2 July 1960. Note the height of the corn, a staple crop grown in the Albemarle-Pamlico region by Native Americans since prehistory. (Daily Reflector Negative Collection [#741], Special Collections Department, J. Y. Joyner Library, East Carolina University, Greenville, NC)

in an early will in which a "Negro" was given to each of two sons (1691–92). Furthermore, slaves by that time had a market value: another will instructed that "6000 pounds of pork" be sold to buy a "Negro" (1694).[3]

The Anglican Church and other denominations here tolerated, if not condoned, the institution of slavery, with one important exception. The Quakers, who predominated in the Albemarle region during this period, held strong antislavery views. Over more than a century in this area they relentlessly agitated for the freedom of slaves. For example, they were known to purchase people of color, including Native Americans, in order to give them their freedom, but such ploys were thwarted when this practice was, in effect, made illegal. Later, Quakers played a major role in the Underground Railroad prior to the Civil War.[4]

Enslavement of the indigenous people by white settlers in the Albemarle-Pamlico region was surprisingly widespread, although not a common practice. The earliest record may be an early inventory that simply listed "one Indian woman slave" (1680). Especially noteworthy in this context was a will in Bath County that instructed that a man's "Indian slave be freed" (1704–5). Ironically, this was the eve of the bloody Tusca-rora War. Without warning on 22 September 1711, some 500 warriors killed about 150 colonists in the Bath area and took white women and children into bondage. The founder of New Bern, Baron Von Graffenried, who was himself captured about two weeks earlier, observed, "Oh what a sad sight to see . . . the poor [white] women and children captives. My heart almost broke."[5]

Local Indians had carried out a similar surprise attack on a neighboring tribe in this region more than 125 years earlier (1584), and that attack also involved the capture of (native) women and children. In point of fact, since prehistory capture of the enemy during native internecine skir-mishes was a recognized spoil of war that replenished the victor. Thus, slavery in its various forms existed in the Albemarle region for many hundreds, if not thousands, of years. Furthermore, at one time or other all three peoples—Native American, African American, and European American—experienced enslavement in the Albemarle region.

After the Tuscarora War, most Indians lived quietly as "free coloreds" in a few designated reservations, such as one at Lake Mattamuskeet (officially established by the Colonial Council in 1715) or in dispersed pockets ("Indian Towns") scattered throughout the region. However, en-slavement of Indians persisted at a low level for decades, being recorded as such in Chowan County (1718), Perquimans County (1723, 1733), Hyde County (1729), Bertie County (1735), Craven County (1746), and Northampton County (1747). In reality, "free coloreds," whether of na-tive or African descent, were at continual risk of enslavement throughout this region until the Civil War.[6]

By the end of the seventeenth century approximately 1,000 slaves lived in the Albemarle region, but slavery here developed slowly compared to Virginia. During the period from 1702 to 1746, an average of only 7.3 slaves were imported each year by ship into all of North Carolina, com-pared to 74 each year during the period from 1749 to 1775. It was begin-ning in the new federal period (1780s) that slavery became big business. For example, during the period from 1784 to 1790 an average of 166 slaves were imported each year into North Carolina. By this time slave labor was needed on a large scale to clear land, to dig drainage ditches and navigation canals, to build roads, and even to drain lakes.[7]

The most notable example of slavery on a large scale in this region was at the immense plantation (Somerset Place) established by Josiah Collins (1735–1819) at Lake Phelps. Conceived in 1784 as the "Lake Company," this was the most ambitious project of its kind in North Carolina. From the outset it was dedicated to modifying thousands of acres of land and water to commercial advantage, most notably digging a six-mile navigation canal to the Scuppernong River.

The entire project at Lake Phelps was dependent on large numbers of slaves. Such was its scale that most of these slaves came directly from Africa. Collins himself went to Boston, "in the latter part of 1784 or early 1785," to arrange a vessel to bring back slaves from Africa. In the following two years, account books and Port of Roanoke records document the importation of several large shiploads of slaves directly from Africa into the Albemarle Sound. The first was in June 1786, when the brig *Camden* brought 80 slaves from Africa, valued at £2,844. The second was in March 1787, again on the *Camden*, with 70 slaves, valued at £7,000. A few months later, in June 1787, the *Jennett* brought 81 slaves, also from Africa. In addition, in September 1786, the sloop *Polly* brought 66 "American" slaves from Charleston. It is presumed that most of these 297 slaves were destined for the Lake Company.[8]

Many of these first-generation African slaves remained at Somerset Place the rest of their lives. Dr. Edward Warren (1828–1893), later surgeon general of North Carolina during the Civil War, made the following firsthand observation from his youth:

> In my early days there were still living [at Somerset Place] several old men who were known as "Guinea negroes," being remnants of the cargoes of African slaves which certain enterprising New England traders had brought into those waters and sold at handsome prices to the neighboring planters. These antiquated darkeys spoke a sort of gibberish, which was a medley of their original dialect and the English language, and to me was perfectly unintelligible. They retained all of their original fetich superstitions and were as uncivilized, even in their old age, as when they roamed in youthful freedom among the jungles of the dark continent. . . . They had retained many of the ideas and traditions of their native land.[9]

According to the Lake Chapel register, "three of the Africans lived to the late 1840s," with "Old Aunt Sally, a Guinea Negro," and "Old Alfred, the last of the guinea Negroes," dying in the 1850s. Descendants of these enslaved people born in Africa still live in the area.[10]

Runaways, Swamp Refuges, and
Maritime Underground Railroad

The swamps of the Albemarle region became refuges for runaway slaves and other fugitives. As early as 1784 an English visitor observed that runaways occurred at that time both in the Great Dismal Swamp and further south in the Albemarle peninsula: "These places are in a great degree inaccessible, and harbour . . . run-away Negroes, who in these horrible swamps are perfectly safe, and with the greatest facility elude the most diligent search of their pursuers."[11]

In the years leading up to the Civil War, the Great Dismal Swamp in particular caught the imagination of writers, poets, and the general public. It was not only a place of mystery but had become increasingly known as a refuge for hundreds of runaway slaves. Some eventually made their way to freedom as part of the Underground Railroad, thanks to the busy docks at nearby Portsmouth and Norfolk.[12] To put this slave refuge into perspective, the only other notable colony of runaway slaves in the United States was in southern Florida, where they were known as the Black Seminoles.

Some runaways existed uneasily on the periphery of the swamps, where they were sometimes employed by local whites, no questions asked. The state government warned that "free men and women sheltering and employing runaway slaves posed a serious danger." In 1848 the General Assembly even enacted a law that required employers in "large sections of the Great Alligator and East Dismal Swamps" to register the names and descriptions of Negro workers and penalized them if they employed runaways.[13]

The "serious danger" was an implicit reference to a raw incident that had occurred some years earlier. In August 1821 small groups of runaways living in swamps in Craven, Carteret, and Onslow counties started an insurrection that spread alarm throughout much of northeastern North Carolina. In organized armed bands, these desperadoes were reportedly "committing degradations including arsons, daytime thefts, jail-breaks, attempted murder and murder." These charges may have been exaggerated, but the white people living near the swamps were genuinely afraid for their safety. In response, a sizeable militia was raised to put a military end to this insurrection before it spread throughout the region; as one account noted, "From mid-August until the end of September 1821, over six hundred militiamen wandered the swamps, pocosins and river banks of Eastern North Carolina in search of a highly mobile band of armed runaway slaves." One unfortunate incident near New Bern summarizes the general nervousness at that time. On the night of August 20 two different groups of armed whites (citizens and militia) inadvertently opened fire on each other, with serious casualties on both sides. Eventually, the insurgency was quelled.[14]

The growing anxiety of whites was exacerbated the following year by a gruesome, high-profile murder of the daughter of a prominent slave owner on the Albemarle peninsula (Tyrrell County). In December 1822 one or more slaves were involved in slitting the throat of Polly Wynne in her home. Three slaves were charged with conspiracy in this crime and hanged. These and other incidents resulted in ever stricter subjugation of the slaves. One such measure was a strengthened system of patrols that closely monitored the comings and goings of slaves on a local level. Penalties for infractions were levied not only against the slave but also against the slave owner. In spite of these patrols, slaves continued to run away from time to time, and descriptions of such individuals were placed in local newspapers by their irate masters.[15]

A few white families, at risk to themselves, actively helped slaves run away. For example, in the summer of 1852 in Tyrrell County a slave woman named Aggy ran away from her master's moderate-sized plantation of seventeen slaves. She took refuge in the home of a local white woman, whose family successfully hid Aggy for about a month. This woman, along with her son, were arrested and found guilty of illegally harboring a runaway. The son happened to be an experienced waterman and, one suspects, was part of the "maritime underground railroad" peculiar to this region. Runaways here had only one realistic means of achieving freedom, by sea from the nearby ports of Plymouth, Washington, and New Bern. Some made it across the Albemarle Sound to the Dismal Swamp en route to the Norfolk area. One slave, for example, escaped from Plymouth and hid in the Dismal Swamp for three months before reaching a schooner in Virginia. In 2004 the Great Dismal Swamp was recognized by the U.S. National Park Service as an important link in the "National Underground Railroad Network."[16]

African American Heritage of Albemarle Region

The Albemarle region, including it tributaries, the Nottoway and Meher-rin rivers, is linked to some of the most notable historical events in African American history. Not only did its Dismal Swamp become a cause célèbre in the nation's imagination, as a refuge for runaway slaves, but this region also produced two black leaders, Nat Turner and Dred Scott, whose antebellum influences shook the entire nation.

In 1831 events in the Nottoway-Meherrin region abruptly forced Southern whites to confront a new reality. In the wee hours of 21 August, a slave by the name of Nat Turner (1800–1831) led an indiscriminate slaughter of local whites. This was the first instance of open slave re-bellion, and it struck fear throughout the South. By the time the rampage was over, a total of fifty-five whites—men, women, and children—had been killed. Turner evaded capture at first by hiding in local swamps, and it was widely thought that he would seek refuge in the Dismal Swamp some thirty miles to the east. He was captured at the end of October and hanged twelve days later.

The Nat Turner rebellion opened a prolonged period of near paranoia that extended south to the Albemarle Sound, and well beyond. Ebenezer Pettigrew observed that "there has been considerable alarm in Craven [County] on account of a supposed conspiracy of the negroes, and from what I learn they had been talking about it. It is a terrible state of things especially for the female portion of the community, to be subjected to such horrible apprehensions."[17]

The two large plantations at Lake Phelps experienced mixed relation-ships with their many slaves during the antebellum period. At the smaller Bonarva plantation, Pettigrew sensed nothing sinister among his own slaves: "We have been much excited here within the last four days, by news of the insurrection in Southampton, Va. I don't believe the negroes here have entertained any such design." However, later, at the much larger Somerset Place, field slaves reportedly conspired to poison the overseer. "Sixteen of the plotters were taken to the Deep South by a slave trader and sold."[18]

In 1857 another slave from the Nottoway-Meherrin region profoundly altered the status of Africans throughout the United States. Dred Scott (c. 1795–1858) had moved from place to place with his master's job as sur-geon in the U.S. Army. His travels included the free state of Illinois and the free territory of Wisconsin, but his master later returned with Scott to the slave state of Missouri. In 1846 with the help of antislavery lawyers, Scott lodged an audacious court case that claimed that he was free because he had lived in a free state ("once free, always free"). This case slowly passed through a series of higher courts, achieving national attention by the time it reached the U.S. Supreme Court. In 1857 the Court ruled against him (7 to 2). They found that men of African descent, whether enslaved or free, are not citizens of the United States under the Constitution.[19]

In response to Nat Turner, Dred Scott, and other events, prominent abolitionists of the day symbolized the Great Dismal Swamp as a runaway-slave refuge. Henry Wadsworth Longfellow set the pace with a poignant poem entitled "A Slave in the Dismal Swamp" (1842), quoted here in part:

In dark fens of the Dismal Swamp
The hunted Negro lay;
He saw the fire of the midnight camp,
And heard at times a horse's tramp
And a bloodhound's distant bay.

Where hardly a human foot could pass,
Or a human heart would dare,
On the quaking turf of the green morass
He crouched in the rank and tangled grass,
Like a wild beast in his lair.[20]

Harriet Beecher Stowe, author of *Uncle Tom's Cabin* (1852), was motivated to write a second antislavery novel, *Dred: A Tale of the Great Dismal Swamp* (1856). This was the fictional story of an escaped slave family who found a sort of communion in these dismal swamps:

So completely had [Dred] come into sympathy and communion with nature, and with those forms of it which more particularly surrounded him in the swamps, that he moved about among them with as much ease as a lady treads her Turkey carpet. What would seem to us in recital to be incredible hardship, was to him but an ordinary condition of existence. To walk knee-deep in the spongy soil of the swamp, to force his way through thickets, to lie all night sinking in the porous soil, or to crouch, like the alligator, among reeds and rushes, were to him situations of as much comfort as well curtained beds and pillows are to us. . . .

"Have you been in the Swamps long?"

"Yes," said [Dred], "I have been a wild man—every man's hand against me, a companion of the dragons and the owls, this many a year. I have made my bed with the leviathan, among the reeds and the rushes. I have found the alligators and the snakes better neighbors than Christians. They let those alone that let them alone, but Christians will hunt for the precious life."[21]

Stowe's religious barb highlighted the fact that many Southerners at that time believed that slavery was justified in the Bible, an issue that had led to church schisms with their Northern counterparts, such as resulted in formation of the Southern Methodist Church (1844) and the Southern Baptist Convention (1845).[22]

Life at the Time of Slavery

In many ways slavery in the Albemarle region is best understood as a local phenomenon, an institution that was integral to the social fabric and local economy. Focusing on a specific community within a wider region yields a more human picture of life at the time of slavery. In this context, the farming community of the lower Alligator River (Gum Neck) is representative in that it lies at the geographical center of the entire Albemarle region. (Moreover, it is my homeland, with which I am intimately acquainted.)

Gum Neck was the largest antebellum township on the Alligator River, with a population of approximately one thousand people, one quarter of whom were slaves (1860). The numerous farmsteads in this sprawling community benefited from having deep black, exceptionally fertile soil. Accordingly, the farms grew in size and productivity, reaching a peak of prosperity about 1830 to 1850. The largest farms operated on a plantation style, in that they were dependent on slaves who lived in adjacent slave quarters. Most of these "plantations" were relatively small, not at all comparable to the immense Somerset Place on Lake Phelps at the other end of Tyrrell County.

The majority of slaves in this community were owned by only a handful of large landowners (see table 3), among them local and state legislators, judges, magistrates, and sheriffs. Collectively, their influence both locally and regionally was greatly disproportionate to their numbers. The most notable slave owner in Gum Neck was Colonel Charles McCleese, erstwhile state senator. In the 1840s his slaves dug a major transportation canal that connected his inland plantation directly to the Alligator River. The McCleese Canal still runs through the heart of this community.

By the 1850s and 1860s some smaller farmers could also afford a few slaves, but most whites in Gum Neck did not own slaves at all, either because they were too poor or on principle. Nonetheless, whether they owned slaves or not, most white people in this community compliantly accepted slavery in their midst.

A minority of whites opposed slavery on principle, but no instance of abetting runaways has emerged in this particular community. However, at least one family moved away to Illinois, a free state, where they expressed strong antislavery views. Furthermore, when the Civil War broke out one-third of soldiers from Gum Neck fought for the Union, a very rough indication of sympathies (coupled perhaps with realism or opportunism).

This community had a system of slave patrols that closely monitored minor infractions on the part of local slaves. The patrollers consisted of two or three young men chosen from slaveholding families within the same community. If a slave committed a serious infraction, he or she came under jurisdiction of the county sheriff and might appear in court. For example, in 1860 one slave man killed another belonging to a dif-

TABLE 3. Major landowners and their slave holdings along the Alligator River (Gum Neck) in 1860

PLANTATION OWNER	SLAVES	SLAVE HOUSES
McCleese, Colonel C.	47	13
Basnight, B. S.	28	5
Spruill, B. A.	23	6
Swain, T.	21	3
Cooper, D.	14	4
Sykes, J.	10	2
Sykes, B. F.	10	2
Liverman family	10	—
Patrick, F.	8	1

ferent owner. His fate was determined at the county court house by a jury of twelve local white men. In this case they found him not guilty of first degree murder (a hangable offense) but did find him guilty of manslaughter. His punishment was thirty-nine lashes at the public whipping post, following which he was sold out of state "so that he may return no more."[23]

The Alligator River communities experienced significant demographic changes in the decade between 1850 and 1860 (see table 4). Most interesting was a decline in the number of slave owners and also in the number of slaves. In Gum Neck itself the number of slave owners had declined almost by 50 percent, and the number of slaves had declined by over 20 percent.

Although these statistics probably indicate that slavery was on the decline here, part of this picture could be explained otherwise. Coinciding with a general decline in population, some of the slave owners had simply moved away. For example, during this period the son-in-law of the aforementioned Colonel McCleese had moved further inland with his family and his ten slaves (valued at $10,800). As the war approached another

TABLE 4. Population changes between 1850 and 1860 along the Alligator River, Albemarle Peninsula

	1850	1860
Tyrrell County		
Whites (slave owners)	3,344 (206)	3,188 (193)
Slaves	1,699	1,596
Free coloreds	105	127
Total	5,148	4,911
Gum Neck Township		
Whites (slave owners)	902 (41)	722 (22)
Slaves	316	248
Free coloreds	22	19
Total	1,240	989

farmer remained in Gum Neck but sent his slaves to more secure territory behind Confederate lines.[24]

When the Civil War broke out, local slaves experienced a period of uncertainty and in some cases serious upheaval. This was exacerbated by the fact that Confederate and Union forces traded control of the area several times during the conflict. The following excerpts capture the mood of that time:

> In early March [1862], six companies of the Sixth New Hampshire were sent to Columbia in search of a Confederate regiment said to be recruiting in the area. No Confederates were found, but a rumor that the local militia was to be called out was used by the New Englanders as reason enough to plunder the town. To the delight of the Negroes, the whipping post was torn down. Then the soldiers broke open the jail, clerk's office, and the dwelling houses of such as were gone from home.

> The Yankees behaved very badly at Columbia. The officers went to the Negro huts and openly invited Negro women to take their children on board their boats. They took off fifty Negro men with them.[25]

These refugees were taken to the Freedmen's Colony on Roanoke Island, but according to a Confederate source,

> the Negroes who have fled to them at Roanoke Island are greatly dissatisfied. Ten days ago two were shot attempting to escape, and later eighteen had gotten a boat and were making off when they fired a shell into it and killed sixteen. The others continued their flight and took the sixteen dead to Hyde County.[26]

After the war was finally over, most former slaves remained in, or in a few instances returned to, their home community and took the surnames of their previous masters. Forbidden schooling and even marriage by law, these destitute people were illiterate and had little family structure, no land of their own, and no financial infrastructure.

At this time the local factor played a critical role. More than a few whites in this community were supportive of these freed men and women, whom they had known all their lives. They offered food and laboring jobs and even sold them parcels of land. One respected freed woman, Nellie Liverman, served for many years as a midwife for most of the white women in her neighborhood, and she even attended the birth of my grandmother in 1896.

A branch of the Freedman's Bank (1865–74) was set up in New Bern and helped a scattering of former slaves throughout the Albemarle peninsula. Many of these bank records have survived to tell the personal stories of the instability of their previous lives as slaves. In an extreme example, a fifty-year-old woman from a neighboring county documented that her father, mother, two brothers, sister, husband, and two children were "sold" or "carried away" individually over a period of thirty years before the war. However, there is no evidence of similar degradations among the 250 slaves in Gum Neck.[27]

In addition to these African slaves, before the war there was another distinct group of "colored people" in Gum Neck. It consisted of several families of "free coloreds," thought by some scholars to be remnants of the original local Native Americans. In any case the two groups had little to do with each other before the war and for nearly a generation thereafter. In due course, however, they increasingly intermarried and slowly merged.

The most enduring legacy of this period concerns the churches. Prior to the war, slaves in Gum Neck attended the same church as white people, in the upstairs gallery of the Free Union Chapel (the only church in the community at that time). After the war, the former slaves were quick to establish a church of their own, Mount Pleasant Missionary Baptist Church (1866), whose congregation is still very active. Interestingly, today the five local churches in this community have remained voluntarily segregated, as is the case throughout most of the South.

As a final footnote to the war, the last Civil War veteran to die in Gum Neck was a ninety-one-year-old black man. David Freeman (1842–1934) had fought for the 35th U.S. Colored Infantry on the Union side. Reportedly, "Uncle Dave" took his own surname, literally meaning "free man."

Reconstruction, Segregation, and Civil Rights

In the years of Reconstruction immediately following the Civil War, Gum Neck produced, improbably, a state governor with ties to the Ku Klux Klan. Thomas Jordan Jarvis (1836–1915), who became governor in 1879 (and later U.S. senator), was a Confederate veteran who had lost an arm in the conflict. After the war he came to Gum Neck, where he briefly ran a general store. Upon obtaining a license to practice law, he became a successful politician, but his reported affiliation with the Ku Klux Klan tainted his administration.[28]

The Ku Klux Klan was active in this region at two other periods: in the 1920s and, again, in the 1960s. In the 1920s a group of outspokenly conservative men held meetings in a local lodge hall in Gum Neck. Although it was ostensibly a secret society, most of the members were identifiable, for example, when they appeared at a local funeral dressed in their white sheets and hoods. This KKK chapter came into ridicule with local young people and gradually died out, though the Klan had a resurrection during the civil rights conflict of the 1960s.

By the end of the nineteenth century traditional politicians regained control of state government, and the legislature reversed certain key policies. For example, it restricted voter eligibility. In 1902 a new electoral roll was implemented such that it consisted of men who could claim descent from an individual voter registered in 1867, effectively excluding nonwhites. Segregation of the races was another institutionalized policy with far-reaching consequences in this region.

This political success coincided with the revival of a romanticized Confederacy. At the outbreak of the Civil War there was strong Union support here, but by the turn of the century this support had virtually disappeared. In August 1902, among much fanfare and widespread support, an imposing monument was dedicated to the sacrifices of local Confederate soldiers. This structure still stands proudly at the Tyrrell County courthouse in Columbia, to most residents a nostalgic tribute to a bygone era. Ironically, the fine print reads, "In appreciation of our faithful slaves."

The Great War had a disproportionate impact on the young black men of the Gum Neck community. They served in the military as equals with whites—equal perhaps, but still segregated. Nonetheless, upon returning home, they brought distinction and, as with local whites, a view of a wider world. That black men viewed their contributions, in both world wars, with immense pride can be seen today in numerous military inscriptions on local headstones.[29]

Following World War II, racial discrimination became an increasingly contentious issue throughout the Albemarle region. In 1947 a "mob" of more than two hundred white men of Tyrrell County gave a small group of mainly white outsiders, who had been working and living with local blacks, twenty-four hours to leave town. They left the next afternoon, at

Ku Klux Klan burning a cross in Greenville, North Carolina, 18 October 1965, at the peak of civil rights strife in the Albemarle-Pamlico region. (Daily Reflector Negative Collection [#741], Special Collections Department, J. Y. Joyner Library, East Carolina University, Greenville, NC)

which time the local police chief reportedly said, "It's a good thing the students left, there might have been violence."[30]

The Civil Rights Act of 1964 led to the integration of schools piecemeal throughout the South. When those in Norfolk finally integrated, some families sent their children to live with relatives in Gum Neck, where they attended the still-segregated school in Columbia. The overwhelming majority of whites here were adamant that integration should not be enforced, especially so quickly. Profound social change was being thrust on them faster than many whites could handle.

Racial tension was running high, and local recruitment into the Ku Klux Klan surged. Matters came to a head in August and September 1965 at the courthouse in Plymouth. Initially the problem was voter registration, not school integration. The *New York Times* reported that Washington County had just been singled out as "one of 26 counties covered by the Voting Rights Act passed by Congress last month. Out of a county-wide population of 8,000 whites and 8,500 Negroes, 3,600 whites and 800 Negroes are registered voters."[31]

Martin Luther King's Southern Christian Leadership Conference organized protest demonstrations in Plymouth in early August, and in response, many KKK recruits were sent to the area. According to the *New York Times*, "Following a Klan rally, civil rights workers were attacked in the downtown business district. Twenty-seven Negroes and white supporters were beaten."[32] Then followed an incident some days thereafter in which one Klan member was shot and another stabbed, neither fatally. Inevitably, this violence made national headlines.

Peaceful but remarkable protests were later staged at Swan Quarter, county seat of neighboring Hyde County. In one incident protestors showed up clutching squawking chickens for publicity, with considerable success. The police simply put all the protestors in jail, along with their chickens! The *Washington Post* brought the nation's attention to this incident with the headline, "25 Students, Squawking Chickens Jailed in North Carolina During Protests."[33]

Locally, civil rights representatives in the 1960s spoke occasionally in Gum Neck, on Friday evenings at the African American church. The presence of unprecedented numbers of cars parked outside the church at these times contributed to white consternation. Furthermore, about this time black and white children of this community were forced to integrate and were bused together the fifteen miles to Columbia.

In the end, however, agitation was very limited in this old community, where everyone, whites and blacks alike, had known one another literally for generations. Racial relations were not perfect, but sensible people on both sides prevailed and a sense of neighborliness returned. Interestingly, in the 2008 presidential election 49 percent of the votes in Tyrrell County went for the African American candidate, Barack Obama, signifying significant white support.

$\mathscr{9}$ *Armed Conflict*

A Recurring Theme

In these days when American wars are fought in some vague place half-way around the world, we need to be reminded that for most of human history armed conflicts took place near home. The Albemarle region is no exception. In fact, wars have been a recurring theme in the long history of this region. Disparate Indian tribes battled intermittently among themselves throughout prehistory until confronted by a common enemy, invaders from Europe. Then, various colonial powers competed for local dominance, settlers fought for independence, and bloodiest of all, Americans fought among themselves on the same home territory.

The people and conflicts changed over the 450 years of recorded history, but local geography repeatedly imposed constraints on combatants. Specifically, the extraordinary waterways, swamps, and barrier islands of the Albemarle region have dictated again and again the nature and outcome of armed conflict in this region.

Depending on circumstances, the Albemarle region has demonstrated the fine line between impenetrable defense and inevitable defeat. It is no accident that the region that shielded America from Spanish takeover in the early colonial period was the same region that resulted in the first significant Union victory in the Civil War. Similarly, Albemarle waterways that were so effective in getting supplies to naval facilities at Norfolk in 1776 and 1812 became, in the form of the Albemarle and Chesapeake Canal, a "fifth column" leading directly into Norfolk in the Civil

War. (In this context, modern military strategists should take note of our vulnerability from intracoastal waterways generally.)

In many cases the outcome was determined not so much by superior arms but by local resources, primarily access to meat and grain by an army or navy. British ships laying siege offshore crumbled when vital supplies were depleted on board. Conversely, getting clandestine supplies of crops and livestock to home-grown rebels prolonged the conflict here during the Civil War. Counterattempts by Union forces to feed themselves and to stop food from getting to the enemy increased the suffering of the local civilian population.

Finally, military presence in this region has had unintended environmental consequences, sometimes irreversible. By far the most profound has been construction of war canals, which had little regard for storm surges, salt entry, and invasive species into pristine freshwater wetlands (see chapter 10). More recently, local bombing ranges have repeatedly ignited forest fires in spite of generous use of herbicides. Low-flying aircraft produce ear-splitting noise pollution and result in a remarkable number of crashes in local swamps and waterways. A recent new threat, discussed in chapter 12, is a jet training base in the midst of one of the nation's most important sites for overwintering waterfowl. How can the United States defend itself abroad by destroying its most precious assets at home?

Brief History of Albemarle Wars

An understanding of prehistoric conflicts between Native Americans vying for supremacy of the Albemarle region suffers from paucity of direct archaeological evidence of weapons and strategy. Recently, however, arrowheads were found in the skull and rib cage, respectively, of two individuals in undated graves in the South River section of Carteret County. In the 1580s the colonists at Roanoke Island gave the first historical insight into the use of surprise tactics against neighboring tribes.[1]

The strategic importance of the Albemarle region was recognized in the Age of Exploration, when the Spanish dominated the New World. In the 1580s the Elizabethans chose Roanoke Island not only as a colonial foothold but also as an English base of operation for espionage, logistics, and naval stores. Lying behind a barrier island, Roanoke Island was hidden from Spanish privateers who were continually skirting the coast. Furthermore, it was accessible only via a few inlets that were notoriously difficult to negotiate. After a successful campaign against the Spanish in the Caribbean and Florida, Francis Drake sought refuge here before returning to England, in time to ensure defeat of the Spanish Armada.

When settlers came in numbers to the Albemarle region, many indigenous inhabitants became hostile, culminating in the bloody Tuscarora Wars (1711–15). As natives, they knew the local terrain intimately and used the swamps to full advantage against the newcomers. They were particularly adept at disappearing into pocosins by canoe after surprise attacks. For example, in April 1713 the Mattamuskeet Indians

> being in number about 50 had fallen on the inhabitants of Alligator River and . . . had killed and taken 16 or 20 of the inhabitants. . . . [This swamp] is about 100 miles in length and of considerable breadth, all in a manner lakes, quagmires, and cane swamps, and is, I believe, one of the greatest deserts in the world, where it is almost impossible for white men to follow them. . . . [The colonial authorities sent troops] but fear it may be to no purpose, they having the advantage of such dismal swamps to fly into.[2]

About this same time this region was known throughout the American colonies as a haven for pirates and privateers. The numerous shallow inlets and coves of the Albemarle and Pamlico sounds served their nefarious purposes well. Such lawlessness reached a peak at the beginning of the eighteenth century.

The most notorious pirate active in these waters was Edward Teach, better known as Blackbeard, whose flagship was the *Queen Anne's Revenge,* a former French slave vessel. He brazenly attacked shipping throughout the Caribbean and along the Carolina coast. Blackbeard was adroit at navigating in the shallow waters of the North Carolina sounds and frustrated British warships in pursuit. In June 1718 Blackbeard was pardoned by colonial governor Charles Eden, for reasons that are still contentious. After residing briefly in Bath on the Pamlico River, Blackbeard returned to piracy. However, he was finally defeated near Ocracoke on the Pamlico Sound and was beheaded on 22 November 1718. The elimination of Blackbeard in 1718 "was also virtually the end of piracy in America."[3]

Elimination of piracy roughly coincided with establishment in the Albemarle-Pamlico region of a system of Royal Customs, with assigned

British naval officers, specifically at the ports of Roanoke (Edenton), Currituck, Bath, and Beaufort. From the beginning of the federal period the U.S. Coast Guard has continued a presence in these same shadowy waters. In this context, the "revenuers" at the Coast Guard facility at Elizabeth City were particularly active in the 1930s along the Alligator River, source of illicit East Lake Whiskey.

During the Revolutionary War (1776), and again in the War of 1812, the Albemarle region played a critical role in the national effort. In both conflicts the British maintained effective blockades of Norfolk and other ports of the Chesapeake Bay. However, "the British navy discovered it was virtually impossible to maintain a siege on this dangerous coast [Outer Banks], far from bases of supplies." The result was that vital American shipping was able to slip through the inlet at Ocracoke and proceed uninterrupted to the Albemarle Sound, from which provisions could be taken overland to Norfolk and Portsmouth. Conversely, the Dismal Swamp Canal was motivated in part "by the desire to furnish Norfolk with a backdoor escape route."[4]

This strategic underbelly in support of Norfolk was firmly blocked early in the Civil War by the Union navy, which used the waterways of the sounds and the new Albemarle and Chesapeake Canal against the Confederates. The need for safe passage of shipping to the naval conglomerate at Norfolk was again exposed during World War I when American ships were torpedoed off the Outer Banks by German U-boats. This led, in the 1920s and 1930s, to construction of the Alligator-Pungo canal, last link in the nation's inland waterway system and discussed in detail in the next chapter.

Vulnerability to Salt Shortages

Throughout the colonial and antebellum periods salt was the main method of preserving meat and fish. However, there were virtually no natural sources of salt available to farmers and fishermen in the Albemarle region, or indeed anywhere in North Carolina, and large quantities had to be imported from abroad. The majority of this all-important commodity came from the West Indies, most notably Tortuga and the Turks and Caicos Islands, which had exported salt from its natural *salinas* since the 1680s.[5]

Salt was not always used as a preservative in the Albemarle-Pamlico region. For hundreds, if not thousands, of years the native people here preserved fish and deer meat by a drying process. Typically the item was positioned individually on slats or sticks near an open fire, benefiting also from the preservative properties of smoke. Such fish or meat was stored for later consumption and possible use for trade with tribes living farther inland.[6]

The earliest account of salt being used as a preservative in the Albemarle region was in September 1665. In a letter of that date John Colleton, Lord Proprietor, debated sending a ship to Collington Island, at the eastern extremity of the Albemarle Sound, with "salt to fetch thence 30 tones of hoggs flesh" (wild pigs were found on the island). The salted pork was to be sent to Barbados, the sale from which would purchase slaves and servants to build a plantation on Collington Island. Fifty years later (1711) salt was being imported from Tortuga into Graffenried's new colony at New Bern at the mouth of the Neuse River. A half century later still (1768) a total of 6,660 bushels of salt were imported that year into the port of Beaufort, Carteret County.[7]

Throughout the colonial period salt was indispensable for preserving fish and meat, but the American colonies as a whole were vulnerable in that they had grossly inadequate sources of their own. During the prolonged war for American independence the British cut off the colonies' normal supply of salt from the West Indies, and colonists in North Carolina suffered accordingly. Alarmist predictions were raised: "Without salt the colonists could not survive. . . . If there is no salt it will require but little force to subdue and starve the Province." By September 1777 Carteret County was already desperate for salt because of British incursions:

We shan't have a single vessel . . . and will prevent our getting any further supply of salt or any thing else from the West Indies. . . . There was a vessel *Gibbins* came last week into Beaufort from Providence, with a load of salt, and I have just heard there is 2 or 3 vessels more, came in there also, with salt. . . . The enemy . . . have already done considerable damage at [Ocracoke], by taking away a brig, and running ashore a sloop, loaded with salt . . . but she had on board 1200 bushels of salt. . . . The people at the inlet were concerned about the salt so they extinguished the fire and saved the salt. But the vessel was ruined.[8]

In 1787–88 severe shortages of salt curtailed river herring fishing on the Chowan River to the extent that local merchants and fisheries pleaded with wholesale salt merchants at the key port towns. One fishery offered 50 barrels of herring for 400 bushels of "Turks Island salt if the salt can be delivered at his ware house pretty soon." Another anticipated catching 1,000 barrels of river herring to be delivered during the six-week period from 1 April to 15 May, the price of the fish pegged at 16s. 6d. per barrel (after cost of salt is deducted). To fulfill this order he needed 400 bushels of fine salt and 300 bushels of Turks Island salt, at 3s. per bushel. Similarly, a merchant on the nearby Meherrin River urgently needed 1,000 bushels of salt but observed, "I find that West India goods have got verry scarce . . . for there was never so great a scercity since my liveing here—salt in particular."[9]

The scarcity of salt at this time inflated the price of corn, which provides an insight into the local economy of the 1780s. As one account noted, "The amazing scarcity of salt has obliged people to feed their hogs much longer than they intended, & consequently there will not be so great a quantity of corn at our market as was expected . . . so that I think it would be as well to buy now as much as you think we shall have occasion for in the course of the season." (This economic dynamic is similar to the inflated price of corn with recent biofuel production).[10]

With war against Britain increasingly likely, efforts were made to encourage local production of salt in North Carolina. Thus, in 1775 the Third Provincial Congress passed a bill offering "a bounty of 750 pounds to any person who shall erect and build proper works for manufacturing common salt on the seashore." Robert Williams of Carteret County had a head start. According to some sources, he was "familiar with the process of obtaining salt from seawater, having made a study of the process used in France, Portugal and Spain. . . . Shortly after arrival in the County from England in 1763 he constructed a salt works of ten acres of land" near Beaufort. Using sun evaporation on eighteen salt beds in the salt marsh, he proposed producing between 10 and 25 bushels a day in hot, dry weather, but his project failed. More successful was Richard Blackledge from Fork of the Tar River (today's town of Washington), who used a boiling method plus evaporation, on Core Sound. His process, however, required quantities of local wood for boiling purposes.[11]

The military significance of salt was also a strategic factor ninety years later in the Civil War. General William T. Sherman himself observed, "Salt is eminently contraband, because of its use in curing meat, without which armies cannot be subsisted." Early in the war the rebel state of

North Carolina appointed a "salt commissioner." His early focus was at Currituck Sound near Corolla (Whale Head). Here, until pushed out by federal forces, boiling pans, fueled with quantities of wood from trees two miles away, produced roughly 200 bushels of salt a day.[12]

Key Military Targets: Meat and Grain

During actual warfare the need for fresh provisions, especially meat, was a theme often repeated in the military history of the Albemarle region. The pirate Blackbeard's flagship *Queen Anne's Revenge* sank in these waters in 1718 and was rediscovered in 1996. Among the two thousand recovered artifacts were animal bones, mostly from immature pigs, obviously on board as a source of fresh meat for his men.

In the seventeenth and eighteenth centuries hostile Spanish, French, and British ships periodically approached the treacherous Outer Banks in search of fresh meat. In a war with Spain in 1741–42 and again in 1747–48 the Spanish took cattle and hogs from Ocracoke Island. One account noted that thirty years later, during the War for American Independence, "the British navy [were] far from bases of supplies. . . . All the sea banks [were] covered with cattle, sheep and hogs," and "if the armed vessels and tenders are prevented from getting supplies of fresh provisions from this sea coast, it will be impossible for the war to be of long continuance in this Province." In 1778 and 1779 the British carried out several forays onto Currituck and Hatteras, respectively, to get cattle and other livestock. Similarly, in the War of 1812, a British force invaded Ocracoke and Portsmouth and occupied these islands from 12 to 16 July 1813, taking with them cattle and sheep.[13]

In the Civil War, the adage "an army travels on its stomach" was acutely true for General Robert E. Lee, whose army had essentially depleted food supplies in Virginia after two years of fighting. Thereafter, the corn, wheat, and pork of the Albemarle watershed became vitally important to General Lee's war effort. So important were these foodstuffs that Governor Vance of North Carolina issued the following warning to the Confederate secretary of state: "The Roanoke, the Tar, and the Neuse [rivers], embracing the richest corn growing regions of the state, upon which the army of Genl Lee has been subsisting for months" are inadequately protected.[14]

Richer still was the lush farmland of the Albemarle peninsula, which played a significant role in sustaining both sides during the Civil War. The plantations around Lake Mattamuskeet and Lake Phelps, as well the agrarian townships along the Alligator River, were particularly important. According to contemporary observers, "In the neighborhood of Mattamuskeet . . . there is a large quantity of corn, upwards of one hundred thousand barrels, and the people refuse to sell it or to trade in any way with Union men and are very bitter Secessionists." A Union raid plundered this area, confiscating "17 horses, 13 buggies, 1 yoke oxen, 1 schooner (*Snow Squall*), 8 cart-loads of cotton, about 1500 pounds of bacon, about 400 bushels of corn, and approximately 40 slaves who followed the troops to the boat landing."[15]

At Lake Phelps, Collins's Somerset Place and Pettigrew's Bonarva were plundered by Union forces on several occasions. In July 1862 a schooner approached these plantations via the Scuppernong River, confiscating 1,080 bushels of corn, 238 bushes of wheat, and 12 horses. Similarly, in January 1864 a land expedition from Plymouth seized "100 head of sheep and poultry in proportion."[16]

Civil War: Synopsis of Albemarle Campaign

In the Civil War the Albemarle-Pamlico region was particularly vulnerable to the superior Union navy, which dominated its sounds, rivers, and canals early in the war. This was probably not the first time that superiority on the water conquered these wetlands. The Carolina Algonquin, who occupied this region from the north some hundreds of years earlier, were master watermen with superior dugout canoes.

In 1861 these very waterways, which gave this region prosperity and protection in the past, were now used against them. Where once water highways led to lucrative agricultural markets in Norfolk, Baltimore, and New York, they now brought Union gunboats, troops, and occupation. For the first time in recorded history the people of the Albemarle region were cut off from their lifeblood, the water highway itself.

The military battles and occupations of coastal towns in this region have been thoroughly described in several excellent publications on this subject.[17] At one level it is a story of naval battles on the Albemarle and Pamlico sounds. Union forces captured Fort Hatteras in August 1861, followed by Roanoke Island and Elizabeth City in February 1862, New Bern in March 1862, and Plymouth in November 1862. The Union navy now controlled the Albemarle Sound, with local headquarters at Roanoke Island (serving as such for the first time since 1585), as well as the Pamlico Sound, with headquarters at New Bern. This Albemarle-Pamlico campaign under General Ambrose Burnside was the first major victory for the Union, after it had suffered ignominious defeats in Virginia at the outset of the war.

For the most part Union forces occupied these coastal towns for the duration of the war. The notable exception was in April 1864, when the Union suffered a serious setback. The Confederates overwhelmed Plymouth at the west end of the Albemarle Sound, aided by a secret weapon, the ironclad CSS *Albemarle*. This ram had been built clandestinely a safe distance up the Roanoke River. (For the same physiographical reasons, this swampy region at the lower stretches of the Roanoke River had also been a military frontier in the 1580s, an interface between the Carolina Algonquins to the east and a hostile tribe to the west, presumably the Iroquois-speaking Tuscarora who were there two centuries later.)

The battle of Plymouth in 1864 has been described as "the second largest battle ever fought in North Carolina, and the last major Confederate victory in the South."[18] The recapture of Plymouth by the rebels resulted in a chaotic "massacre," including of some African Americans and local Union sympathizers ("buffaloes"). The following months were a period of severe recriminations, as far east as the Alligator River, against individuals who had assisted the Union when it was in occupation. Finally, in October 1864 the Union regained control of Plymouth for the last time when the *Albemarle* was sunk by Union forces.

Apart from the brief, but bloody, reversal at Plymouth, the waters and coastal towns of the Albemarle-Pamlico region were more or less under Union control from 1862. However, Confederate forces controlled much of the farmland and pocosins outside these enclaves. Throughout the war, local militias maneuvered clandestinely through this area, which they knew intimately (markedly reminiscent of the Native Americans against the British during the early colonial period). In addition to attacking Union assets, they also hit isolated farmsteads in search of food and, most ominously, enforced conscripts to the Confederate cause.

The conflict in the Albemarle peninsula degenerated locally into a struggle for grain and livestock. As hostilities dragged on, competing militias on both sides desperately needed these foodstuffs for bare sustenance. Both sides would, if necessary, destroy grain, mills, warehouses, and private boats rather than let the enemy benefit. For this reason, locals were denied the means to fish or gain access to salt needed for food preservation. As a consequence some of the civil population became badly malnourished, especially in the latter months of the war.

The Civil War greatly affected the ordinary people of the Albemarle peninsula. While their sons were away fighting (on both sides of the conflict), these people tried to live "normal" lives but were caught in the interface of two bitter struggles: control of the water highways (communications) and dominance of the land (food). It was a raw time, evoking social ills and personal tragedies that still have an emotive aftertaste.

An account of the wartime deprivations of one community on the Alligator River (Gum Neck) has been published recently elsewhere.[19]

10 *Intracoastal Waterways*

War Canals

The Outer Banks is called the "Graveyard of the Atlantic" for good reason. At no other point along either coast of America has shipping been so hazardous literally for centuries, from shoals, storms, pirates, and other hostile attack. Little-known events during World War I reexposed this vulnerability in a modern world. Few people are aware, for example, that between 5 June and 17 August 1918 a total of ten ships were sunk by German submarines off the Outer Banks.[1]

The need for a more secure inland waterway system was conceived in the nineteenth century, and work toward such an ambitious project had been advancing slowly for decades. As early as 1880 the U.S. Army Corps of Engineers presented plans to the U.S. Congress for an intracoastal waterway from Norfolk through the Dismal Swamp to the Albemarle Sound and then south.[2]

In 1916, prompted by the probable entry of the United States into the European war, the *Washington Post* carried an article entitled "A War Coast Canal from Boston to Mexico":

> One of the most important plans for preparedness in event of war now under consideration by the United States government is the creation, or rather the linking together, of a strategic waterway extending all the way from Boston to Texas just inside our coast line. The War and Navy departments are both most anxious to see the project carried out. To complete this coast canal, already begun, would not take more than five years. All

the plans are made: It only remains for Congress to provide the money. Its cost will be around $200,000,000.

Already the future of the Albemarle peninsula was being determined, as the article continued:

> From the head of Chesapeake Bay to Norfolk is clear sailing. For some years past the army engineers have been opening the water passage from Norfolk to Beaufort, by digging short canals to connect the rivers and sounds along the route. . . . [Even in times of peace shipping] would thus avoid the perilous trip around Cape Hatteras and Cape Lookout, the dangers of which, with incidental wrecks, add much to freight rates."[3]

The earliest inland waterway link in the Albemarle-Pamlico region was completed in 1911. Known at the time as the Boston-Beaufort Inland Waterway Canal, it linked the Neuse River (Adams Creek) with Newport River (Core Creek). World War I interrupted further plans, but immediately after the war the federal government refocused on the need for a safe passage between Norfolk and Beaufort, bypassing the Outer Banks. As originally conceived, the proposed waterway route from Norfolk was via the Dismal Swamp Canal to Albemarle Sound to Alligator River to Lake Mattamuskeet to Rose Bay (a local route first proposed in 1833). Instead, the Corps of Engineers decided on a different route, via the (widened) Albemarle and Chesapeake Canal to Albemarle Sound to Alligator River. From there they proposed an ambitious two-hundred-foot-wide canal to the headwaters of the Pungo River, thereby cutting an eighteen-mile swathe through the pristine swampland of the Albemarle peninsula.

After the war, in 1919, Congress appropriated $500,000 to cut the proposed Alligator-Pungo canal. Constructing the canal through miles of swamp, however, was technically and legally challenging for the Corps of Engineers. At the outset draftsmen had to determine its exact routing, and then lawyers had to acquire land on behalf of the federal government, typically through unwelcome purchases invoking eminent domain at one dollar per acre. Surveyors laboriously marked the rights of way so that woodsmen could clear a path through ancient swamps. These time-consuming preparatory steps had to be well advanced before digging could start.[4]

Steam dredge boat at official opening of the Intracoastal Waterway linking Neuse River (Adams Creek) to Newport River (Core Creek) on 6 January 1911. (Frank C. Salisbury Collection [#99], Special Collections Department, J. Y. Joyner Library, East Carolina University, Greenville, NC)

Alligator-Pungo Canal:
Last Link of the Nation's Intracoastal Waterway

Dredging commenced late in 1922 at Winn's Bay on the Alligator River. For this purpose the Corps of Engineers brought the survey boat *Pungo* and the coal-fired dredge *Currituck* from Norfolk. These vessels moored for long periods on the main river at Gum Neck, the largest community on the lower Alligator River. As administrative base for such a long-term operation Gum Neck enjoyed a boost to its stagnant local economy. This unprecedented project offered much-needed work for casual laborers (including my grandfather) for a period of several years. One local man in a more senior position earned $60 to $65 per month, allowing him to purchase one of the first motorcars here. Furthermore, the half-dozen general stores in the community kept the workmen and vessels in fresh supplies. Some of the engineers, surveyors, dredgers, and other skilled young men from outside met and married girls from this community, most of whom moved away after the canal was completed.[5]

On 5 September 1928 the *New York Times* announced that a national

The Alligator-Pungo Intracoastal Waterway Canal connects the Alligator River with the Pungo River in the Albemarle peninsula. This canal may be a significant conduit for salt from the Pamlico Sound during storm surges. The view faces east from the top of the new single-span "hurricane evacuation" bridge on North Carolina 94 near Fairfield. In the foreground is the opened swing bridge of 1935, shortly before it was dismantled in March 2001. In the background in front of the forest of pond pines (*Pinus serotina*) on the left in the distance is the original, bypassed channel of the upper Alligator River. (Author's photograph)

highlight for that year was "the opening of the Alligator Pungo River section of the intracoastal waterway." Although the respective Alligator and Pungo ends of the canal were finally connected, it was a considerable time yet before the canal was fully navigable for safe shipping, no doubt impeded by the intervening Great Depression.[6]

By May 1935 the Alligator-Pungo canal was essentially completed for full-scale navigation. According to the *Daily Advance*, "Surveyors are now completing their last link in what is to be the longest coastal inland waterway in the world. . . . The government is now setting up beacons, buoys and towers . . . in the Alligator River whose rough waters have doomed many brave seamen. . . . Channel and depths are being charted for the first time."[7]

In the summer of 1935 an epidemic of malaria at Fairfield near Lake Mattamuskeet coincided with the opening of the Alligator-Pungo canal. Other fatal outbreaks of this mosquito-borne disease extended into the mid-1930s to other counties of the northeastern Albemarle region along the route of the intracoastal waterway, namely, Hyde, Tyrrell, Pasquotank, and Camden counties. It is probable that some boats using the newly opened intracoastal waterway brought infected people or invasive mosquitoes from farther south. This is not unlike what happened with another mosquito-borne disease, yellow fever, brought by boat to Bath (1711), New Bern (1789, 1864), and Norfolk (1795, 1802, 1855).

In September 1935 a new 308-foot bridge with a swing span of 200 feet was opened over the canal near Fairfield. Prior to this time the new intracoastal canal presented an obstacle to the few road travelers on North Carolina Highway 94. This was solved initially by a ferry that operated from the mid-1920s until 1935. With improvement in the mid-1930s of the (only) road between Fairfield and Columbia, motor traffic increased noticeably. This drawbridge across the Alligator-Pungo canal functioned for over sixty-five years. Finally, the aging swing bridge was replaced by a single-span "hurricane evacuation" bridge in March 2001, and the historic swing bridge was immediately dismantled.[8]

Environmental Impact: Salt Penetration

The Alligator-Pungo canal is probably the most insidious environmental disaster to hit this region. Most importantly, it connects a brackish water ecosystem to a pristine freshwater wetland, allowing chronic salt penetration far into drainage canals (especially during storm surges and droughts). Furthermore, this canal serves as an unnatural conduit for invasive plant and animal species.

In addition, a significant portion of the headwaters of the Alligator River is now canalized, and the dredged material, deposited voluminously on the canal bank, constitutes an eighteen-mile dike, preventing surface water flow through adjacent swamps. Furthermore, the canal completely bypasses a seven-mile, meandering stretch of the old river course such that it can no longer drain the southern portion of this vast wetland, as it had for millennia.

The worst flood experienced in Albemarle peninsula in the twentieth century occurred on 15–16 September 1933, when an unnamed hurricane passed directly over this area without warning. The unique feature of this storm was the magnitude and duration of flooding. The water rose to unprecedented levels in the lower Alligator River (Gum Neck), submerging this community into a veritable lake, with loss of lives, homes, and livestock. Detailed accounts of this horrific "September Storm" (in which my grandparents' home was demolished by the incoming flood water) have been published elsewhere.[9]

This particular hurricane approached from a rare trajectory, from the southwest rather than from the usual, more benign southeast. Thus, the rains of this category 3 hurricane (maximum winds estimated at 125 miles per hour, pressure 28.26 inches) were first felt near Beaufort during the early morning of 15 September, and the onslaught virtually inundated eastern Carteret County. Various accounts noted that it "swept Carteret County for more than twelve hours without ceasing for a minute," and the tide at Merrimon was estimated at fifteen or sixteen feet, and virtually "all the homes at Cedar Island were washed off their foundations or severely damaged." The flooding in New Bern was the highest ever known, and "a three-quarter-mile-long section of the Neuse River bridge washed out."[10]

In other words, before the full effects of the storm were felt in the Albemarle Sound, the wind had already driven the western part of the Pamlico Sound, including the Pungo River, to unprecedented heights. At this time the water height differential between the Pungo and Alligator rivers would have been considerable, pushing water through the newly constructed Alligator-Pungo canal into the lower Alligator River like a giant garden hose.

As an approximate measure of the amount of water involved, if the Alligator-Pungo canal rose three feet in height, there would be an *additional* 57 million cubic feet of water in the canal itself, and such replenishing water would have gushed into the lower Alligator River for a number of hours. Considering that the Gum Neck community was flooded by approximately 225 million cubic feet of water, it is quite conceivable that a significant amount of this water came from a funneling effect from the Pungo River through the Alligator-Pungo canal.[11]

Thus, the Alligator-Pungo canal undoubtedly increased severity of flooding in the lower Alligator River during the hurricane of September 1933. In this sense the 1933 storm was a forerunner of Hurricane Katrina, which hit New Orleans in 2005. It is widely believed that Katrina's devastating storm surges used the intracoastal waterways and contiguous canals as a "hurricane highway" funneling water into the city. Two years after Katrina the Corps of Engineers recommended closure of the Mississippi River-Gulf Outlet, a mammoth navigation canal.

The long-term environmental consequence of storm surges from the Pamlico Sound/Pungo River is that they can bring water contaminated with salt into the Alligator River, a distance of eighteen miles. That contaminated water can travel such distances via the intracoastal waterway has a precedent elsewhere in the Albemarle region. In April 1917 the tide lock at Great Bridge, Virginia, was discontinued on the Albemarle and Chesapeake Canal. The result was that "salty, polluted, turbid water flowed into Currituck Sound" from Norfolk Harbor, killing aquatic plants that served as duck food. A new tide lock was constructed in August 1932 at the brackish Elizabeth River entrance to the canal, and water quality was restored.[12]

In the 1930s old-timers who had lived along the Alligator River all their lives expressed concerns about increased river salinity, which, they claimed, became noticeable only after the last link of the intracoastal waterway was completed. For the first time, the Alligator River became contiguous with the brackish water of the Pamlico Sound. Today, the lower Alligator River has a noticeable salinity problem that is far worse than it was decades ago, as testified by the once-great stands of salt-sensitive Atlantic white cedar.

Since 1982 the North Carolina Division of Water Quality has maintained an excellent Ambient Monitoring System that records salinity in various waterways of the Albemarle region. In the drought of late 2007 record high salinity (up to 45 percent that of sea water) was measured at the Pungo River end of the Alligator-Pungo canal, having increased progressively over a period of four months. Unfortunately, no routine monitoring of salinity is undertaken at the Alligator River end in the Alligator-Pungo canal. The nearest recording station is some considerable distance away at the mouth of the Alligator River at the highway 64 bridge (where the maximum salinity was 26 percent of sea water during the same period). In other words, after eighty years of the existence of the Alligator-Pungo canal no study has ever focused on it as a source of salt penetration into the upper Alligator River, *especially at times of storm surges.*[13]

The back-to-back hurricanes of 1954 (Hazel) and, especially, 1955 (Connie and Diane) caused salt damage to farmland of the southern part of the Albemarle peninsula (Hyde County). As previously noted in chapter 2, contemporary accounts indicated that "farmers were still reeling from the 1954 hurricanes when Connie and then Diane struck. Hazel put 3,500 acres of crop land [of Hyde County] under salt water. . . . [while] Connie raised the salt soaked land to 8,000 acres" and "drove salt ocean water into the fresh water sounds and her sister hurricane poured more on to that." In addition, "Diane's slow movement to the northwest caused prolonged winds to push salt water out of Pamlico Sound and into the farms and fields of the east," and "much farm land in Hyde County was worthless for years." Such powerful wind-driven surges of salty water inevitably funneled into the Pungo River and the Alligator-Pungo canal.[14]

In September 2005 Hurricane Ophelia brushed this area as a category 1 storm and did not make landfall. However, its winds pushed salt from the lower Alligator River more than two miles via drainage canals into the interior of an adjacent nature preserve. According to one source, such "saltwater intrusion through the canal network is stressing and killing Atlantic white cedar stands, preventing regeneration." The increased salt eventually flushed away over a period of several weeks. Interestingly, a saline layer persisted longer along the bottoms of the canals. One study recommended installation of tide gates on canals contiguous with the Alligator River (and ultimately with Pamlico Sound). Indisputably, man-made canals and ditches throughout the Albemarle region serve as potential conduits for salt penetration miles into freshwater swamplands, and in my opinion, the Alligator-Pungo canal is one of the worst culprits.[15]

Furthermore, the Alligator-Pungo canal constitutes an unnatural link between two freshwater rivers, bypassing the saline waters of Pamlico Sound, a natural barrier to certain salt-sensitive aquatic plants and animals. This canal has been specifically identified by environmentalists as a possible route for the highly invasive zebra mussel (*Dreissena polymorpha*) to disperse southward from Virginia. This boat-fouling, pipe-clogging species was accidentally introduced into North America from eastern Europe in 1986 and has already spread through much of the Great Lakes watershed and beyond.

In this context, the Asiatic clam (*Corbicula fluminia*), from southeastern China, has already established itself in the Neuse, Tar, Roanoke, and Chowan rivers of the Albemarle-Pamlico watershed. Similarly, the wedge clam (*Rangia cuneata*), a more benign species that is native to the coastal Gulf of Mexico, is now established in the Neuse and Pungo rivers and in Currituck Sound (Back Bay). Furthermore, several destructive aquatic plants are now well established in the Alligator River, as well as in the Northwest and North Landing rivers of Currituck Sound. Plants of particular concern are the aggressive common reed (*Phragmites australis*) and the waterways-choking alligator weed (*Alternanthera philoxeroides*). The latter is native to South America.[16]

Revised Mandate: Protected Wildlife Zone

After eighty years the time has come for reassessment of the best contemporary use of the Alligator-Pungo canal. Today, this canal is a dinosaur: modern container vessels are far too large to use it, so it is used infrequently for commerce and mainly by private pleasure craft. The reality is that the Alligator-Pungo canal is of virtually no economic benefit to the people of the Albemarle peninsula through which it passes. At the same time, this world-unique region continues to pay a very high environmental price.

The canal is implicated as a source of increased salinity into a vast protected freshwater ecosystem. And as part of a chain of canals unnaturally linking bodies of water, this canal is a conduit for introducing invasive, economically destructive species that replace native fauna and flora and that are virtually impossible to eradicate. As a major intrusion into future viability of the most pristine and arguably the largest freshwater wetland between Florida and Canada, a radical approach is urgently required. The Alligator-Pungo canal has outlived its usefulness as a war canal, being superseded by road and air links, and should be closed in its current form.

Assuming flood gates are added at the more brackish Pungo end, an attractive option would be to incorporate the Alligator-Pungo canal into a protected wildlife zone. It would be contiguous with refuges already bordering the Alligator River, namely, the Buckridge Preserve, Alligator River NWR, and Pocosin Lakes NWR (Frying Pan). The benefit for local ecotourism could be substantial: natural history experiences via tour boat, paddleboat, and even houseboat.

Changing use of federal waterways to benefit the environment has precedents, as one account concludes: "In the eastern U.S., portions of lands owned by the Corps of Engineers and Tennessee Valley Authority are now managed as wildlife refuges. For example, the Tennessee [National Wildlife Refuge] is land and water owned by the Tennessee Valley Authority now managed as a wildlife refuge under a Presidential Executive Order."[17] Closer to home in the Albemarle watershed is the exemplary Roanoke Canal Museum and Trail.

11 Forests Then and Now

When humans first arrived in the Albemarle region thousands of years ago the most superlative feature here was the hundreds of thousands of acres of primeval forest, unsurpassed in the entire eastern United States. The rich, damp soil and warm climate created a canopy of trees of truly gargantuan size and age. The virgin hardwoods, bald cypress (*Taxodium distichum*), and Atlantic white cedar (*Chamaecyparis thyoides*), interspersed with pond cypress, black gum, red maple, loblolly bay, pond pine, and loblolly pine, constituted a temperate forest ecosystem supremely rich in wildlife.

Cypress trees of the North Carolina coastal plain are truly remarkable in their antiquity. In fact, they represent the oldest known living trees east of the Rocky Mountains. For example, a bald cypress in Pender County, North Carolina, is over sixteen hundred years old, dated by tree rings to AD 372. Ancient bald cypresses also survive along the Nottoway and Blackwater rivers, tributaries of the Albemarle Sound, where one tree is over eight hundred years old, dated to AD 1185. A closely related form, the pond cypress (*Taxodium ascendens*), also reaches great age in this region. Along the shore of Lake Phelps in the Albemarle peninsula lives the largest and possibly the oldest pond cypress tree in the world, dated to around the sixth century AD.[1]

As early as the 1580s the Roanoke colonists, who had come from an already deforested England, identified the ship-building potential of tidewater forests. In the 1600s and 1700s subsequent settlers in the Albemarle region naturally used these trees for building homes, boats, shingles, and fences and as an endless source of fuel. Pine trees were particularly useful for making various marine stores, such as turpentine, pitch, and tar. A reference to "tar kiln" indicates pine trees were being exploited along the Alligator River prior to 1783.[2]

In 1839 the noted agriculturist Edmund Ruffin of Petersburg, Virginia, visited Somerset Place plantation on the shore of Lake Phelps. A very astute observer, he commented on the enormous size of cypress trees (up to 80 feet high) in the vicinity of the lake. Many of these large trees had been killed by the usual practice of ring cutting to reclaim farmland, but they had stood for 50 to 100 years before eventually falling in hurricane-force winds. Ruffin's host, Josiah Collins, had counted more than 800 rings in some of these trees when they were cut in cross section. Being aware of even larger cypresses on his plantation, he had concluded that some were more than 1,000 years old.[3]

Furthermore, Ruffin and Collins concluded that at least one generation of cypress trees lived and died along Lake Phelps before the current crop. This was based, for example, on an exceptionally large dead cypress (33 feet in circumference) that was still standing but itself was above an old prostrate cypress log whose wood was still good. In addition, it was observed that "these 'ground logs,' as they are called, [were] so numerous under the swamp, that it would seem as if the trunks of the more ancient forest, thus buried, were as many as the trees now standing above them."[4]

Apart from patchy land clearances for agriculture and relatively small-scale shingling, log cutting, plank production, and boat building, the forests of the Albemarle region remained essentially unharvested well into the nineteenth century. Then, after the Civil War, came wholesale, mechanized exploitation of the rich timber tracts by several large lumber companies from outside. This relentless exploitation was a direct consequence of the Civil War itself.

More ominously from the long view, there has been a general pattern of nonsustainability, which has also been experienced in agricultural and waterway practices. That is, large out-of-state corporations, as well as various governmental agencies, have exploited the natural resources of the Albemarle region for their own short-term ends but have left a significantly diminished legacy for each successive generation.

About 1870 in northeastern North Carolina there were 200,000 acres of the evergreen conifer, Atlantic white cedar. Locally known as "juniper," this was the most commercially valuable tree in the region. Today, only about 10,000 acres are left, that is, only about 5 percent of the original, and half these remaining tracts are on the remote east side of the Alligator River. Somehow, the tallest individual white cedar tree in North America, in excess of 100 feet, survives like a beacon in the heart of its ancient range, in Pettigrew State Park, Tyrrell County.[5]

Tracts of bald cypress, some of which exceeded one thousand years in age, suffered even worse by logging. This water-tolerant species grows so slowly in the tidewater region that a tree normally has to reach two to three hundred years in age before it produces marketable heartwood. Regeneration of a mature cypress tract here would take more than ten human generations.

More than any other individual, John Lonsdale Roper (1835–1921), a Union soldier, was responsible for decimating the unharvested forests of the Albemarle region. During the Civil War Captain Roper of the 11th Pennsylvania Cavalry was stationed primarily in Virginia, where he became "familiar with the great timber tracts in southeastern Virginia and the adjoining part of North Carolina" (according to a later account). In 1865 he moved to Norfolk and started a lumber empire of enormous scale, including much of the Albemarle peninsula.[6]

As early as 1873 Roper began to cut this timberland under the auspices of the Eastern Land, Lumber, and Manufacturing Company. About 1887 Roper established the Roper Land and Lumber Company at Lee's Mill on Kendrick's Creek in Washington County. Owing to this company's success, the town boomed in the early decades of the twentieth century, and it was renamed Roper, after the "Yankee" soldier who gave them jobs and momentary prosperity.

Roper Lumber Company grew into one of the largest timber companies in the United States. It bought up or leased enormous tracts of forests throughout the region and had mills throughout North Carolina and Virginia. Roper even had his own railroad, the Albemarle and Pantego Railroad, which went from Mackey's Ferry through Roper to Belhaven. In addition to Roper Lumber Company, other notable companies exploited timber on this peninsula, including East Lake Lumber Company, Dare Lumber Company, and most importantly, Richmond Cedar Works (replaced in the 1950s by West Virginia Pulp and Paper Company).

For the first time the Albemarle region was faced with big, outside corporations whose influence was awesome. By way of example, in 1919 the *Independent* reported that "the Dismal Swamp canal is almost a thing of the past. It exists now largely because it is to the interest of two big lumber corporations, the Richmond Cedar Works and the John L. Roper Co. The canal serves these companies in that it holds the water on their millions of acres of juniper timber."[7]

Although a full economic and social history of the lumber industry of the entire tidewater region lies outside the scope of this book, it is fair to say that these companies with their heavy investment and mechanization made a profound impact on the environment of these wetlands. History will assess whether a fair balance was achieved between much-needed local employment, on the one hand, and decimation of the tidewater's most outstanding natural resource, on the other.

Logging on the Albemarle Peninsula

In the years following the Civil War logging became the mainstay for many people struggling throughout the Albemarle region. The leading authority on forestry in northeastern North Carolina observed in 1894, "Lumbering has been one of the leading industries in these counties [i.e., the Albemarle peninsula] for a great many years, the numerous canals and streams which penetrate the region affording great facilities for removing timber." A total of 47.9 million board-feet were cut in Hyde, Tyrrell, Washington, and Dare counties in 1893 alone.[8]

Logging was particularly important along the Alligator River, where it was a way of life for several generations, until the 1960s, by which time the original canopy was all but gone. A brief account of the social and environmental impact of logging along this river will serve as a microcosm of events occurring throughout the region.

From the 1880s the Alligator River abounded with tugboats and barges, reflecting the ascendency of logging as an insatiable local industry. Little is recorded about the identity of these early commercial vessels or their captains, but in 1888 the tug boat *Nellie Prior* towed juniper logs from here to Richmond. It was captained by a Canadian by the name of James Evans. In 1893 Evans became chief engineer of Old Dominion Line's passenger steamer *New Bern*, plying between New Bern and Norfolk.

Construction of railroads elsewhere in the country created a huge demand for railway ties such that a railroad tie factory was established in the community of Alligator. Its proprietor, William Thurston (1847–

1896) was a Civil War veteran who had come down from Virginia after the war and married a local girl. In 1880 his factory employed twenty-six people (eleven whites and fifteen blacks, the youngest being thirteen years old).

Similarly, the coal industry in Pennsylvania created a demand for sturdy posts to support mine shafts. In 1898 a barge from the Alligator River (Gum Neck) transported a load of such "mine props" to Philadelphia. On this particular barge was seventeen-year-old Robert W. "Captain Bob" Jones (1881–1977), a local legend embarking on his first job on the water, as cook for twelve dollars per month.

A tragedy involving a sawmill at a local landing on the Alligator River provides a snapshot of life here at the end of the century (1896); according to the *Economist and Falcon*, "There was a boiler explosion at a mill in Gum Neck, Tyrrell County, that killed one white man and two colored men. The white man was Richard Daniels from near Fairfield, Hyde County. . . . The loss is about $5,000." By poignant irony, fifty-one-year-old Daniels had survived being wounded in the Civil War only to be killed in this boiler accident not far from his home.[9]

This sawmill at Cherry Ridge Landing was the property of (Massachusetts-born) Captain Frank Hussey, who had married a local girl and settled. He died a year or two after the explosion, but a large sawmill continued operating here for at least another fifteen years. One notable employee in this sawmill, in 1910, was an intriguing fifty-six-year-old African American, Mathew Perkins, who grew up as a "free colored" on the Dismal Swamp Canal at South Mills, Camden County. There, most unusually, this man of color had received an education a few years before the Civil War.

Buffalo City: The East's Largest Ghost Town

The Alligator River has the improbable distinction of having the largest ghost town in the eastern United States. Hidden in swamps up Mill Tail Creek, Buffalo City was the stuff of legends. Its raison d'être was 168,000 acres of Atlantic white cedar and bald cypress trees on the isolated mainland of Dare County.

Buffalo City originated in the aftermath of the Civil War when some enterprising New Yorkers purchased tens of thousands of acres of rich timberland along the eastern Alligator River. As the *Atlanta Constitution* noted,

"A syndicate of New York capitalists has just purchased a big tract of land in North Carolina. This land was bought of a syndicate in Norfolk and the original grant was given by George III of England. The property is thickly covered with pine, juniper, cypress and other valuable timber" (1885).[10]

The modern era of this ambitious enterprise actually began in 1904 when Dare Lumber Company leased land from East Lake Lumber Company, and logging operations commenced two years later. At its peak in 1920, when the end of World War I brought general prosperity to lumber enterprises throughout the region, Buffalo City was a boom town. It was a permanent community in excess of two thousand residents, including "five hundred non-English speaking Russians."[11] The "city" had well-laid-out streets lined with trim houses, a ten-room hotel, a well-stocked store, its own lodge hall, a cemetery, a post office, a doctor, and a school. To support such a large-scale logging operation, there were two barge-lined docks and eighteen miles of main line and spur railway running through the swamps.

Buffalo City was served by East Lake Landing, where John B. Pinner (1859–1936) operated the largest store on the Alligator River for over thirty years. In fact, the *Dare County Times* reported that "it contained one of the largest docks, warehouses and store complexes in the entire coastal area. Here the mail boats docked, and here supplies of all kinds were stocked. The warehouse was a hundred feet long, holding merchandise for the store as well as cargo waiting for shipment. . . . It sold everything. Over the big store were rooms to rent to travelers." Once merchandise was disembarked, however, it was still a rough journey by horse and cart over the "pole road" to Buffalo City.[12]

Buffalo City declined abruptly in the 1920s, and, according to the *Dare County Times*, by 1939 it was "a shingle center. . . . Where one hundred or more families, their houses and boardinghouses, once stood, there now remain but a dozen or more tenantable buildings, with less than two score permanent inhabitants." In the end, the swamps got their revenge by relentlessly reclaiming this once thriving community until it disappeared completely. Today, not a single building remains.[13]

Richmond Cedar Works

The mighty Richmond Cedar Works (RCW) was the last major company to cut the remaining stands of unharvested white cedar in the Albemarle peninsula. At the turn of the twentieth century this aggressive Virginia-based lumber company started purchasing and leasing large tracts of swampland in the region. Such acquisitions commenced on both sides of the Alligator River prior to 1907 and continued until at least the 1920s. From the outset this aggression created problems for local residents. Most irritatingly, RCW frequently disputed boundaries with local landowners, and its litigious lawyers were quick to resort to court action against anyone who stood in its way.

By about 1920 RCW had become the foremost employer (and landowner) along the Alligator River. Most of the employees, white and black, were young men from nearby Gum Neck who worked for about $5.50 per day. Some had simply transferred from the declining lumber operations at Buffalo City and at nearby Frying Pan.[14] Their jobs were quite diverse, with titles such as store keeper, paymaster, railway engineer, mechanic, track (section) layer, track (section) maintenance, fireman (skidding machine), engineer (skidding machine), saw filer, and gate tender.

Richmond Cedar Works established its base of operations at Northwest Fork of the Alligator River, a deepwater dock where tug-driven barges received timber cut in nearby swamps. Its administrative headquarters was on the adjacent, low-lying section of the old Columbia road on the outskirts of Gum Neck. Here RCW created a self-contained logging village that included a commissary, a boarding house, housing for workmen, a railroad network, a machine shop, and a prominent sawmill that served as a local landmark.

The RCW logging operation thrived here in the 1920s and 1930s and continued well into the 1940s. A testament to the number of people associated with this logging camp was that it was one of only a few stops for a short-lived bus service on North Carolina Highway 94 between Columbia and Engelhard in the late 1930s and 1940s. During World War II this logging camp was stretched to full capacity. For example, in June 1945,

> forty Barbados Island workers, imported by the War Manpower Commission to ease acute labor shortages in essential activities, have arrived in Tyrrell County and are now employed by the Richmond Cedar Works Company, which operates logging and a sawmill in Gum Neck community of the county. The men are provided with housing facilities. Some work in the log woods and some in the sawmill which is now in operation 24 hours daily.[15]

Richmond Cedar Works affected many families (including my grand-father), who were grateful at the time to find any employment, especially during the Depression years. The following is a brief account of its logging operation, based primarily on memories of the dwindling number of people who worked or grew up there.

Integral to RCW's logging operation was a sizeable tram network that penetrated into "Sea Going Woods" in the river swamp of the Alligator River. The main line and its spurs served to take men into the woods to cut and transport felled timber on a large scale. Near the terminus of the tram was a large, busy sawmill. Adjacent to both was the machine shop and garage. The logging, tram, sawmill, and machine shop were administered from the nearby main office, which was more or less at the "commissary." The latter was a general store that sold just about anything the workmen or their families would need, "from clothes and shoes to flour and canned goods." It even had a "candy show case" where children could choose from the penny selection.[16]

The commissary was a real company store, in the worst sense of the word, in that it issued credit to its workers, perhaps too freely. Anyone could use cash in the commissary, but the (indebted) workmen used "pluck," a kind of currency in the form of tokens of different sizes. Pluck could be used only in this commissary. In retrospect, RCW has a tarnished reputation locally. Some say it purposely "kept employees indebted to the company so the men could not quit." This was a veritable swamp version of Tennessee Ernie Ford's coal-mining aphorism, "I owe my soul to the company store."[17]

Near the commissary was a company-owned boarding house for its employees. In the mid-1920s this "Sam Everton Boarding House" was managed by a local man whose wife was recognized for her cooking. In those days of muddy roads preceding the arrival of motor cars, some of the senior men actually commuted on a weekly basis within the sprawling Gum Neck community. For example, for several months in 1925 (until he got a car) the chief engineer of the tram, West Weatherly (1887–1928), boarded here during the week and returned on weekends to his home five miles away. The bulk of the nonlocal workmen, the loggers and tram and sawmill workers, black and white, stayed in makeshift shanties, supplied by the company. Often the men brought their families with them, for shorter or longer periods.

There was a small lane adjacent to the tram track that went west some distance into the white cedar swamp. There were rumors of an illegal still up that lane, and occasionally men returning home after work were seen carrying five-gallon jugs or bottles, obviously prohibited moonshine. In fact, many of the laborers who worked here in the 1930s did drink, typically with one another away from critical eyes. A few of them developed serious drinking problems, to the detriment of their families. At least one unsolved murder, with racial overtones, was attributed to hard drinking one Saturday night in 1939.

Northwest Fork was a relatively deepwater dock on the Alligator River where it intersects North Carolina 94. It bustled in the 1930s and 1940s with commercial, mainly logging traffic. Foremost were tugboat-powered barges that RCW filled with logs to be taken to South Mills on the north shore of the Albemarle Sound. The best known of these tugs was the *Lucille Ross*, an old seventy-foot wooden steam tug whose story adds to the mystique of the Alligator River as an extinct water highway.

The *Lucille Ross* was built in 1893 by Brewster Shipbuilding Company of Baltimore and was owned by RCW when World War I broke out. In April 1917 the vessel was taken over by the U.S. Navy to serve in the war effort. As part of the Naval Coast Defense Reserve it operated out of Norfolk throughout the war, serving as a shore and harbor patrol boat, assisting during customs inspections and occasional towings. In addition, it carried supplies to coastal lighthouse ships in the Chesapeake Bay and Atlantic. After the war it was returned to RCW, in June 1919. The *Lucille Ross* eventually made its way to the Alligator River, where it became an integral part of the local logging industry for many years. At least some of its crew were local men from Gum Neck (including my father, who served as its cook just before World War II).[18]

West Virginia Pulp and Paper Company

In 1953 a change occurred on the Albemarle peninsula that fundamentally affected the economy and ecology of this region. Richmond Cedar Works was bought out by the huge West Virginia Pulp and Paper Company (Westvaco). In all, Westvaco acquired 300,000 acres in Dare, Hyde, and Tyrrell counties, reportedly for $10 per acre. As one can infer from the respective company names, "Cedar" versus "Pulp," the nature of the forests of the Albemarle peninsula had been transformed in fifty years.

During surges from passing storms, salt can penetrate into small canals a distance of up to two miles. To retard such salt penetration, conduits with unidirectional flaps have been installed at the Buckridge Preserve. This canal was dug by the West Virginia Pulp and Paper Company in the 1950s and leads directly to the Alligator River. The road seen above the conduit was made from dirt excavated from the canal and is itself a barrier to water flow through adjacent swamps. (Author's photograph)

The much-prized stands of mature white cedar were virtually gone, and no significant regeneration had occurred in the interim.

Westvaco was the first "modern" company in these swamps in that it operated on roads with log trucks rather than on rivers with barges. Westvaco set up its Alligator River headquarters, complete with an airstrip, near the erstwhile RCW base at the edge of the swamp, but in this case Westvaco was located directly on the "new" paved highway (North Carolina 94). By this time most of the (few) main road arteries throughout the Albemarle region had been paved.

Logging practices had also changed immensely since RCW was at its peak. Instead of using trams through the swamps, Westvaco built a network of straight dirt roadways through great tracts of land. These also served as fire lanes. In addition, numerous drainage canals were dug, the spoil constituting raised dirt lanes for vehicle use.

Westvaco pioneered the commercial value of planting fast-growing softwoods, especially loblolly pine (*Pinus taeda*), in intensely managed wetland forests. Although lowering the water table might have been desirable for loblolly pines, fire became an increasing problem, hence the airstrip. It was rumored locally that these planes were also used at times to watch for suspected arsonists. The greatest forest fire in the South's history occurred here in 1955.

In 1973 Westvaco sold its 300,000 acres in the Albemarle peninsula, reportedly for $100 an acre, to Malcolm McLean, who created First Colony Farms. In 1975 First Colony sold timber rights to its white cedar to Atlantic Forest Products. By the early 1980s the Atlantic had harvested most of the remaining 2,000 of white cedar, at Buck Ridge on the bend of the Alligator River.[19]

In retrospect, these great lumber enterprises, Dare Lumber Company, Roper Lumber Company, Richmond Cedar Works, and to a lesser degree Westvaco, for a while created bustling boom towns amid the once pristine forests of the Alligator River. These self-contained communities are now totally extinct, true ghost towns. In each case the companies are long gone, and the lumbermen are also gone—what has been left behind is a deforested swampland devoid of its centuries-old canopy of mature white cedar and cypress. There is no better example, perhaps anywhere in the United States, of the way short-term gain by big corporations can impoverish the next generation of local people and degrade ecosystems to points where they may not recover.

12   *Droughts and Forest Fires*

For tens of thousands of years forest fires occurred naturally in what is now northeastern North Carolina and southeastern Virginia, independently of human disturbance. Such fires were linked to the juxtaposition of two naturally recurring phenomena, droughts and lightning. The significance of lightning in starting fires in the past can be extrapolated from contemporary studies. Forestry research over recent decades has demonstrated that lightning-induced forest fires are surprisingly common, especially in summer.

Throughout North Carolina in the thirty-four-year period between 1970 and 2005, there were a total of 2,657 forest fires that were ignited by lightning, an average of 74 such fires statewide each year. During the five-year period ending 2005, the Albemarle peninsula had an average of 60 forest fires each year. Over 10 percent of these fires (6.2) were caused by lightning each year, mainly in July and August. Lightning caused the Dare County fire of August 1957, which burned 75,000 acres. More recently, in June 2008 lightning started a large fire in the Pocosin Lakes NWR that burned over 40,000 acres. The smoke and haze was witnessed as far away as Norfolk and Richmond.[1]

The earliest documented forest fires in the Albemarle basin occurred more than ten thousand years ago. During the Paleo-Indian period "natural forest fires . . . appear to have been frequent on the high elevations" along the Nottoway River in the vicinity of the Clovis quarry (Williamson Site). Another such fire occurred about three thousand years ago at Rockyhock, a Carolina Bay on the north shore of the Albemarle Sound, near the Chowan River. The existence of this fire was inferred from a temporary change in vegetation in which the water-tolerant black gum declined, followed by the growth of pocosin shrubs.[2]

Tree Adaptations to Droughts and Fire

Every forester knows that various tree species are adapted to recurring forest fires, and some even thrive on it. In the pocosins of the Albemarle peninsula, the pond pine (*Pinus serotina*) is particularly adapted to occasional fires. Its cones are serotinous, that is, they require fire to release the seeds that may lie dormant for several years. Other tree adaptations include sprouting from stumps (pond pine, cypress, black gum, tupelo), thick bark (pines), opportunistic colonization, and natural elimination of low limbs. Some species are adapted to smaller, more frequent burns, whereas others benefit from larger, infrequent fires. In this context, it should be noted that droughts also benefit some plant species even in the absence of fire. For example, cypress, black gum, and other water-tolerant species can take root when the swamp floor is relatively dry, allowing seedlings to get established before standing water returns.

By way of perspective, cyclical droughts and resultant forest fires were not only normal in the Albemarle region but were sometimes beneficial, even necessary over the long term to maintain this wetland. Unfortunately, humans have profoundly disturbed this delicately balanced ecosystem by creating artificial drought conditions (by land drainage), thereby greatly accelerating the frequency and intensity of major fires.

Humanity Tips the Balance

Even in prehistory, the native peoples in this region undoubtedly caused occasional forest fires when conditions were very dry. One possible mechanism lies in their tradition of fire hunting for deer in annual autumn hunts. In the case of the Virginia Algonquins this was a communal activity in which fires were set around a herd of deer in a circle four or five miles in diameter, thereby concentrating the animals for the kill. Then, "the hunters would move on to another area the next day and go through the same procedure again."[3]

The number and severity of forest fires, however, accelerated after English settlers came to the Albemarle region. This was due foremost to

The wetlands of the Albemarle-Pamlico region vacillate between submerged swamps and dry woodland, depending on seasonal precipitation. The black gum (tupelo) swamp (*Nyassa sylvatica* var *biflora*) in the Buckridge Preserve on the Alligator River, typical of the Albemarle-Pamlico region, is pictured filled with water on the top (in March 2007) and under drought conditions on the bottom (in October 2007). Each autumn local bears climb these black gums to eat gumberries in abundance.

relentless draining of peat-rich pocosins for agriculture and, more recently, forestry. This lowering of the water table has been environmentally costly, sometimes with catastrophic and fatal consequences.

A case in point is the great pocosin at the middle of the Albemarle peninsula, where a drainage policy that started in 1780 led to the "largest forest fire in the south's modern history" two hundred years later. Because of the remoteness of these swamps little is known to outsiders about what has been happening here. However, the incredible fire history in the vicinity of Lake Phelps is one of the best examples in the United States of humanity's chronic mismanagement of wetlands.[4]

About 1786 the Lake Company (Josiah Collins), which owned over 100,000 acres, proceeded to drain much of Lake Phelps to turn the lakebed into arable land. Hundreds of slaves were imported for the purpose of digging a network of drainage ditches and canals, not the least of which was the Collins Canal (1788), which connected to the Scuppernong River.[5]

Within a decade of lowering the water table came the first inferno. Following a dry period in the spring of 1791, the swampland between Lake Phelps and Pungo Lake caught fire to a degree never before recorded. The extent of this uncontrollable fire was captured vividly in a letter of 15 April 1791 by Charles Pettigrew, who lived on the north shore of Lake Phelps:

> I shall not attempt a full description of the fire, & the thunder and smoke that issued from it. It would seem to be borrowed from some of our travellers, who have undertaken to describe the bursting of a volcano from some of the burning mountains. . . . It appeared yesterday as if every thing but the Lake itself would be drawn into the general conflagration. We seem to be the center where the fires were aiming to unite from every quarter.
>
> The atmosphere you know was clear, & the wind from north west—But when the fire got into the cypress grounds, it announced its own approach, by such crackling & thundering & columns of smoke as were truly frightful. The cloud grew very heavy. The air grew dark. I can compare it to nothing but the total eclypse of the sun which we had a few years ago. The ashes & coals from the burning reeds, & other combustable mater, were scattered every where so that Mr. Trotter thought it advisable to throw water over the roof of the mill & all about it—The cloud at lest became so thick & ponderous to the eastward that its pressure on the atmosphere gave us ye wind out from thence, which rendered it still more

alarming, & redoubled our apprehensions—but divine providence . . . checked its progress by a shower of rain, just when it had got nearly thro' to my high grounds. The shower is very propitious to our planting business this morning for we were very dry.[6]

Pettigrew received the following letter in reply from Edenton, on the other side of the Albemarle Sound: "I perceived about ten days ago that, The Prince of the powers of the air, had been let loose upon you; my garden was covered with the burnt tops of reeds, which I was very confident came from your quarter."[7]

In the spring of 1799 a similar fire burned for several days in the much-drained Great Dismal Swamp on the north side of the Albemarle Sound. Human ignition was certain; as one source noted, "In clearing land, the planter often sets fire to the woods; sometimes the conflagration passes the intended limits."[8]

Fifteen years after the 1791 fire, following an unusually prolonged drought in the summer of 1805 and spring of 1806, another significant fire burned in the vicinity of Lake Phelps. The nearby pocosins were dry for eighteen months, and the water level in Lake Phelps had fallen by four feet.[9]

In 1806 Ebenezer Pettigrew made firsthand observations from his plantation at the lake:

It was perhaps never known to be so dry as it is this spring—From the dryness fires have broken out & done immense mischief, burning over the whole face of the earth & in some places trees of 2 & 3 feet diameter up by the roots in others every bush reed & stick smooth leaving but few trees of any kind standing, the juniper swamps it is said are entirely ruined. In them it has burned the trees down, & then burned them up, so that they are quite clean—At one time there was so much smoke in the atmosphere that it was disagreeable to the eyes even in the house. . . .

When at last the rains again saturated the swamp, and the superabundant water flowed hence into the lake, the water of the lake was at first so deeply colored as to stain cloth that was washed in it, and it was feared that its previous quality was lost forever. But this condition was merely transient; and it was not long before the water was restored to the state of purity which it had before, and has since retained.[10]

The same drought brought a great fire to the Great Dismal Swamp in 1806. This infamous fire burned for months, with cinders seen as far as

Norfolk, Virginia. It destroyed much timber in the Dismal Swamp, as well as large quantities of shingle ready for sale.[11]

In the spring of 1880 a series of large forest fires broke out along the eastern seaboard from North Carolina to Pennsylvania, no doubt due to extensive drought conditions at the time. In the tidewater region a great fire was started in an unspecified location in the North Carolina swamps by careless brush burners about 9 April and raged for over two weeks, by which time it had reached the outskirts of Norfolk. On the Albemarle peninsula a shingle cutter, Zachariah Owens (1815–1880), noticed smoke while working in the forest and rushed back to his home at Clabber Point on the Alligator River. Before he could get his family to safety, the fire overtook Zachariah, his wife, and their three children, who were all fatally burned. Heavy rains on 27 April brought the tidewater fires under control.[12]

"South's Largest Woods Fire": 1955

Starting in 1953 the West Virginia Pulp and Paper Company (Westvaco) acquired 300,000 acres in Washington, Hyde, Tyrrell, and Dare counties and proceeded to drain great swathes of these swamplands. Two years later the area in the vicinity of Lake Phelps experienced the greatest forest fire ever seen in the southeastern United States, followed by one of similar significance in 1985 and again in 2008.

The pocosins in the vicinity of Lake Phelps achieved national attention in the greatest swamp inferno ever known in the United States. A catastrophic forest fire, described in front-page headlines at the time as the "South's Largest Woods Fire," started near Lake Phelps on the night of 29 March 1955.

Fanned by strong, changeable winds, the advance of the fire was extremely fast and unpredictable. Furthermore, the ground was soft, with very few accessible roads or trails for use of tractors and other heavy firefighting equipment. The smoke was so dense that surveillance planes had to fly at six thousand feet.[13]

On 4 April the *New York Times* reported, "State forestry officials called on the Coast Guard, Army and Marine Corps today for help in battling an eastern North Carolina forest fire that had become a 'major emergency situation.' The blaze in Hyde and Tyrrell Counties is reported to have swept over about 240,000 acres since it began last Tuesday."[14]

In southern Tyrrell County the fire threatened Kilkenny and burned especially the low region of the Alligator River between Kilkenny and Gum Neck. The *Statesville Record and Landmark* reported that "in the east the fire was checked on a line near NC Highway 94 between Fairfield and Columbia and in the south along a canal and road between Lake Mattamuskeet and US 264." At one point flames approached Ponzer and, jumping southward across the Alligator-Pungo canal (Inland Waterway), even threatened Rose Bay.[15]

After more than eight days, with the help of some rain, the fire was finally brought under control, but it had to be closely monitored for some weeks thereafter. The final assessment was that 203,000 acres were burned, at an estimated loss of three to four million dollars. Westvaco alone lost more than 100,000 acres of timberland. An investigation at the time concluded that the fire was started by arsonists, according to one newspaper account: "N.C. seeks arsonists who set forest fire. . . . There is 'no question' but that the fire was deliberately set." However, neither proof of arson nor the culprit(s) was ever found.[16]

Another forest fire in this area resulted in an air crash with two fatalities. The fire started between Lake Phelps and Gum Neck on 25 April 1961. By the next day it had burned over seven thousand acres owned by Westvaco. Fighting the blaze on the ground was a force of ninety men, including thirty firefighters from Westvaco, along with fifteen prisoners and forest rangers from around the state. In addition to the ground force, four small planes, one owned by Westvaco and three by the state, were fighting from the air, including bombing the fire with water. The next day Westvaco's chief forester, John D. Earle (1914–1961) was overseeing the fire in the company's single-engine plane when it crashed in the swamp near the paper company's shop and airfield in Gum Neck, killing Earle and the pilot, a local man.[17]

A severe drought in 1985 was a prelude to yet another major forest fire in this same area. This one was comparable in scale to the legendary inferno of thirty years earlier. It started on Easter Saturday (6 April) and particularly threatened Gum Neck. It is not often that this small community warrants coverage in the *Los Angeles Times*, which reported that "a four-mile-wide fire swept up North Carolina's parched coast, scorching 80,000 acres of woodlands, but firefighters made a determined stand at the Alligator River and saved the town of Gum Neck, a crossroads community of 200 persons." Smoke was visible for fifty miles, and several water-bearing helicopters were brought in to fight the fire. In Gum Neck itself the focus of the fire was in the river swamp in the vicinity of Northwest Fork of the Alligator River, especially threatening homes and the church along the nearby Old Columbia Road.[18]

In addition to the fire itself cinders were falling throughout other communities a considerable distance from the fire. Of foremost concern was that the cinders would ignite the asphalt tile roofs typical of the region, so that about thirty-five people from Gum Neck were evacuated to safety. So widespread was this fire that cinders also threatened homes much further north, including Scuppernong Township. In one case a local farmer slept on his lawn for three consecutive nights, keeping the roof and sides wet with water pumped from an adjacent pond. By 9 April the fire was under control, but the *Washington Post* noted that "the outbreak in Washington, Hyde and Tyrrell counties still poses a threat to un-burned adjacent areas. . . . Mostly contained means it is not spreading." Smoldering into underlying peat, a phenomenon peculiar to these poco-sins, continued for at least a week.[19]

In all, just short of 100,000 acres burned in the Pocosin Lakes fire of 1985. Amazingly, before and after images of the entire area burned in this fire were captured by satellite. Analysis of these images with ad-vanced spectral technology twenty years later concluded that this fire burned with greatest intensity in the eastern portion of the pocosin, specifically where pond pines form the canopy (62 percent of total burned area). The eastward march of the fire was stopped abruptly by the North-west Fork of the Alligator River.

A factor that finally brought the fire under control was intentional raising of the water table by reverse pumping of water into agricultural ditches. Ironically, the water level in Lake Phelps lowered to such an extent that it led to one of the most remarkable archaeological discoveries in the United States. Thirty dugout canoes, one radiocarbon dated to five thousand years ago, were found submerged in the lake bottom (as dis-cussed in chapter 1).[20]

Forest Fires from Military Aircraft

Since the 1960s U.S. Air Force, Navy, and Marine Corps aircraft have been significantly detrimental to the environment of the Albemarle pen-insula. In particular, the heavily wooded mainland of Dare County on the east side of the Alligator River has a peculiar fire risk from practice bombs dropped onto the Air Force bomb range. From 1965 to 1970 there were 138 fires (averaging half an acre) on this range. One of these fires, in April 1966, burned 3,600 acres. The Air Force Bomb Range Fire of 22–26 May 1971 "was ignited by a practice bomb dropped at 1028 e.s.t." The fire raged uncontrolled for four days and burned 29,300 acres. To minimize such fires the military in Dare County used various fire-suppression measures, including "herbicides." This avowed use of herbicides might give credence to local rumor that the military in Dare County has used Agent Orange, a powerful cancer-causing defoliant widely employed in Vietnam.[21]

In addition, a surprising number of training aircraft have crashed in the swamps of the Albemarle peninsula, with fatalities and burned forests. As early as 1965 two military planes reportedly collided near what is now the Gum Neck pumping station. During the period from February 1986 to June 1988 at least five military planes crashed in the Alligator River area, an average of one every five months. Some of these were involved in night-training exercises. More recently, about 1997, several local witnesses saw a military plane crash on a marsh at the mouth of Gum Neck Creek on the Alligator River. The area was immediately cordoned off and the plane soon removed. Inexplicably, I have found no newspaper record of this crash.

In January 2008, in response to a bitter seven-year, David-and-Goliath struggle on the part of locals, environmentalists, politicians, and the federal judiciary, the U.S. Navy withdrew major plans for a 30,000-acre, $230 million Outlying Landing Field (OLF) in the middle of the Albemarle peninsula immediately adjacent to the wildfowl-rich pocosin lakes.[22]

Unfortunately, the OLF threat has now moved to five new proposed sites still within the waterfowl-rich Albemarle region. In North Carolina these are the Sandbanks Site (Gates County) and the Hale's Lake Site (Camden and Currituck counties); and in Virginia these are the Mason Site, Dory Site, and Cabins Point Site (Southampton, Sussex, and Surry counties). All these vulnerable sites are rich in wildlife and are incurring very strong local resistance.[23]

For more than two hundred years spectacular forest fires have plagued the pocosins of the Albemarle region. These fires are linked to massive land-drainage programs in the 1780s and again in the 1950s. Remarkably, the ensuing major fires in the Albemarle peninsula, in 1791, 1806, 1880, 1955, 1961, and 1985, all occurred in the month of April. This suggests that all these fires were manmade since lightning-induced fires occur primarily in the months of July and August. The exception was the most recent fire, 5–12 June 2008, which was attributed to lightning.[24]

All the fires mentioned here were associated with a dry spell, that is, conditions were ripe for ignition. However, that is not the full picture: prior to human disturbance the pocosins were perpetually wet, whereas now the water table is artificially lowered and the ground is significantly drier than normally would be the case. Finally, there is one additional factor that causes such spectacular fires in the Albemarle peninsula: the ground itself burns. The significance of the underlying peat is discussed in the next chapter.

13 · From Peat Mining to Wildlife Refuges

The Albemarle region of southeastern Virginia and northeastern North Carolina holds some of the largest deposits of peat in temperate North America, comparable in area to that in Ireland. The Albemarle peninsula in particular "has the largest and deepest peat soils in North Carolina" and contains nearly half the peat for the entire state. Similarly, the Great Dismal Swamp north of the Albemarle Sound also has rich deposits. In both regions the depth of the peat generally ranges from one to seven feet, but it can be up to fifteen feet, or more, in certain areas.[1]

These pocosin peatlands are unique and constitute a once-living record of plant life here thousands of years ago. Partially decomposed leaves, twigs, tree trunks, and stumps have all been preserved under the anaerobic conditions of swamp water. Peat is the geological predecessor of coal, and like coal, the fundamental element is basically carbon that was removed from the atmosphere by photosynthesis long ago. In other words, over geologic time plants in these wetlands removed significant quantities of carbon dioxide from the atmosphere and stored it as peat for thousands of years. In modern jargon, the Albemarle peninsula is an environmentally valuable "carbon sink," perhaps the largest in the eastern United States.

The age of these peat deposits is relatively young, coinciding with the rise of sea level associated with the end of the last ice age. In the Albemarle peninsula, for example, the average age of the peat was radiocarbon dated at 4,500 years (range 1,715 to 8,895 years). These pocosins have produced on the order of 535 pounds of carbon per acre each year throughout this period (0.06 kg per square meter per year), roughly about 10 percent of their annual photosynthesis. The richest form of peat in these pocosins contains up to 60 percent carbon.

By way of caveat, however, this invaluable carbon sink is strictly dependent on the peat staying submerged in stagnant water such that oxidation does not occur. Humanity's disturbance of this region, especially by land drainage, has released great quantities of carbon into the atmosphere and led to land subsidence and release of toxic chemicals such as mercury.

Peat Oxidation: Land Subsidence

Under certain conditions water can be a superb preservative. The key is the absence of oxygen, an element necessary for life, as well as the absence of microorganisms that normally decompose organic (carbon-based) material. Stagnant water of tidewater swamps is typically anaerobic, that is, all the dissolved oxygen has been used up. Thus, leaves, limbs, and trees that fall into such water are barely oxidized. Other factors are at work, of course, but one can generalize that the spongy organic soil (peat) underlying these massive swamps is attributable foremost to being submerged in standing water for thousands of years.

When this water is removed, either naturally via droughts or by humans for land drainage, great quantities of (unoxidized) organic material are exposed to oxygen, a highly reactive element. This material will then inevitably oxidize ("burn"). This oxidation process may be slow, whereby the organic components of the soil will gradually return to carbon dioxide, or related oxide gases (methane is not an oxidation product), and eventually "disappear" (subsidence). Alternatively, it may oxidize quickly in the form of fire. Either way human activity has tipped the balance, and peat is quickly disappearing from these wetlands, releasing large quantities of "greenhouse gases" into the atmosphere. The entire process can be reversed if the water table is raised to original levels (i.e., if land drainage is stopped).

When swampland is cleared for cultivation, and subsequently drained, a barely perceptible process commences within organic soil (peat) that does not occur in mineral soil. Organic soil, affectionately called "black gold" by farmers, literally disappears over time. This soil subsidence was observed at Somerset Place at Lake Phelps as early as 1839 by the pioneering agronomist Edmund Ruffin of Petersburg, Virginia (see chapter 11). In the process of clearing land here, trees were killed by ringing and left in place for up to several decades. These trees and stumps constituted a marker by which the soil level could be measured over many years, as one account concluded: "In the land cultivated this year [1839] for the first time, though drained long before, the mark of the former surface can be fixed by the dead trees and stumps whose roots are now so far naked as to make it evident that the surface is already two feet lower than formerly." On Ebenezer Pettigrew's adjacent plantation, Bonarva, a similar marker had measured a surface subsidence of three feet. Today, "the deep organic soil of the Collins plantation north of Lake Phelps no longer exists."[2]

Ruffin was before his time in his observations in 1856: "But no one formerly, and few even now, would suppose that the rotting away, and waste of soil would proceed farther, and much farther [than simple settling], by the complete decomposition, and resolving into the primary gaseous elements, and escape into the air of much of the vegetable parts of the swamp soil. This is the natural and gradual operation . . . [and] final results as seem to me inevitable."[3]

Under prolonged drought conditions the organically enriched soil of these wetlands becomes tinder dry, ripe for ignition either from lightning or human cause. Such fires can burn far more intensely than a typical forest fire because not only the trees but the ground itself literally burns. Underground smoldering can continue for weeks or months, sometimes leaving a depression that will eventually fill with water.

The question of whether any of the great pocosin lakes formed by peat fires lies outside the scope of this book, but it is quite possible. In bottomland near the Scuppernong River cleared for cultivation, the fields were flat except for some ponds of one-half to two acres. When the ponds were drained the exposed soil revealed charcoal and ash, evidence of a former fire.

This ground-burning phenomenon was observed firsthand following the 1806 fire in the vicinity of Lake Phelps. In a particular part of the land adjoining the Collins Canal, the soil continued "slowly burning for twelve months altogether." In the same region the 1985 fire burned an average layer of organic soil approaching four inches throughout the entire area of the fire, with peat burn depths greater in parts. In the Great Dismal Swamp more recent fires again demonstrated the burning capacity of organic soil. Following the severe drought of 1930, a resultant fire burned to a depth of six feet in the northeast corner of the current swamp.[4]

First Colony Farms: Peat Mining Threat

In the 1970s agribusiness took over the Albemarle peninsula, where land ownership was held disproportionately by a handful of large corporations, including Mattamuskeet Farms (35,000 acres, owned jointly by John Hancock Mutual and American Cyanamid) and Shima Farms (7,500 acres owned by a Japanese firm, Shima American Corporation). However, by far the largest landowner was First Colony Farms (375,000 acres), which owned about one-third of the entire peninsula.

First Colony Farms was the brainchild of wealthy entrepreneur Malcolm P. McLean (1913–2001), a maritime legend attributed with developing containerization, thereby transforming the shipping industry worldwide. From humble beginnings in North Carolina, he founded Sea-Land, Inc., which he eventually sold for a sizeable amount. With some of the proceeds he acquired First Colony Farms, a departure from his usual investments. He also purchased United States Lines for a reported $111 million. This he built into one of the largest shipping companies in the world, valued in excess of $1 billion.[5]

In mid-1973 McLean, then based in New York City, responded to an advertisement in the *Wall Street Journal*. By 23 August 1973 he had purchased West Virginia Pulp and Paper Company's holdings of 287,000 acres in the Albemarle peninsula for $28.7 million ($100 per acre). In addition to this land, McLean also acquired adjoining property, including Atlantic Farms (40,000 acres), to consolidate 375,000 acres in Washington, Tyrrell, Hyde, and Dare counties.[6]

McLean's plans for First Colony, already the largest "farm" in North Carolina, were extraordinarily ambitious. He wanted to make it one of the most productive farms in the eastern United States. Land reclamation began in 1974 aimed at planting corn, winter wheat, and soybeans, plus pasture grasses for a large, self-contained hog and cattle enterprise. That year alone, 24,000 acres of "almost worthless" pocosin were ditched and drained, according to one report: "Draglines and bulldozers are at work over wide areas, digging drainage canals and ripping up trees and other vegetation, then pushing up the resulting debris into long windrows. A process of irreversible change has been set in motion." In addition, First

Colony leased its vast timberland to the forestry giant MacMillan-Blodell, Inc., whose subsidiary, Atlantic Forest Products, decimated remaining stands of Atlantic white cedar.[7]

Reminiscent of the failed drainage of Lake Mattamuskeet in the 1920s, the biggest problem faced by First Colony's farming operation was the difficulty of working with the deep organic muck (peat) that dominates much of the peninsula. As one account noted, "From the beginning, the First Colony project has been bedeviled by the 5- to 6-foot mantle of 'woody' peat that covers about half of the farm. The big stumps, tree trunks, and limbs found throughout the soil profile—preserved there for thousands of years by the peat's acidity—can wreck farm machinery and make cultivation of row crops impossible." Corporate farming ceased expanding here after only a few years. By 1978 farming had become eclipsed by another project of even greater ambition.[8]

In 1973 the energy crisis rocked the United States. The federal government pushed for unexploited domestic sources of energy, including the burning of peat as fuel to generate electricity or to produce methane gas or methanol. Ever astute, McLean recognized the potential of the vast peatlands under his massive First Colony Farms. In the spring of 1978 he embarked on a feasibility study to determine the scope of a peat-mining operation at the farm. Toward this end he acquired special peat-mining equipment from the Soviet Union and Finland and commissioned a geological assessment of energy assets.

These studies concluded that First Colony had "recoverable reserves of peat at more than 400 million tons. This is believed to be enough to fuel four 400-megawatt power plants for 40 years or an 80-million-cubic-foot-per-day gasification plant for nearly 50 years. The heating value of First Colony peat is 5200 BTU's per pound at 50 percent moisture, or almost 40 percent that of bituminous coal." After committing about a million dollars, the "First Colony peat development project represents to date [1978] the biggest effort actually to demonstrate in the field, methods for mining and using U.S. peat deposits as an energy resource."[9]

In 1980 the state issued First Colony a license to mine peat on six thousand hectares (fifteen thousand acres) near Lake Phelps.[10] In 1983, the *New York Times* reported that Peat Methanol Associates, a consortium with First Colony, had announced plans for a "$540 million plant, the first in the country for converting peat to methanol for use in raising octane levels in gasoline." Local county officials were attracted to an anticipated nearly 50 percent increase in property-tax revenues and the aspiration of 350 full-time jobs when the plant was fully operational. Furthermore, the consortium issued assurances that the environment would not be affected by the proposed peat mining.[11]

However, local citizenry and environmental groups were united in their concern that peat mining on such a massive scale in the Albemarle peninsula would be seriously detrimental to the environment, particularly to sensitive shellfish nurseries in brackish water of the Pamlico Sound. It did not help that the U.S. Army Corps of Engineers determined that the peat-mining area was not in a "wetlands," as defined by the Clean Water Act. In effect, it authorized "the filling without federal or state environmental review of wetlands that had low water flows or were isolated from major river systems." The National Wildlife Federation, along with a number of local groups, filed a lawsuit against the Corps of Engineers. The court found that the land in question was indeed "wetlands" and fell within the Clean Water Act. The court also ruled, even after appeal, that a federal agency had failed "to exercise its authority with respect to wetlands." This led to an out-of-court settlement whereby the Corps of Engineers would tighten wetlands regulations.[12]

Significantly, this was the first time in three hundred years when local citizens of the Albemarle peninsula united against the federal government and big corporations in order to protect their unique wetlands. Their newly formed North Carolina Coastal Federation (www.nccoast .org) and other local groups raised awareness to their plight and received national coverage on the *CBS Evening News* and PBS's *MacNeil-Lehrer Report*. Little did they know then that similar "people power" would be indispensable twenty years later in a successful, hard-fought campaign against the U.S. Navy's proposal to build an Outlying Landing Field in the same area (discussed in chapter 12).

In spite of these tighter environmental hurdles, plus a 100,000-acre forest fire in this area in the mid-1980s, First Colony continued with its plans for mining peat. Then, global events overtook the project. On 24 November 1986 McLean Industries, which owned First Colony Farms, which in turn owned United States Lines, filed for bankruptcy in New York City. International freight rates had plummeted, leaving McLean Industries with debts in excess of one billion dollars, and First Colony Farms was tied up in litigation.[13]

In August 1989 a parcel of 104,293 acres still owned by First Colony came up for auction in a Manhattan bankruptcy court. The Conservation Fund, a private, nonprofit organization based in Arlington, Virginia, bid $7 million in order to save these wetlands from development, but a Japanese consortium led by Nissho Iwai Corporation reportedly outbid them at $8.1 million, with the intention of mining the peat. At the last minute "in a tense, exciting session" the Richard King Mellon Foundation of Pittsburgh saved the day by authorizing purchase of the land for a reported $8.8 million.[14]

Another parcel, a 15,000-acre site in northern Hyde County south of Lake Phelps, was the subject of proposals to North Carolina Power for peat mining as late as April 1990, but these did not materialize.[15]

Albemarle Wildlife Refuges

As recently as 225 years ago the Albemarle region was an incomparable natural wetland unsurpassed anywhere east of the Rocky Mountains. This wilderness contained vast forests dominated by gargantuan Atlantic white cedar and ancient bald cypress and replete with deer, bears, cougars, wolves, and alligators. Each winter the lakes and marshes were home to immense populations of arctic waterfowl. Each spring the rivers teemed with unimaginable numbers of river herring returning home from the Gulf of Maine. Each summer the water-saturated pocosins added incrementally to already huge deposits of peat, as these wetlands had done for thousands of years. To complete the cycle of life in this unique ecosystem, tropical storms replenished vital water each autumn.

Then came a relentless onslaught by settlers and developers who modified these wetlands almost beyond recognition, mostly in the past one hundred years. In spite of humanity's environmental short-sightedness over many years, the Albemarle wetland maintained a resilience rarely experienced in most of America. Most importantly, the region's deep pocosin muck created unworkable pockets that allowed disjunct swamp refugia to survive.

The region's bountiful waterfowl tipped the balance in favor of saving much of this vast wetland for future generations. They were the catalyst for the first designation of a handful of wildlife refuges in the Albemarle region in the 1930s, and it was the waterfowl again in 2008 that ultimately defeated the U.S. Navy's attempt to establish a very unpopular Outlying Landing Field (OLF) in the pocosins.

Starting with the Lacey Act, signed by President William McKinley in 1900, the nation slowly became aware of the need to protect wildlife at the interstate (federal) level.[16] In the 1920s the U.S. government responded to the vulnerability of waterfowl migrations across state and even country jurisdictions by passing the seminal Migratory Bird Conservation Act of 1929. This led to a number of key sites on the Atlantic Flyway being designated as waterfowl refuges.

The first of these refuges in the Albemarle-Pamlico watershed was established in 1932 when 16,411 acres of mainly brackish marshes in Hyde County were set aside to form the Swanquarter National Wildlife Refuge (NWR). In 1934 a total of 50,180 acres encompassing nearly all of previously drained Lake Mattamuskeet formed the Mattamuskeet NWR. As a Great Depression project, the Civilian Conservation Corps converted the water-pumping station, once the world's largest, into a hunting lodge that operated until 1974. In 1938 over 9,000 acres of Back Bay, a freshwater marshland in Virginia contiguous with Currituck Sound, were set aside as the Back Bay NWR. More than twenty years passed before even waterfowl gained further protection in this region. Then, in 1960, 8,219 acres straddling North Carolina and Virginia between Back Bay and Currituck sounds became Mackay Island NWR. In 1963, 12,230 acres encompassing the Pungo Lake area became the Pungo NWR. (A few additional refuges, such as Pea Island NWR in 1937, were located on the Outer Banks, a saltwater ecosystem that lies outside the scope of this book.)

The state of North Carolina took a wider view of conservation in this region, beyond the specific needs of waterfowl, and set aside a few areas deemed to be of outstanding natural significance. In 1939 the state took a ninety-nine-year lease on some 17,000 acres at Lake Phelps. This area, which had come under the federal Scuppernong Farms Resettlement Project of the Great Depression, included 16,600 acres of water (Lake Phelps) along with more than 1,200 acres of land at the north rim of the lake. This leased package became the Pettigrew State Park, the sixth state park in North Carolina. In 1947 the federal government converted the lease into a gift to the state. In 2005 more than 2,500 acres along the nearby Scuppernong River were added to the state park as its "Scuppernong Section."

In 1973 the state accepted a donation of 919 acres in Gates County to form Merchants Millpond State Park. This initial gift included the 760 acres of a 190-year-old mill pond, to which the Nature Conservancy soon added an additional 925 acres of woodland. Today this state park encompasses more than 3,250 acres of unspoiled riverine swamp, which harbors what is probably the northernmost (but recently established) population of alligators in the world. In 1974 local residents of Beaufort County persuaded the state to acquire 1,208 acres on the north shore of the Pamlico River to form Goose Creek State Park. This park protects one of the most northern populations of the dwarf palmetto (*Sabal minor*).

Ironically, it was actually the Internal Revenue Service that transformed these wetlands into a region dominated by vast wildlife refuges. Between 1974 and 1990 the IRS struck deals to give tax relief to corporations that donated lands for conservation. As a result, with the intervention of the Nature Conservancy and the Conservation Fund, nearly four hundred thousand acres have been set aside in the Albemarle region.

The first was the Great Dismal Swamp, which, almost unbelievably, was still in private ownership and vulnerable to exploitation as late as 1974. Furthermore, at this time the U.S. Army Corps of Engineers owned the water rights to Lake Drummond to control water levels in the Dismal Swamp Canal. To the detriment of the swamp, the water was most needed for commercial use in shipping on the canal at times of drought.

What started as a local campaign in 1962 culminated more than twenty years later in the Dismal Swamp Act of 1974. The initial campaign is attributed to Alva Carter Duke of Richmond, soon joined by William Ashley of the Izaak Walton League and other key individuals. Together they tirelessly raised public awareness of the environmental significance of the Dismal Swamp, first in the Virginia state capital and then in Washington, DC. At the time, the land was owned by a large lumber company, Union Camp Corporation, which ultimately was receptive to conserving this unique swamp if it could be done on commercially realistic terms. The Nature Conservancy, then relatively new, played a key role in negotiating with the IRS to value the land for tax purposes prior to donation. On 30 August 1974, President Gerald Ford signed the bill that accepted the gift of 49,097 acres from Union Camp and formed the Great Dismal Swamp National Wildlife Refuge. Today, this refuge contains 111,000 acres, of which 38,000 acres are located in North Carolina. In 1974 the state of North Carolina brought 14,344 contiguous acres into the state park system as the Dismal Swamp State Natural Area.[17]

The national significance of the Great Dismal Swamp NWR is that it pioneered the concept of conserving an entire ecosystem, not just water-fowl haunts or specific habitats for endangered species. The secretary of the interior was authorized to "manage the area for the primary purpose of protecting and preserving a unique and outstanding ecosystem." In this context, the Dismal Swamp refuge was recognized as one of the remaining remnants of what was once well in excess of one million acres of a unique wetlands ecosystem in southeastern Virginia and north-eastern North Carolina.[18]

Over the next fifteen years more than 240,000 additional acres, south of the Albemarle Sound, were added to the national wildlife refuges in the Albemarle watershed. These two parcels, in 1984 and 1990, resulted from the First Colony Farms debacle discussed earlier.

The Prudential Life Insurance Company had formed a partnership ("Prulean Corporation") with First Colony Farms to develop a large tract of land east of the Alligator River into a farm. According to the *Raleigh News and Observer*, with intervention of the Nature Conservancy, "that venture was abandoned and the company instead capitalized on a tax writeoff for donating the land"; and thus, in March 1984, Prudential donated 114,259 acres to form the Alligator River NWR, which was "valued at $50 million," and "was the largest conservation gift in history at the time." Contiguous tracts of land were systematically added so that to date this refuge has 152,260 acres in Dare and Hyde counties. This refuge has achieved national attention because it was chosen as the site for the reintroduction of the red wolf. (The Alligator River NWR sur-rounds the 46,000-acre site constituting the U.S. Air Force bombing range on mainland Dare County. This land was initially leased from Westvaco in 1965 but later compulsorily acquired from First Colony Farms in 1978.)[19]

On 3 July 1990 the Richard King Mellon Foundation ceremoniously donated 93,000 acres, acquired in First Colony's bankruptcy auction in New York City, to the secretary of the interior to form the Pocosin Lakes National Wildlife Refuge. At its formation, this refuge administratively incorporated the 12,000-acre Pungo NWR mentioned earlier. Today, the Pocosin Lakes NWR contains over 110,000 acres, extending westward from the Alligator River. This sprawling refuge in Tyrrell, Washington, and Hyde counties gets its name by being contiguous with three of the pocosin lakes—Lake Phelps, Pungo Lake, and New Lake (Alligator Lake) —that dominate the Albemarle peninsula.

About this time, 20,978 acres in the rich bottomland swamps of the lower Roanoke River were set aside as the Roanoke River NWR (1989). In addition to preserving "the largest inland heron rookery in North Carolina," this refuge has a mandate to preserve nurseries for river herring and other fish.[20]

In June 1999 the North Carolina Division of Coastal Management purchased 18,652 acres (18,377 acres plus two adjoining tracts acquired through the Nature Conservancy) on the southwest portion of the Alligator River. This refuge became the Emily and Richardson Preyer Buckridge Reserve (historically known as "Buck Ridge"). According to the North Carolina Department of Environment and Natural Resources, this reserve "contains one of the largest stands of Atlantic white cedar still in existence in the state." In 2002, 8,210 additional acres (Roper Island) on the Alligator River were added to the Buckridge Preserve. Most recently, in April 2008, the North Carolina Wildlife Commission, with assistance from the Nature Conservancy, added 8,476 acres at the northwest portion of the river (Second Creek). As the *Raleigh News and Observer* reported, "the acquisition marks the first time in state history that an entire river has been protected."[21]

In 1999 the Conservation Fund acquired another site in Tyrrell County, namely, ten thousand acres in the northern part of the county bordering the Albemarle Sound. This was a mitigation project to offset road construction losses by the North Carolina Department of Transportation. Named the Palmetto-Peartree Preserve, this site protects the endangered red-cockaded woodpecker (*Piscoides borealis*), which makes its nests in living pine trees.

In 1930 not a single acre had been set aside specifically for preserving wildlife in the Albemarle-Pamlico watershed. Today, well over half a million acres serve as dedicated wildlife refuges in this area alone (table 5). If the Croatan National Forest (159,886 acres) in Craven and Carteret counties is also added, a total of about 1,130 square miles are now devoted to wildlife conservation here. This is greater than the land area of the entire state of Rhode Island and is a tribute to the uniqueness of these wetlands. Fittingly, over 615 square miles (70 percent) are located on the pocosin-rich Albemarle peninsula.

This environmental revolution is a remarkably recent phenomenon. In fact, nearly 80 percent of all the refuges were acquired since 1973, and most of those in the sixteen-year period between 1974 and 1990. The

TABLE 5. National, state, and private wildlife refuges in the Albemarle-Pamlico watershed, 2008

	ACRES
Federal NWR	
Alligator River	152,260
Dismal Swamp	111,000
Pocosin Lakes (including Pungo NWR)	110,000
Mattamuskeet	50,180
Roanoke River	20,978
Swanquarter	16,411
Back Bay	9,000
Mackay Island	8,219
TOTAL FEDERAL	478,048
State Areas	
Pettigrew	20,300
Alligator River:	
Buckridge (including Roper Island)	26,862
Second Creek	8,476
Dismal Swamp	14,344
Merchants Millpond	3,250
Goose Creek	1,208
TOTAL STATE	74,440
Conservation Foundation	
Palmetto-Peartree	10,000
TOTAL WILDLIFE REFUGES	562,488

overwhelming impetus for this transformation is attributable to the U.S. Department of the Interior, whose holdings account for nearly 85 percent of the refuges, in the form of National Wildlife Refuges under the U.S. Fish and Wildlife Service.

These vast wildlife refuges in the Albemarle area are unique in the eastern United States. They promise not only to conserve the remaining wildlife but, slowly, to restore these wetlands to their former water wilderness. Ambitious projects are already focusing on restoring normal hydrology as a matter of priority. Resaturating these pocosins will in turn retard future forest fires and restore the earth to suitability for reforestation of Atlantic white cedar and bald cypress. These hardwoods are slow-growing trees, so it will be one hundred years or more before the pocosin forests return to anything like their former glory.

Ironically, however, not since the original "Albemarle Countie" was administered from London by the king of England has the Albemarle-Pamlico ecosystem been so administratively distant from the people who live here. Today, for example, the U.S. Fish and Wildlife Service administers its vast holdings in the Albemarle watershed from two different regional offices, each located five hundred miles away in opposite directions. The Dismal Swamp NWR and Back Bay NWR, for example, are administered from Hadley, Massachusetts (Northeast Regional Office), whereas the others are run from Atlanta, Georgia (Southeast Regional Office). To put this into perspective, more federal refuge land exists within the Albemarle-Pamlico watershed alone than in all the rest of the thirteen states (from Maine to Virginia) that constitute U.S. Fish and Wildlife's entire northeastern region. From sheer size alone, there is a compelling case for the Albemarle ecosystem to be consolidated into its own region, directly under the Department of the Interior.

As currently structured, fourteen disparate refuges—federal, state, and charitable—occupy different parts of the Albemarle watershed. Each has its own history, biology, priorities, and budgets. Yet each one constitutes a significant part of the same unique ecosystem. Each of these refuges, however, has the same straightforward mandate, namely, to preserve the animals and plants for future generations. Unfortunately, none of these refuges exists to preserve the rich human heritage that is integral to the Albemarle region. With regard to cultural history, perhaps the best known is the Great Dismal Swamp, whose diverse past includes the abundant Archaic Indians on its western edge, George Washington's Canal, the Underground Railroad, Lake Drummond Hotel, which straddled two states, and much more.

Less known, but no less rich in heritage, is the Albemarle peninsula. After a visit through the refuge land of this peninsula, outsiders might be forgiven for thinking that virtually nothing historic happened here. They could not conceive of America's first naturalists exploring these wetlands in the 1580s, the enduring Indian settlements at Lake Mattamuskeet, the bustling antebellum water highway on the Alligator River, slavery and the tragic events of the Civil War, or the East's largest ghost town (Buffalo City). Surely, the next phase beyond today's refuges is to integrate this rich cultural heritage with an equally rich natural history. Perhaps it is time to consolidate America's most historic wetlands into the U.S. National Park System, where cultural heritage is on equal footing with wildlife.

14

Lost Heritage

LAST RIVER HIGHWAY

Much of the Albemarle region was virtually inaccessible by road until relatively recently. The vast swampy Albemarle peninsula was particularly isolated, especially the remote communities along the Alligator River. Indeed, one of these, Kilkenny, was described as late as the 1930s as "one of the most isolated villages in North Carolina." Although indeed isolated by land, these communities had good communications by water for hundreds of years, a river way of life that disappeared in the twentieth century with ascendency of the motorcar.[1]

The farmers and fishermen of these communities along the Alligator River depended fundamentally on the water highway between Fairfield (Lake Mattamuskeet) and Elizabeth City. For generations a succession of familiar scheduled steamers, *Dickerman, Lizzie Burrus, Soon Old,* and *Alma,* left Fairfield in the morning several times a week, stopping at the deep-water Cherry Ridge Landing (Gum Neck) and smaller docks along the way, and terminated eventually at Elizabeth City, from which one could continue on to Norfolk or catch the next scheduled steamer to New Bern.

Little has been written about this bygone aspect of the Albemarle region, especially on the Alligator River. Its very remoteness sustained this lifestyle longer than virtually any similar water highway in the eastern United States. With the advent of proper roads, bridges, and trains even the Alligator River slowly declined as a water highway, and an ancient and romantic tradition finally ended in the mid-1930s.

Steamboats were a way of life on the Albemarle-Pamlico waterways. Shown is the *R. L. Myers II*, which plied the Tar River between Washington and Greenville, 1897. (Courtesy of the North Carolina Division of Archives and History)

The very old community of Gum Neck was the largest on this river. Its original landing of the colonial period was located up narrow Gum Neck Creek, but it slowly became inaccessible to larger boats. In due course it was replaced for commercial traffic by a deep-water landing directly on the river itself at Cherry Ridge, a couple of miles upstream. This occurred about 1845 when a refurbished canal linked the river to Fairfield at Lake Mattamuskeet. For about a hundred years Cherry Ridge Landing was the economic hub of the Alligator River. Throughout this period, apart from the Civil War years, when it was burned intentionally, this landing was the lifeline for locals to transport their fish and farm produce, and themselves, to and from Elizabeth City and beyond.

Cherry Ridge Landing was probably typical of many other landings that at one time dotted the Albemarle and Pamlico sounds and their river tributaries. Its main distinction is that it was bustling after most of the other river ports had closed because of better communications via road and train. A brief account of this time warp in the 1920s is a rare glimpse into a bygone age:

The routes of these early steamboats [on the Alligator River] ran like this: They each had separate days to come into Gum Neck at Cherry Ridge Landing. Weather conditions controlled the punctuality of these runs. The Albemarle Sound got pretty rough at times. . . . Fairfield was the home port for these boats. A boat would leave there at 1:00 o'clock AM, get to Kilkenny about daylight, pick up freight and passengers there, then go to Deep Point to collect fish from a campsite before moving on to Cherry Ridge Landing at Gum Neck, arriving there about 9:30 AM Mr Joe McKinney (with a walrus mustache) was Dock Master or whatever you call the man in charge of all that shipping, etc.

These steamboat days were extra special days. Things were happening, and news from the outside world was always welcome, and someone interesting might get off the boat to spend some time in Gum Neck, hopefully. . . . It usually took the rest of the day to get all the merchandise off the boat and get reloaded to depart at 5:00 PM for other parts and return to Elizabeth City. . . . There were barrels, boxes, crates and bags all containing commodities for our [general] stores. Huge blocks of ice for the stores and some homes and for the fishermen slid all over the docks before they were corralled. . . . Windows, doors and finer things were ordered from Sears Roebuck & Co. . . . Some times there were houses, all pre cut, complete with nails on these boats, they came from Sears Roebuck & Co . . . and there were always things like fence wire or furniture, etc. . . . After the unloading of the imports, then the exports went on. There were usually eggs, chickens, ducks, geese, hogs, fish, molasses and stock peas (soy beans). These things went to Elizabeth City, Norfolk, Baltimore and New York. . . . The checks for them came to the senders by mail.

The activity at "Cherrige" was lively and I always wished that I was a boy so I could go with Papa every week to that exciting event. The only time little girls were allowed to go to the landing was when they were with their family going on a boat trip.[2]

In fact, the author of this account, Louise Weatherly (1913–2005), made the boat trip to Elizabeth City twice:

Our first visit to my grandparents was by way of the *Alma*. I don't remember very much about it except the big box of food we packed. Aunt Addie gave us Devils Food Cake, which I wasted over the rail. . . . There were bedbugs (chinches) on that boat. . . . After we had eaten supper (from the box) we were supposed to sleep while crossing that big sound. But not much. . . . Grandpa met us at the docks in Elizabeth City very early in the morning. He was in the surrey with fringe on top, driving a beautiful black horse . . . way to gooo![3]

Then, about 1925 Louise made a second trip:

> When I was almost twelve years old, we went to see my grandparents the second time. . . . Again we sailed on the *Alma*—and the commotion and activity was just as I remembered, with one exception: I think there were more hogs on board this time than anything else. Your state of mind was controlled by the winds. . . . The stateroom seemed smaller than before. I guess it was because we were bigger. You got so wrinkled staying in the bunks. I stayed outside on the deck as much as possible.[4]

The office for the steamboats was located at Cherry Ridge Landing itself, where several local men, in succession, served as shipping agents, including Bill Liverman (1876–1969) and later Joe McKinney (1880–1929). It was not a particularly safe job, according to one account: "One day in July . . . a woman named L— M— wanted to go on the boat. [Bill Liverman] wouldn't sell her a ticket, he told us long ago, because she was drunk. She went home and got a gun, and came back and shot him. . . . When he returned to work several weeks later, he wore a pistol on his hip in plain view to show one and all that he was fully prepared to defend himself should the need arise."[5]

History of Scheduled Steamboat Service

The earliest known scheduled passenger service on the Alligator River was the *M. E. Dickerman,* based at Elizabeth City, from which it plied the eastern Albemarle Sound on a weekly schedule. An advertisement of 1888, headlined "Steam Line Connections at Elizabeth City," announced that it also served Gum Neck, Kilkenny, and Fairfield: "Steamer *M. E. Dickerman* (for freight and passengers), Tuesday and Friday for Old Trap, Shiloh, Manteo, Roanoke Island, East Lake, Fort Landing, Newfoundland, Gum Neck, Kilkenny, Fairfield, and for Jarvisburgh, Newberne's Landing and Powell's Point Fridays only."[6]

On the morning of 6 August 1895 a most remarkable sight chugged down the Alligator River toward Cherry Ridge Landing. The steamer *Lizzie Burrus* was arrayed in celebratory flags and bunting, which Captain Flavius Spencer (1859–1931) displayed in honor of Colonel William S. Carter (1833–1902), president of the Fairfield Canal Company. A widower, Colonel Carter had remarried the previous evening at the Method-ist church in Fairfield, and he and his bride were on their way to Elizabeth City to transfer to the steamer *Neuse* for a prolonged Southern honey-moon.[7]

With the rise in Confederate nostalgia, Colonel Carter would have been remembered with deference by some old-timers for the leadership role he had played locally in the Civil War some thirty years earlier. In August 1862, when a Union naval boat proceeded up the Alligator River to Fairfield, the Yankees searched some of the houses of the enemy, and "in Col Carter's house [they] found a large silk Confederate flag." Colo-nel Carter of the Thirteenth Militia Regiment was the pragmatic leader of local rebels when Hyde County was "occupied" by the Yankees.[8]

The *Lizzie Burrus* meant different things to different people of the river. For some, it was a reliable means of getting locally produced crops, meat, or fish to market, whereas for others it was a means of receiving a variety of goods, from shoes to gravestones, ordered from Elizabeth City and beyond. To the few who could afford to subscribe, it meant receiving the latest weekly issue of the *Economist*, published in Elizabeth City. The few copies were widely circulated within the community. The *Lizzie Burrus* burned sometime between 1901 and 1903. The warehouse at Fair-field also burned, in 1901, but it was rebuilt.[9]

The obscure steamer *Soon Old* burned in harbor at Fairfield and was replaced by the larger *Alma*. Launched on Christmas Day 1898, the *Alma* was owned and operated by the aforementioned Captain Spencer, who became president of the Fairfield Canal, as well as chairman of the board of the First Citizens National Bank of Elizabeth City. The vessel was named after his youngest daughter, Alma L. Spencer, who was born the same year the boat was launched.

After the *Lizzie Burrus* and *Soon Old* burned, the *Alma* became the main steamer between Fairfield and Elizabeth City, and it was familiar to a generation of people on the Alligator River. This floating institution offered employment to local young men and boys as young as fourteen, black as well as white. The *Alma* burned in 1918, "was rebuilt, burned again in Elizabeth City, was rebuilt and then burned a final time in Fairfield."[10]

Captains in charge of passenger and freight boats on the Alligator River had to be licensed professional men who knew the river and their boats well. After Captain Spencer, Albin Williams (1886–1960) served as the captain of *Alma,* and later still was the legendary Bob Jones (1880–1977). "Captain Bob" was originally from Gum Neck but had spent most of his maritime career on the waters of the Chesapeake Bay. About 1916, not long after he started working in Elizabeth City as a water pilot, Captain Spencer offered him a position on his boat, the *Alma.* Soon thereafter, Jones moved his family to Fairfield, where he lived for more than forty years. Captain Bob operated commercial boats between Fairfield and Elizabeth City until about 1936, when improved roads finally brought an end to local traffic on the Alligator River.[11]

Navigational skill on the part of the captain was especially critical in negotiating the seven-mile stretch between Fairfield Canal and Kilkenny, at the headwaters of the river. In the early 1890s the Corps of Engineers surveyed this meandering stretch with the view of making it shorter and more navigable. Toward this end, the Corps proposed in November 1894 to dredge thirteen specific cuts (thirty feet wide, eight feet deep) across sharp bends in the river. There is no evidence that these cuts were actually made. However, the Corps's map of the river clearly discloses an already preexisting cut ("Hussey's Cut") about a mile down water from Fairfield Canal.[12]

Another tricky part of the Alligator River was at its wide estuarine mouth, where an unseen bar was an ever-present danger. The problem was addressed in the following notice published in the *New York Times* a few weeks before the maiden launch of the *Alma*: "Alligator River Beacon Light . . . Notice is hereby given by the Lighthouse Board that on or about Dec. 1, 1898, a fixed white lantern light will be established, 16 feet above mean high water, on the structure recently erected in about 5 feet of water on the easterly end of the shoal making out about 1 mile from Long Shoal Point, westerly side of the mouth of the Alligator River." It was about here that a barge sank during the epic hurricane of September 1933: "Two Negroes and two white men were drowned in Tyrrell County when the storm capsized a lumber barge on Albemarle Sound."[13]

James Adams Floating Theatre

In the days before cinema, young people of the Alligator River rarely, if ever, attended live theater. Instead, the live theater came to them. The James Adams Floating Theatre was essentially a large, 132-foot barge built for the purpose in 1914. It was two decks in height, not counting the pilot's deck, and contained a theater with a balcony, reportedly for African Americans. During the warm months this innovative and popular showboat made the rounds of communities lining the sounds and rivers of the Albemarle region. It would overwinter in larger towns such as Elizabeth City. While on the Alligator and Scuppernong rivers it was towed by the *Mamie G*, a "steam screw vessel" captained for a while by a local man, Charlie Sawyer (1887–1961).[14]

One can almost imagine the excitement when, about 1915, the Adams Floating Theatre first docked at Cherry Ridge Landing. It had come up from New Bern and Bath, and afterward it would proceed on to Columbia. Gum Neck was relatively populous at that time so, depending on the season's schedule, the showboat might stay docked for up to several days. The full cast of actors and support staff had to eat, much to the benefit of local general stores, which supplied groceries at each stop.

A young boy later recalled, "The plays were excellent and educational, and the actors and actresses were outstanding. The plays were mostly classics and lasted about two hours. There were dramas, musicals, and comedies—something different each night. Tickets cost 35 cents. Refreshments were sold, and Cracker Jacks cost 5 cents." In a cash-strapped farming community such as Gum Neck, it was quite acceptable to pay with garden produce in lieu of money. Impeded only by some puritanical parents, teenagers would flock to see the live performances or, later, a silent film.[15]

The James Adams Floating Theatre was in service for a remarkable twenty-seven years, during which time it became an institution as it plied inland waters from Chesapeake Bay to South Carolina. In April 1925 Edna Ferber spent four days on it while gathering background material for her novel *Showboat*. This floating theater was destroyed by fire on 15 November 1941 on its way to Savannah. There is a recent movement to restore the floating-theater tradition in the Chesapeake Bay.[16]

Closure of Ferries: Rise of the Motorcar

At the beginning of the twentieth century bridges were still a novelty in much of the Albemarle peninsula. In fact, at that time there was not a single bridge across the Alligator River. Instead there were three ferries, one near the head of the river (Fairfield), one midway at its major fork, Northwest Fork (Gum Neck), and one across the mouth of the river (to East Lake). One by one these ferries were replaced by bridges, a process that took another sixty years to complete. The fate of the ferries was inexorably linked to the final demise of the once bustling water highway that flourished throughout the Albemarle region.

FAIRFIELD FERRY (terminated 1904). At the turn of the century the only way to get from Fairfield to the isolated community of Kilkenny by land required crossing the headwaters of the Alligator River via a hand-pulled ferry. This was located about where the Fairfield Canal enters the river. In November 1904, an observer of the Disciples Church "reported directly from the field: Kilkenny is now opened up by bridge and road, and should be encouraged to build a [church] house of suitable size."[17]

NORTHWEST FORK FERRY (terminated 1921). The precarious, muddy "road" between Kilkenny and Gum Neck involved crossing the North-west Fork via another hand-pulled ferry. Then, in 1921 a bridge was built across the river at this point (now North Carolina 94). The new bridge was manned by a local tender. It was a swing bridge that mainly allowed passage of Richmond Cedar Works logging barges and tugs, rather than steamboats.

ALLIGATOR RIVER FERRY (terminated 1962). For many decades a ferry crossed near the mouth of the Alligator River to East Lake Landing. In fact, this was the only way to get a vehicle from Tyrrell County to main-land Dare County and onward to the Outer Banks. This well-established ferry route was totally disrupted during the hurricane of September 1933. Tides had reached between four and five feet, enough to destroy a floating bridge at Alligator community. Early in the morning of the storm the ferry *Tyrrell* was blown out of its dock and sank, thus ending communications with Dare County. At the other terminus across the river at East Lake, "the [John B.] Pinner pier was washed away." After this storm ferry service resumed for another thirty years.[18]

The new Alligator River bridge opened amid a formal celebration on 10 May 1962, only eight weeks after the devastating Ash Wednesday Storm discussed in chapter 3. This three-mile, toll-free crossing was a swing bridge that opened primarily for the larger water traffic on the intracoastal waterway. For the first time, a vehicle could be driven in a few minutes across this wide expanse of the river. This further opened the Outer Banks to tourism, a process that started in the 1830s. The down side, however, is that this bridge ended forever a centuries-old tradition of scheduled boats on the Alligator River.[19]

15 Urbanization and Depopulation

Silkworms, Artificial Silk, and Technology

In March 1540 the de Soto expedition observed the Apalachee Indians of northwest Florida (Tallahassee) making fine cloth spun from the bark of mulberry trees: "And they know how to process it and spin it into thread and to prepare it and weave it." The women wore white cloaks from this cloth and made a fine appearance.[1]

Some forty years later the Roanoke colonists were first to report the presence of mulberry trees in the Albemarle region, and they were quick to propose that the area would be ideal for silkworm cultivation. As early as 1711 settlers already had ambitious plans for creating a silk industry in New Bern. The British even passed an Act of Parliament to encourage silkworm culture in the colony (1769). French Huguenots, who had experience with silkworm culture, were particularly encouraged to bring their skills. Unfortunately, the native mulberry (mainly *Morus rubra*) proved unsuitable for silkworm culture.[2]

In the 1830s a silkworm mania again attracted investors to sericulture. In 1836 plantation owners Josiah Collins and Ebenezer Pettigrew, both of Lake Phelps, jointly undertook large-scale culture of an imported mulberry (*Morus multicaulis*), a species considered ideal for culturing silkworms. By 1839 they had in cultivation forty thousand such mulberry saplings, which they planned to sell wholesale to markets in Baltimore and elsewhere. For whatever reason, this curious silkworm enterprise on the Albemarle peninsula dissolved in 1842.[3]

Nonetheless, the mulberry tree was to have great economic impact on the lives of people in the Albemarle region. In Europe, just before World War I, research on mulberry leaves and bark resulted in a new technology that exploited cellulose from wood products and cotton to produce, among other things, a man-made fiber (rayon), known also as "artificial silk." This cellulose-based technology evolved into big business by World War I.[4]

In America, this cellulose industry had its early roots along James River, Virginia, an area that has several times played a pivotal role in the history of the Albemarle region. As discussed in chapter 4, planters first migrated from James River settlements to the Albemarle region starting in the mid-1600s. Many of their descendants returned generations later, in the 1920s and 1930s, as economic migrants to work in the new silk factories.

The town of Hopewell is on the James River very near the headwaters of the Albemarle basin (Blackwater-Chowan River). During World War I it was home of a DuPont factory that produced "guncotton munitions" from the same cellulose technology. This "guncotton plant" employed some draft-deferred men from the Albemarle peninsula, including George Hussey, son of the local boat captain mentioned in chapter 11. After the war, DuPont closed its plant, with devastating effect on Hopewell. However, in the early 1920s several industries were attracted to the old DuPont site. The biggest was Tubize Artificial Silk Company, which located here from Belgium in 1921.[5]

Before long, Tubize had established an Albemarle ghetto in Hopewell, as one migrant from the Albemarle observed, "after DuPont had closed [Tubize] brought a different group of workers into the community. And as best I can remember most of them came from North Carolina. . . . When Tubize opened they recruited. They sent recruiters down to North Carolina, South Carolina and they recruited people off of farms. . . . I remember one block of the B Village section and everyone from that block came from North Carolina." The record shows that many men and their families from the Albemarle peninsula answered the call for a better life in Hopewell. The men, their wives, and even their children found employment in Hopewell, especially in the "silk plant," and some settled here indefinitely.[6]

The wife of one such emigrant wrote fascinating letters to family back home on the Alligator River (Gum Neck), describing their journey and new life. On 1 November 1922 the whole family had taken the train from

Elizabeth City at 6 AM and at noon arrived at Petersburg, ten miles away (according to an account in the Tyrrell County *Times*): "I found every thing like they promest. . . . People is coming hear from everywhere. . . . Mr George Hussey lives here." She recounted details of their jobs (the older children earned $8.00 to $13.90 a week), rent ($9.00 a month, including lights and water), snuff (only "Big G"), street cars, medical treatment, pneumonia epidemic, and the friendliness of the people. Her own church denomination from back home, Disciples Church, was absent.[7]

The Depression hit Hopewell badly, and the silk plant closed in 1934, "following a controversial strike." However, the town's fortune once again revived toward the end of the decade. By the late 1930s a third crop of laborers from the Albemarle peninsula were employed in Hopewell. By this time roads were so improved that some men were able to commuted, returning to their families as often as possible.[8]

Great Depression

In the mid-1920s, for the first time since before the Civil War, prosperity was once again palpable in the Albemarle peninsula:

Columbia [county seat of Tyrrell County] is about to take her place among the peppy, progressive, aggressive, up and coming towns of North Carolina and she's going to celebrate. . . . Columbia will stage one of the biggest road and bridge celebrations ever held in Coastal Carolina on Wednesday, September 7, 1927. She invites the world to come over Route 90 to join with her on that date to have a real picnic. . . . There will be a brass band, airplanes, parades, beauty show, speaking; a continual round of festivities from early morning till late at night.[9]

The new bridge over the Scuppernong River, the focus of the celebration, finally linked Columbia by road to the rest of the state. This bridge was integral to an ambitious plan of road building and bridge construction throughout the Albemarle region.

At this time Columbia enjoyed a good hotel (Columbia), "one of the biggest general stores in eastern North Carolina" (Davis & Coffield), McCleese retail stores, a cinema, a car dealership, a gasoline distributor, a hospital, a drug store and a soda fountain, a lawyer, a boat freight company, an electric light plant, and even the Cohoon Telephone and Telegraph Company. The roads and sidewalks in town were paved for the first time, complementing the new brick stores that replaced the old wood buildings.[10]

The rural population was sharing in the urban prosperity at this time, enticing many people to move to town, where life was even better. As one account notes: "The rural population of Tyrrell County has shown real prosperity in recent years. Tyrrell County farmers don't come to town with cow dung on their boots anymore. They come in automobiles, wearing as good clothes as town folks wear and have the appearance of being better fed."[11] At this time, even the lower Alligator River (Gum Neck) had telephones connected to the exchange in Columbia some twenty miles to the north, even before there was a proper road. There was no rural electrification, of course; that did not come here until 1948.

Unfortunately, this last grasp for prosperity was short-lived. The Great Depression of the 1930s hit this area very badly, and in a sense much of the Albemarle region never recovered. The backdrop of this period was the deepening economic depression, which was affecting the whole nation, with a growing uncertainty not unlike the global recession that started in the autumn of 2008.

President Roosevelt's New Deal programs penetrated even into the most remote communities here. Most importantly, the Works Progress Administration (WPA) offered much-needed employment to many rural breadwinners until at least 1939. The National Recovery Administration (NRA) was campaigning for a minimum wage (twenty to forty cents per hour), a maximum work week (thirty-five to forty hours), and no child labor, for whites and blacks. Local businesses that signed up for this code of practice flew the "Blue Eagle" banner.

The Emergency Relief Administration for North Carolina recorded that the counties of the Albemarle region were among the most depressed at this time, according to a contemporary report: "The tidewater country is an area of very high relief case load due partially to the severe storm of 1933 and to the depressed conditions of the fishing industry."[12] In 1934–35 Tyrrell County was ranked first in average benefit relief of all North Carolina's one hundred counties. Unfortunately, malaria was also prevalent in these eastern counties at this time, leading to yet another ambitious program of land drainage.

In the 1930s the state intensified efforts to build roads and bridges in the Albemarle region and thereby improve communications between neighboring counties. Some young men worked for lengthy periods with the State Highway Commission before landing a coveted place on the federally funded Civilian Conservation Corps (CCC). Locally, the CCC played a major role in transforming Lake Mattamuskeet into a wildlife refuge. The scarcity of jobs, combined with limited federally funded placements, did not help local race relations. For example, in June 1934 the CCC quota for Tyrrell County was thirteen *white* boys.

As the Depression began its grip, the owner of the Elizabeth City Buggy Company (Walter Pool Wood) visited the lower Alligator River on business by boat in December 1930. A newspaper account of his trip gave a prophetic glimpse of this community before an impending new road (North Carolina Highway 94) was built:

> People there [Gum Neck] complain of a lack of cash, in common with those of other places, he says, but everyone appears to have enough of foodstuffs on hand to last through the winter and then some. Every barn is stocked with corn and stock peas and the family larder is so well filled with good things that Mr Wood threatened or promised, as the case may be, to go there if things got any worse in Elizabeth City. . . . Gum Neck is at least one section where old time courtesy and hospitality still holds, says Mr Wood. Everyone at whose home you stop asks you to have dinner, and means it; offers you a place to spend the night—if they have only one chair in the house it's yours to sit in—and they mean all that too. But Gum Neck, now readily accessible only by boat, is about to lose its isolation, he says. The right of way for the new road to Columbia via Kilkenny is being cleared and the road itself will soon become a reality.[13]

Whereas the Depression was a temporary phenomenon, a more fundamental change to life along the Alligator River was taking place. This was the rise of the automobile and construction of a modern road to the outside world. Probably no single event in the history of the Alligator River had a greater negative impact on the social fabric than the new all-weather road between Fairfield and Columbia that opened in 1935. It was the inevitable death knell for the river way of life. Inland waterway traffic and for a while logging barges continued on the river, but the majestic passenger and freight service on the Alligator River was forced to cease, forever. For this and many other river communities of the Albemarle region, the following prediction made in 1935 turned out to be opposite from what really happened: "If good roads were constructed in the county it would cause the county to become more thickly populated."[14]

Depopulation

In some ways, the story of the Albemarle region in the mid-twentieth century was reverse that of the mid-eighteenth century, up to ten generations earlier. More people left this region to find a new life in Virginia than originally came here from Virginia during the colonial period. The result of this sustained economic migration to Virginia and elsewhere from 1920 to 1960 is that fewer people live in parts of the Albemarle peninsula today than the number of Native Americans living here before the Roanoke Colony. Examples include mainland Dare County (Dasemunkepeuc) and Buck Ridge and possibly Gum Neck (Tramaskecook) in Tyrrell County.

The Albemarle region of the 1960s has changed radically from its golden age, a comparable period one hundred years earlier when slave-based farming was flourishing and the water highway transported crops to lucrative northern markets. The Civil War was a major setback from which this area really struggled to recover. After that war agriculture was still the major source of income, but young men turned increasingly to fishing, lumbering, and merchant marines to supplement their incomes. Then the great lumber enterprises, such as at Buffalo City, offered paid employment. However, as the white cedar (juniper) and cypress, along with herring, were exhausted, many men did not return home.

World War I and the Great Depression drove working men and their families to seek jobs in urban areas such as Elizabeth City, which by this time was bustling with various shipyards, factories (e.g., Taft Airplane Corporation) and mills (notably Avalon Hosiery Mill). When World War II broke out most young men were called up and left the area, many for good. A disproportionate number of these farm boys became career soldiers, and after the war others, including my father, took military-related jobs, especially around Norfolk, whose fine harbor had sustained shipping and naval defense since colonial days.

In less than two generations urbanization had transformed most of the Albemarle region into suitcase communities of aging parents and grandparents. Ghost towns dotted the once bustling waterways. For example, along the Alligator River were the now vanished settlements of Buffalo City, East Lake, Frying Pan, Buck Ridge, Head River, and New Lake, as well as remnant communities of Kilkenny and even Gum Neck and Fairfield. Few places in America suffered such an abrupt reversal of fortunes.

The water highway of the Albemarle-Pamlico waterways was key to this unique agrarian society so recently lost, a time when the populace was undoubtedly more content. One by one these water routes were superseded by motorcars and trains. The last water highway to go, in the mid-1930s, was on the Alligator River between Lake Mattamuskeet (Fairfield) and Elizabeth City, as discussed in chapter 14. Concomitantly, in May 1935 a new road (North Carolina 94) was opened between Fairfield and Columbia, at last spanning the Albemarle peninsula. Symbolically, village post offices closed, and the mail now came by road instead of by boat.[15]

Only three years later a major bridge was built across the Albemarle Sound, an engineering feat inconceivable twenty years earlier. The Albemarle Bridge officially opened on 25 August 1938, amid great fanfare:

> Citizens of the Albemarle section of Northeastern North Carolina will join in a public celebration on Thursday to dedicate the new $1,500,000 bridge across Albemarle Sound that will facilitate travel between two large groups of coastal counties. . . . For the first time in its history North Carolina has a direct route to Northern and Eastern markets for the farmers living south of the sound. . . . The bridge worked a miracle of union, and there is no longer a North Albemarle and a South Albemarle. There is just The Albemarle.
>
> Seven counties will cooperate in the dedication ceremonies, starting with a parade from Edenton to the middle of the bridge. Fourteen children in Colonial costumes will open a decorative gate, symbolic of the formal opening of the three-and-a-half-mile-long structure that will replace the ancient ferry.[16]

The formal opening was "attended by approximately 10,000 people with four brass bands and floats from nine counties. Tyrrell (County)'s float honored its native general, James Johnston Pettigrew [1828–1863]." It says a lot that Pettigrew's fatal charge at Gettysburg was remembered here seventy-five years after his death.[17]

Thus, very shortly before the outbreak of World War II, trucks rather than boats took all produce from farming communities of Lake Mattamuskeet, Lake Phelps, and the Alligator River all the way to Elizabeth City and onward to Norfolk. Ironically, for the people of the Albemarle peninsula the roads led only in one direction, away to nearby towns and cities, and many people slowly left. However, the old communities are still considered "home" to the emigrants, and family ties to this land remain remarkably strong. Homecoming celebrations in churches and communities still feature prominently on the annual calendar throughout the Albemarle region. Furthermore, a sense of history runs very deep throughout the Albemarle region, a measure of the generational stability here. For example, the three counties that comprise most of the Albemarle peninsula publish arguably the most comprehensive, award-winning genealogical and historical Web sites in the entire nation.[18]

Today, in spite of this being one the poorest regions of North Carolina, surprisingly few people live directly off the land that sustained them here for more than ten generations. Throughout the Albemarle region agriculture is primarily dominated by a very few large corporate farms, whose modern mechanization employs few local people. The farms consist of vast fertilized and sprayed fields, often diked to keep out flood water. The crops are monoculture, often genetically engineered and restricted to soybeans, potatoes, wheat, corn, and, of course, hogs.

Poignantly, age-old family farmsteads with well-tended vegetable gardens, chickens, and milk cows have virtually disappeared throughout the region, as have country stores, community schools, and a growing number of churches. But the exhausted swamps themselves have had a reprieve, in the form of huge wildlife refuges that have sprung up since the 1970s and 1980s (see chapter 13).

Epilogue

The journey through the tidewater region of Virginia and North Carolina in the preceding chapters has recorded environmental and human events over some fifteen thousand years, the approximate period that people have lived here. From this history, we can safely predict that well into the future this region will continue to experience periodic megastorms, droughts, and forest fires. However, superimposed on these events will be an intrusive rise in sea level that will eventually inundate much of the current Albemarle peninsula.

Regarding the "tidewater culture" unique to this region, the future is much less certain. To maintain the integrity of this culture, the Albemarle people must surely veer away from dependence on corporate farming, logging, and coastal resorts. Instead, they should look toward a more sustainable compromise with their unique environment and heritage, most compellingly via ecotourism.

Sea Level Rise

There is a general consensus today that our climate is growing warmer, resulting in extremes of weather, but as environmental historians we must be cautious. With the perspective of hundreds of years of records, as discussed in these pages, it may be premature to conclude that recent weather patterns are somehow out of the ordinary. In the Albemarle region, for example, there have been other significant periods of warming. For example, the Roanoke Colony, as well as the Jamestown Colony, were both settled during such hot, dry periods.[1]

More recently, the decade of the 1930s was a period of global warming and was associated with increased hurricane activity on the Atlantic seaboard, "Dust Bowl" drought in the Great Plains, and as discussed in chapter 2, worldwide die-back of eelgrass (*Zostera marina*). In fact, until perhaps very recently, 1933 was the most active year for tropical storms on record. This manifested itself in the storm of September 1933, which was the worst to hit the Albemarle peninsula in the twentieth century (see chapters 3 and 10). Going further back, the 1840s was another period of intense tropical storm activity in the Albemarle region, and its effects, in the form of famine, were felt here, as well as in Ireland (see chapter 4).

Nonetheless, the recent past does seem to be a period of warming, with a significant projected rise in sea level. In this context, the low-lying Albemarle region has been identified as among the most vulnerable localities in America to coastal submergence.[2] This being the case, perhaps it is best to accept the inevitable and refrain from building expensive defenses or further development in this vast zone of submergence. Expenditure should focus on minimizing salt intrusion by blocking man-made conduits of brackish water (intracoastal waterways and contiguous drainage canals), as discussed in chapter 10. Fresh water is the region's most precious commodity, and it is being continually replenished from tropical storms, if we let them.

Ecotourism

One of America's oldest rural societies is itself at risk of extinction. This "tidewater culture" is unique in America and has a remarkably ancient heritage. It comprises people who have lived here since at least the earliest colonial times and who still retain what is often described as an Elizabethan dialect. Those of European and African descent have lived here for more than 350 years, having settled here from the 1600s, contemporary with Jamestown and Williamsburg. Intermixed with both races are many of Native American descent, whose ancestors lived here thousands of years before that.

The colonial period here was unusually influential in the history of the Carolinas and Virginia. This region experienced an antebellum golden age, when a system of water highways was integral to a bustling agrarian lifestyle. Slowly, life here became increasingly difficult for an accumulation of reasons, including the Civil War, the Great Depression, the ascendency of the motorcar, and urbanization. The population dwindled as people migrated elsewhere in search of livelihoods.

The strength of today's Albemarle region lies in its unique freshwater wetlands, surrounded by an incomparable assemblage of relict colonial fauna. Today's vast wildlife refuges in this area unwittingly undermine local heritage and provide little local employment, though this is not meant as a criticism. In fact, only a few dozen people are employed by the refuges. Understandably, many of these positions are taken by skilled foresters and biologists who have no historical connection to the area.

Nonetheless, pioneering efforts in ecotourism, such as Historic Albemarle Tour, Partnership for the Sounds, Ecotourism–Tyrrell County, Inner Banks Xpeditions, Red Wolf Coalition (evening howling), are under way in the Albemarle peninsula.[3] However, in my opinion, the infrastructure for ecohistorical tourism here is currently inadequate for what is needed in the twenty-first century. Accommodation is sparse, and access to the exciting wildlife is very limited. Only the most robust canoeists and wildlife enthusiasts will seek the undeniable beauty in these swamps. Perhaps that is the way it should be, but the local economy may continue to unwind.

If tourism is to sustain local employment in this swampy region for future generations, we may need a radical approach. Ideally, what may be needed is an ecohistorical visionary, like John D. Rockefeller Jr. was for Williamsburg or Malcolm McLean was for First Colony Farms, with the foresight and capital to create a rural Williamsburg.

Foremost, significant investment is needed in infrastructure and innovation far greater than is currently being spent. By way of example, the two major wildlife refuges on the Albemarle peninsula, Alligator River NWR and Pocosin Lakes NWR (over 260,000 acres between them), have annual budgets of $4.0 million and $2.1 million, respectively (2007). In sharp contrast, First Colony Farms and partners were prepared to invest somewhere between $300 million and $540 million to mine the peat in precisely the same area in the 1980s.

Investment in ecohistorical tourism on the order of $300 million to $500 million could allow a world-class experience. To minimize impact on the wildlife, the emphasis should be on the rich human heritage unique to the Albemarle, including, for example, the Clovis culture of the warm thermal strip at the end of the ice age,[4] an Algonquin Indian village as known to the "Lost Colonists," seventeenth- and eighteenth-century colonial settlements (including rice culture), nineteenth-century plantation life and Maritime Underground Railroad, Civil War, herring fishery, the East's largest ghost town ("Buffalo City"), and steamboat life, including reconstruction of the James Adams Floating Theatre.[5] Colonial wildlife, such as alligators, wolves, and bears, could be more accessible to the public in a confined seminatural setting, a showpiece for Thomas Hariot's prescient natural history of 1588.[6]

Such attractions, like Williamsburg, would emphasize historical accuracy interpreted as living history by trained Albemarle people. Furthermore, they could be coordinated synergistically with existing attractions, for example, in the Albemarle peninsula, Paul Green's *The Lost Colony* (since 1937, America's "first and longest running historical outdoor drama"), Fort Raleigh National Historic Site, Somerset Place State Historic Site, Davenport House, and North Carolina Estuarium.[7]

NOTES

Citations starting with "RTS" and followed by a number and/or initials refer to pagination and interviewee as found in the author's original notebooks. Copies are filed with the Tyrrell County Genealogical and Historical Society, Columbia, North Carolina, and the Joyner Library, East Carolina University, Greenville, North Carolina.

Introduction

1. McAvoy 1992; McAvoy and McAvoy 1997, 2003; Oaks and Coch 1963; E. Berry 1907; Russell et al. 2009; Haire et al. 1996, 14, 41.
2. Sawyer 2007a, 2007b, 2008a, 2008b, 2009.
3. Martof et al. 1980; Palmer and Braswell 1995; Meyers and Pike 2006.
4. For example, Kirk 1979; Rose 2000; Royster 2000; Simpson 1997, 1998.

1. Ice-Age Enclave

1. Oaks and Coch 1963; S. Olson 1977; Gaskell 2000; Russell et al. 2009; Hobbs 2004; Riggs and Ames 2003; Beyer 1991; Cronin et al. 1981.
2. Clark, Mitchell, and Karriker 1993.
3. McAvoy 1992; McAvoy and McAvoy 1997, 2003; Flanagan 2000, 16; Russell et al. 2009.
4. Firestone et al. 2007; McAvoy 1992; McAvoy and McAvoy 2003; E. Berry 1907; Russell et al. 2009; Davis 2006. See also *Science* 323 (2009): 26, 94; *Nature Geoscience* 2 (2009): 202–5.
5. Kirk 1979, 44, 48, 49, 50, 54; Scarry and Scarry 1997; VanDerwarker 2001.
6. Eastman 1994a, 6. Note that care is advised in interpreting the absolute ages of these canoes from radiocarbon technology, in that samples taken from the heartwood of an old tree may be hundreds of years older than the outside when the tree was cut.
7. Rountree 1989, 34.
8. Hyde County, *High Tides* 25 (Spring 2004): 2, 3; Eastman 1994a, 19; Eastman

1994b, 56–63; Ruffin 1839, 728; Quinn 1991, 1:104–5, 432–33, 461; Hulton 1984, 73, 118, 119; Rountree 1989, 32.

2. Relict Fauna

1. See, for example, Linzey 1998; Palmer and Braswell 1995; Martof et al. 1980; Radford, Ahles, and Bell 1968; Clark, Mitchell, and Karriker 1993; Stephenson 2002, 58 (photo of seal on Meherrin River); USDA n.d. The eastern diamondback rattlesnake and Venus flytrap are currently known as far north as Craven County and Beaufort County, North Carolina, respectively.

2. Russell et al. 2009.

3. Richmond 1963; Beyer 1991, 182–83.

4. O'Brien and Doerr 1986; Meyers and Pike 2006; Scarry and Scarry 1997; VanDerwarker 2001.

5. Smith et al. 1990; Sturman 2005, 312; Brickell 1737, 133, 179.

6. *North Carolina Times* (New Bern), 24 Mar. 1864; *Daily Reflector* (Greenville, NC), 24 Nov. 1886, 12 Sept. 1894, 27 Mar. 1895, 6 Aug. 1901, 19 Aug. 1959, 14 June 1960; *Washington Gazette* (Beaufort County, NC), 12 June 1884.

7. Janson 1935, 314.

8. *Daily Advance* (Elizabeth City, NC), 16 and 18 May 1935.

9. Palmer and Braswell 1995, 271; RTS (LJC, 69).

10. Rose 2000, 166, referring to Richmond 1963.

11. Stephenson 1995, 95.

12. Brickell 1737, 133, 179.

13. The Albemarle peninsula population of alligators extends to latitude 35°55' N, whereas the Chinese alligator population of Anhui Province extends to 34°40' N.

14. *Daily Reflector* (Greenville, NC), 29 July 1959. A photo of the killed alligator is in the Joyner Library, Special Collection, *The Daily Reflector* Collection, #741.18.c.63.

15. Rountree 1989, 49, citing Strachey 1612, 72; Hodge 1910, 299.

16. Quinn 1991, 1:358, 432; Hulton 1984, plate 43, figs. 9, 15, 74.

17. Strachey 1612, 126.

18. Lawson 1967, 150.

19. Brickell 1737, 202.

20. Whan and Rising 2009; Rogers and Hammer 1998; "2004 Annual Report of the North Carolina Bird Records Committee," Carolina Bird Club, www.carolinab irdclub.org. For an excellent discussion of the current status of the trumpeter swan in the eastern United States see *Birding* 34 (4) (2002): 338–45.

21. Salter and Willis 1972, 10.

22. Forrest 1999, 116.

23. Ruffin 1861, 151.

24. Dunbar 1958, 35, 148, citing G. R. Weiland, "Currituck Sound, Virginia and North Carolina," *American Journal of Science,* Series 4, 4 (19) (1897): 76–77.

25. Dunbar 1958, 148, citing E. Dean, "Currituck County," *The State* 18 (2) (1950): 3. (Dunbar added, "Currituck was undeserving of Dean's superlative statement, but the area did become very popular with sportsmen after the Civil War.")

26. L.S. 1868.

27. *New York Times,* 24 May 1956; Barnes 2001, 112; M. Berry 2006.

28. *Daily Independent* (Kannapolis, NC), 15 and 19 Aug. 1955; *Statesville Record* (Statesville, NC), 22 Aug. 1955.

29. Short, Muehlstein, and Porter 1987.

30. Petrie and Wilcox 2003; Atlantic Flyway Tundra Swan Research, North Carolina Wildlife Resources Commission, www.ncwildlife.org.

31. *Virginian-Pilot* (Norfolk, VA), 27 Apr. 1995.

32. Ibid.

33. "New Navy Study Says Washington County Landing Field Preferred," *Statesville Record* (Statesville, NC), 23 Feb. 2007; U.S. Public Law 110-181, 28 Jan. 2008, Repeal of Authorization for Construction of Navy Outlying Landing Field, Washington County, NC; *Raleigh News and Observer*, 22, 23, and 27 Jan. and 1 Feb. 2008.

34. Quinn 1991, 2:782; Brickell 1737; *Atlanta Constitution*, 26 Dec. 1885 (quote); Kirk 1979, 349–51; Linzey 1998, 298; Rose 2000, 27, 28.

35. Quinn 1991, 1:81, 100, 356–57; Lawson 1967, 120–21; Byrd 1728, 44, 45, 51, 64, 81, 82, 114 (quote), 116 (most of Byrd's encounters with buffalo were west of the Albemarle region); Brickell 1737, 108; Linzey 1998, 296–98.

36. Collins 1991; Linzey 2008.

37. Quinn 1991, 2:603; Sentry 2003, 361.

38. Linzey 1998, 284; Powell 1958, 62; Tyrrell County, *Branches* 11 (Nov. 2006): 6, citing M. W. Lambeth, *Memories and Records of Eastern North Carolina* (1957).

39. *Virginian-Pilot* (Norfolk, VA), 5 Nov. 2007.

40. RTS (EPW, 64, 300); "Wildlife Refuges Hope to Fight Invasive Species with U.S. Money." *Virginian-Pilot* (Norfolk, VA), 5 Nov. 2007.

41. McAvoy and McAvoy 2003, 174.

42. Scarry and Scarry 1997; VanDerwarker 2001, 4, 5, 12, 15, 37, 41; Ward and Davis 1999, 219; Rountree and Turner 2002, 67.

43. Leonard et al. 2002.

44. Quinn 1991, 1:357.

45. Ibid., 247, 356–57; Hulton 1984, plate 32, figs. 23, 35 (oddly, John White's publisher, Theodor de Bry, did not depict this dog in his subsequent engravings); Columbus 1988, 1:42, 120, 136.

46. "Tracking America's First Dog." *Smithsonian Magazine*, Mar. 1999; "Did Carolina Dogs Arrive with Ancient Americans?" *National Geographic News*, 11 Mar. 2003; www.carolinadogs.com.

47. Smith 1612, 349 (which is almost identical to Strachey 1612, 125–26); Powell 1973, citing Thomas Wilson 1728; Byrd 1728, 566.

48. Lawson 1967, 124.

49. Brickell 1737, 119.

50. Sturman 2005, 267, 274–75, 297.

51. Brickell 1737, 119.

52. *Colonial Records* 23:288 (1748); Tyrrell County, Court Minutes, 1761–1770; Tyrrell County, Deed Book 4, Pt. 1, 224 (300), "Wolf Pit Branch, 22 Mar. 1763"; Tyrrell County, Deed Book 1:96.

53. Perquimans County Court Records, 6 Apr. 1782.

54. Ruffin 1839, 519; Kirk 1979, 331; Rose 2000, 232; *Virginian-Pilot* (Norfolk, VA), 16 July 1997.

55. Wilson et al. 2000; Nowak 2002.

56. Linzey 1995.

57. *Charlotte Observer*, 5 Oct. 2003.

58. Flood and Parker 2006.

59. *International Wolf*, Winter 2007 (entire issue devoted to red wolf recovery

program), International Wolf Center; *Red Wolf Journal,* Winter 2008, U.S. Fish and Wildlife Service.

60. Kirk 1979, 331–40; Rose 2000, 25–27; Linzey 1998, 235–40.

61. Scarry and Scarry 1997; VanDerwarker 2001.

62. Quinn 1991, 1:330, 356.

63. Kirk 1979, 332; Ruffin 1839, 701.

64. *Atlanta Constitution,* 26 Dec. 1885; see, for example, Hellgren and Vaughan 1989; Hellgren, Vaughan, and Stauffer 1991, citing also D. M. Hardy, "Habitat Requirements of the Black Bear in Dare County, North Carolina," master's thesis, Virginia Polytechnic Institute and State University, Blacksburg, 1974.

65. Wellman, 1980, 48; "Trial and Conviction of a Baptist Minister for Murder— His Suicide," *New York Times,* 5 Dec. 1853, reprinted from *North State Whig* (Washington, NC), 30 Nov. 1853.

66. Kirk 1979, 334; Tyrrell County, *Times* 6 (Oct. 2000): 55.

67. "Looking Back Fifty Years," *Tar Heel* (Elizabeth City, NC), 20 Aug. 1909.

68. A black coyote was captured alive on the Albemarle peninsula (Beaufort County) in September 2008. K. Wheeler, Red Wolf Coalition, personal communication.

69. Culver et al. 2000; Lee 1977; Heist, Bowles, and Woolf 2001; *Chicago Sun-Times,* 16 Apr. 2008.

70. J. Smith 1612, 360.

71. VanDerwarker 2001, 21, 22, 41; Hutchinson 2002, 34, fig. 2.6; Hulton 1984, plate 48; Quinn 1991, 1:357 (quote).

72. Brickell 1737, 115; "An Act to Encourage Destroying of Vermin," New York Historical Society, BV North Carolina, Laws (1727), 301–3, available online at the Colonial Records Project, Historical Publication Section, Acts, North Carolina Office of Archives and History, Raleigh, www.ncpublications.com/Colonial/editions/Acts/vermin.htm.

73. Albemarle County Records 1678–1737, Misc. Records, 27, 295, 307, 347, 348; Tyrrell County, Court Minutes, 1761–1770, 304 (Feb. 1769).

74. Letter from Governor Tryon to Earl of Shelburne, 28 Mar. 1767, *Colonial Records* 7:445; Tryon 1980–81, 1:440–41, 513, 601.

75. Janson 1935, 340.

76. Clark, Lee, and Funderburg 1985.

77. Herbert Hutchinson Brimley Papers, 1861–1940, North Carolina State Archives, Private Collections (14 Dec. 1939).

78. "Deer Season Opens in Tyrrell County," *Daily Advance* (Elizabeth City, NC), 6 Sept. 1933; Kirk 1979, 347–49; Linzey 1998, 290–91.

79. Caption (2007) to public exhibit of *Puma concolor,* North Carolina State Museum of Natural History, Raleigh.

80. North Carolina State Museum records.

81. EPW to RTS (RTS, 8, 18F, 50); DSL to RTS, 6 Feb. 2001.

82. D. S. Lee, North Carolina Museum of Natural History, personal communication (quote); Lee 1979; Downing 1981; Downing 1984.

83. I interviewed the woman from Fairfield whose childhood memories are discussed in the text on 20 March 2001. RTS (HSO, 140, 141).

84. Case Numbers 42-87 and 43-87, Clinical Necropsy Report, Southeastern Cooperative Wildlife Disease Study, Athens, GA.

85. RTS (ER, 68a).

86. Culver et al. 2000; O'Brien et al. 1990; www.panthersociety.org; *National Wildlife Federation et al. v. U.S. Department of the Army*, Civil Action No. 03-1392, U.S. District Court for the District of Columbia.

3. Water's Environmental Facets

1. Stahle, Cleaveland, and Hehr 1988, 1517; Havholm et al. 2004, 980; Stahle et al. 1998, 564; Powell 1958, 62; News Release, North Carolina Department of Agriculture, 12 Sept. 2007. For a general account of long-term variations of precipitation and temperature, respectively, see also Woodhouse and Overpeck 1998; and DeGaetano and Allen 2002.

2. Lawson 1967, 187; Williamson 1812, 1:176; Tyrrell County, *Branches* 10 (Apr. 2005): 4, reprinted from Tyrrell County, *Swamproots* 3 (1976); Royster 2000, 261, 542; Morgan 1995, 314; Goerch 2003; *Democratic Pioneer* (Elizabeth City, NC), 3 and 17 Feb. 1857; Tyrrell County, *Times* 4 (Oct. 1998): 7; *Tar Heel* (Elizabeth City, NC), 20 Aug. 1909; Tyrrell County, *Branches* 1 (Oct. 1996): 14; Tyrrell County, *Times* 1 (Oct. 1995): 24; *Carteret County News-Times*, 5 Dec. 1974; Tyrrell County, *Swamproots* 4 (1977), 35; Long 2001, 160; White and Haire 2004, 33.

3. Driscoll, Weissel, and Goff 2000; Locat et al. 2009; Oaks and Coch 1963.

4. *Boston Gazette*, 5 May 1735; *Boston Weekly News Letter*, 8 May 1735; U.S. Geological Survey, Earthquake Hazards Program, North Carolina; *New York Evening Post*, 18, 23, and 26 (quote) Dec. 1811; *Pennsylvania Gazette*, 25 Dec. 1811, 5 and 18 Feb. 1812; Nuttli 1973. I am grateful to Chris Meekins for finding original sources to the 1735 earthquake.

5. Stockton 1986; Cloud 1996, 132, 177; *Daily Advance* (Elizabeth City, NC), 25 June 1936; RTS (MG, 136), RTS (FW, 87); Talwani and Schaeffer 2001. See also Driscoll, Weissel, and Goff 2000.

6. Gay-Lord 2001, 1–2 (Lee's Mill); see also "A Brief History of Roper," Roper, NC, Web site, www.vergie.com/roper.html.

7. *Daily Journal* (New Bern, NC), 22 Aug. 1899.

8. Barnes 2001; Maiolo et al. 2001; M. Berry 2006.

9. Whitehead 1981, 451, 469; Beyer 1991, 189, citing R. T. Kaczorowski, "The Carolina Bays: A Comparison of Modern Lakes," Ph.D. diss., Geology Department, University of South Carolina, Columbia, 1977.

10. Pearce 2000.

11. Dunbar 1958, 215–18.

12. *New York Times*, 24 May 1956; see also Barnes 2001, 37.

13. Tryon 1980–81, 2:772–73; Maiolo et al. 2001, 238–39; Burkholder et al. 2006.

14. *Daily Advance* (Elizabeth City, NC), 9 and 13 Oct. 1930.

15. *Daily Advance* (Elizabeth City, NC), 19 Sept. 1933.

16. Barnes 2001, 76–77.

17. *Philadelphia Inquirer*, 19 Dec. 2005.

18. Stick 1952.

19. Stick 1987.

20. Bureau of Sport Fisheries and Wildlife 1958–64, 13.

21. Titus 2002; Titus and Richman 2001; Riggs and Ames 2003.

22. Hayden 1888; *Boston Daily Globe*, 12 Apr. 1889.

4. Period of European Colonization

1. Strommel 1965, 1, 2.
2. Quinn 1991.
3. Fox n.d., chap. 18, "Two Years in America, 1671–1673."
4. Powell 1958; Pelt 1996, 20, 21; *Colonial Records* 1:215–16; Lawson 1967, 200.
5. *Colonial Records* 1:401, 407, 479, 493, 610, 618, 715.
6. Gardener 1990, 72; Andrews 1967, 158.
7. "Journal of a French Traveller" 1921, 737.
8. Hulton 1984, 86, 106; *Colonial Records* 2:39–42, 45; 25:313 (1755), 379 (1758); 23:641 (1764), 792 (1770); Tyrrell County, P&Q Court Minute, 1778, 98; Haire et al. 1996, 13–20.
9. Janson 1935, 314.
10. Ellis 2004, 119, 121.
11. Powell 1958, 62–64.
12. *Colonial Records* 3:28; Franklin 1926, 555, 572.
13. *Daily Advance* (Elizabeth City, NC), 17 July 1917, reprinted in White and Haire 2004, 112.
14. Lemmon 1988, 521–614. Specific quotations are from, in text sequence, 521, 530, 525, 530–31, 532, 559, 560, 565–66, 574, and 614.
15. *Daily Advance* (Elizabeth City, NC), 25 and 27 June 1945.

5. Agricultural History

1. Whitehead 1965, 881.
2. Fearn and Liu 1995; Hutchinson 2002, 29.
3. Quinn 1991, 1:337–50, 422; Ruffin 1839, 700; Peacock, Haag, and Warren 2005.
4. Otis 1878, 68–69; Strachey 1612, 127; Wright 1911, 429, 430.
5. Andrews 1967, 16.
6. Lawson 1967, 50–51, 145–46.
7. O'Rourke 1970, 61–62, fig. 12, which illustrates the stuffed specimen of a passenger pigeon now in Trinity College, Dublin; *Cincinnati Enquirer,* 24 Mar. 2000.
8. Dunbar 1958, 32–34.
9. *Colonial Records* 23:288, 538, 617, 784, 914, 133; 24:749, 912, 958; 25:312, 476; Simpson 1998, 148–50.
10. Lemmon 1971, 303, 304, 519, 617, 489.
11. Lemmon 1988, 40 (quote), 209, 316, 556, 559, 561; Ruffin 1839, 728.
12. Quinn 1991, 1, 2:344 (no wheat trial at Roanoke), 837; Harrison 1941, 11, 67–68, 356, 362.
13. Lefler 1955, 102; Lawson 1967, 70, 80, 88, 114.
14. *Pennsylvania Gazette* (Philadelphia), 28 July 1768; see also M. L. Wilson, "Survey of Scientific Agriculture," *American Philosophical Society, Proceedings* 86 (1943): 54–55, citing the Society's fragmentary *Minutes* of 18 May 1768 ("Hessian fly").
15. Hyde County, Will of Abraham Easter: "one wheat hand mill" (1751); Hyde County, Deed: Thomas Smith to Benjamin Smith (1762); Hyde County, Will of Lydia Slade: "to son Samuel, . . . my crop of corn, wheat and all" (1765); Hyde County, Will of John Carawan Sr.: "to son William, . . . crops of corn, tobacco and wheat" (1770).

16. Lemmon 1971, 289, 355, 441, 497, 522, 624; Lemmon 1988, 32, 209, 470; Ruffin 1839, 728 (quote).

17. Census of Agriculture, 2004, Agricultural Statistics Division, North Carolina Department of Agriculture.

18. Lefler 1955, 102; Lawson 1967, 81; Sturman 2005, 285.

19. Royster 2000, 217, 272, 283.

20. Ibid., 217, 319, 351, 371.

21. Kell and Williams 1975, 104, 121 (citing Clark's *State Records* 22:745), 125 (citing Saunder's *Colonial Records* 10:798–801), 132 (citing *North Carolina Gazette*, 13 June 1778).

22. Lemmon 1971, 303, 304.

23. "Long Tom (Indian)'s Rich Patch," Hyde County Deed Book A, Part 1, pp. 213–16, in Garrow 1975; Albemarle County (Pasquotank Precinct, then including Tyrrell County), Will Book 3, Will #47, Secretary of State Papers, Will of William Ludford of "Alligator," 2 Aug. (?) 1732.

24. Lemmon 1971, xv, 90, 118, 155, 167, 229, 239, 386, 403, 414, 416 (quote).

25. Ibid., 166.

26. Ibid., 561 (quote); Ruffin 1839, 729.

27. Steen 2003, 23; see also *Independent* (Elizabeth City, NC), 27 Mar. 1936; "I Abel Liverman . . . am indebted to C. B. Jones for $6 secured by . . . all my crop of corn and rice," 4 Sept. 1879, Jones Family Collection #890, Joyner Library, East Carolina University, Greenville, NC.

28. Levi Branson's *North Carolina Business Directory for 1884*, Raleigh, NC, Hyde County; *Washington Gazette* (Washington, NC), 12 June 1884; State Board of Agriculture 1896, 402 ("to which the drained swampland"); *Tar Heel* (Elizabeth City, NC), 4 Dec. 1903 ("He has modern machinery").

29. *Winston-Salem Journal*, 10 July 2005, www.journalnow.com/.

30. Shurtleff and Aoyagi 2004.

31. Wolf and Lehman 1926.

32. *Winston-Salem Journal*, 10 July 2005, www.journalnow.com/.

33. Columbus 1988, 1:86n; see also ibid., 2:100, 134; Smithfield Foods, "History of the Pig," www.smithfieldfoods.com; Ewen 1996; Ewen and Hann 1998, 53, 67, 90.

34. Quinn 1991, 1, 2:162, 163, 176, 187, 219, 386, 501, 503 (quote), 549, 603, 735, 736, 742, 747, 782, 786–87.

35. Rountree and Turner 2002, 148, 156.

36. Sturman 2005, 298.

37. Powell 1958, 6–7, 62.

38. Brickell 1737, 55.

39. Franklin 1926, 565.

40. "Journal of a French Traveller" 1921, 736.

41. Tryon 1980–81, 2:364.

42. Franklin 1926, 568.

43. Stith, Warrick, and Sill 1995; www.pulitzer.org; Pollution Information Site (http:// scorecard.org).

44. North Carolina Riverkeepers and Waterkeepers Alliance, www.riverlaw.us.

45. Census of Agriculture, 1997, 2002, National Agricultural Statistics Service, U.S. Department of Agriculture.

46. *New York Times*, 30 Nov. 1999.

47. Maiolo et al. 2001; *New York Times,* 19 and 22 Sept. 1999, 17 Oct. 1999, and 30 Nov. and 7 July 2004; Burkholder et al. 2006.

48. American Rivers Foundation, www.americanrivers.org; North Carolina River-keepers and Waterkeepers Alliance, www.riverlaw.us; Burkholder et al. 1992, 2006; Glasgow et al. 2001; Environmental Protection Agency 1998; *Daily Advance* (Elizabeth City, NC), 15 Aug. 2008.

49. "Journal of a French Traveller" 1921, 735.

6. *Sturgeon, Herring, and Other Fisheries*

1. McPhee 2002, 170. "Spearfish Moon" probably refers to New England Algonquins.

2. Stephenson 1995, 65–88; Dawdy 1995; Carraway 2008, 166–69.

3. VanDerwarker 2001.

4. U.S. Fish and Wildlife Service, "The Coastal Program Strategic Plan," Southeast Region, 2007, part 2, p. 13, citing Smith 1907, vol. 2.

5. VanDerwarker 2001, 16, 35.

6. Quinn 1991, 1:359.

7. *Colonial Records* 3 (1): 90; *Daily Reflector* (Greenville, NC), 12 July 1882, 9 Sept. 1885, 19 Apr. 1893, 16 May and 24 Apr. 1894; Armstrong 1999, 3, citing Leary 1915; Dunbar 1958, 78.

8. Armstrong 1999, 7 (citing *Roanoke News,* 1908), 19; Stephenson 2007, 35; Ausbon 2007, 64, 265 (pagination refers to original manuscript); *Daily Advance* (Elizabeth City, NC), 9 Sept. 1933; Hyde County, *Messenger,* Apr. 1935; *Daily Reflector* (Greenville, NC), 8 May 1959, 28 May 1964; Stephenson 2007, 131 (photo).

9. "Shortnose Sturgeon," North Carolina Wildlife Profiles, www.ncwildlife.org; Armstrong 1999, 21.

10. North Carolina Division of Marine Fisheries, personal communication.

11. Fay, Neves, and Pardue 1983.

12. Rao and Raghuramulu 1996.

13. Once open inlets leading to the Albemarle Sound were (Old) Currituck Inlet (1585–1731), Musketo Inlet (1585–1671), Carthys Inlet (1585–?, 1798–1811), and Roanoke Inlet (1585–1811). Dunbar 1958, 218.

14. Quinn 1991, 1:fig. 5; Hulton 1984, 108.

15. Tyus 1974.

16. "North Carolina Fishery Management Plan, River Herring, February 2007" (draft), www.ncdmf.net, 132; "Trophy Largemouth Bass Management at Lake Phelps," North Carolina Fishing News (2007), www.ncwildlife.org (quote).

17. Hulton 1984, plate 43, fig. 17; Quinn 1991, 1:435.

18. "Journal of a French Traveller" 1921, 735, 738.

19. Stephenson 2007, 17; Leary 1915, 174; Tryon 1980–81, 2:251.

20. Keith 1952, 1:272 (22 Mar. 1787).

21. Tryon 1980–81, 2:413 (30 Nov. 1769); *Colonial Records* 8:153–54.

22. *Daily Economist* (Elizabeth City, NC), 27 Oct. 1905; Dunbar 1958, 75.

23. Perry-Wynns Fish Company Records, 1949–2002, Collection MC304, North Carolina State University Libraries Special Collections Department, Raleigh; *Daily News* (Washington, NC), 23 Jan. 2009; Stephenson 1995, 2002, 2007.

24. Zehmer 2007, 142.

25. Lemmon 1971, 589, 638, 643, 645, 658, 662.

26. Zehmer 2007, 119, 131, 139, 142; Tyrrell County, 1891 Tax List, p. 26 (Delinquents).

27. I am particularly grateful to the late Walter C. Basnight (1913–2001) of Gum Neck for sharing his early experiences of herring fishing on the Alligator River. Text quotes in sequence are from Ausbon 2007, 64, 77, 256, 297 (original pagination); RTS (WCB, 35, 77, 78, 80; EPW, 48, 95; LJC, 70).

28. Zehmer 2007, 142.

29. RTS (WCB, 35, 77, 78, 80).

30. "North Carolina Fishery Management Plan, River Herring, February 2007" (draft), www.ncdmf.net.

31. Dunbar 1958, 73–76.

32. L.S. 1868; *Atlanta Constitution*, 26 Dec. 1885.

33. Winkler and DeWitt 1985 (quote); *Ecotoxicology and Environmental Safety* 47:54–58 (2000); Rose 2000, 249; North Carolina Division of Water Quality, Basinwide Assessment Report, Pasquotank River Basin, Mar. 2006, Station FT-2 (Lake Phelps), 23, 41–42; DiGiulio and Ryan 1987.

34. Bear Pocosin Web site, http://www.bearpocosin.org.

35. "Atlantic White Cedar Project," North Carolina Department of Environment and Natural Resources, Division of Water Quality, Nonpoint Source Management Program, n.d.

36. Dunbar 1958, 27, 68, 79, 85, 137, 138, 216; Eastman 1994a, 25; Eastman 1994b, 15, 16, 19, 29, 32, 34, 35, 36, 50; Sturman 2005, 290; *Atlanta Constitution*, 18 Nov. 1886; Luther 1975, 274; Carraway 2008, 76, 119–21.

37. *New York Times*, 24 Jan. 1891.

38. Dunbar 1958, 80.

39. McAvoy and McAvoy 1997, app. E; Eastman 1994b, 78 (quote).

40. VanDerwarker 2001; Rountree and Tucker 2002, 139, 227.

41. Quinn 1991, 1:362; "Where Are We Digging Now?" Historic Jamestowne Web site, http://historicjamestowne.org/the_dig.

42. Janson 1935, 318.

43. True 1887, 493–503; Dunbar 1958, 83; Coker 1906.

44. *Daily Advance* (Elizabeth City, NC), 11 and 13 June 1935.

7. Antebellum Golden Age

1. Combs 2003, 22–23, citing "James Iredell, Sr., Port of Roanoke, 1767–1776," Charles E. Johnson Papers, Private Collections, North Carolina State Archives.

2. Lemmon 1971, 345–46.

3. Royster 2000, 422; Tazewell and Fridell 2000, 50.

4. Royster 2000, 287, 288, 292, 299, 300, 332, 340, 342; Ramsey 2000; Hinshaw 1948; Tazewell 1990; Watson 1998, 42.

5. Tazewell and Fridell 2000.

6. Tazewell 1984.

7. Janson 1935, 380; North Carolina Land Company 1869, 130.

8. *Colonial Records* 24:861–62.

9. Numaoka 1998, 98–120; Lemmon 1971, 63–64; Lemmon 1988, 16, 481, 536, 601.

10. The earliest reference to Alligator Lake may be that in the will of Samuel Spruill, written 25 May 1765 (Tyrrell County Will Book 1, p. 59): "Alegator Lake the part next to the river new pattent land" (South Fork Township); Alligator Lake is conspicuously absent in John A. Collet's *A Compleat Map of North Carolina, 1770*. The timing of settlement is corroborated by Dunbar family tradition, which claims that the first child born at New Lake was John Cohoon (1777–1847), in February 1777, "about six weeks after arrival of his parents," "New Lake, Hyde County, NC," *Washington Progress*, 19 Nov. 1889, 3, reprinted in *High Tides*, Hyde County Historical and Genealogical Society, North Carolina, Spring 2004, 48; Tyrrell County, Deed Book 6, p. 125, State Grant no. 375 ("William Howard Patent"). See also Hyde County, Deed Book 21, p. 343, and Book 26, p. 54; Tyrrell County, Tax List, 1794; Tyrrell County, Will Book 3, p. 7; Will of Thomas Dunbar Sr., dated 15 Nov. 1841, probated April Court 1844; New Lake Issue, Hyde County Historical and Genealogical Society, North Carolina, Spring 2004. Note: This publication refers to *The New Lake Dunbars* by Sybble Smithwick and Nelson Wynne Allen (privately printed).

11. "Old ditch Dunbar" in Will of Thomas Dunbar, 15 Nov. 1841; North Carolina Land Company 1869, 70, 130. For an excellent account of boundary changes in Tyrrell and Hyde Counties see "The Formation of Hyde and Our Neighboring Counties 1696–1921," in Harris 1995, 73–110.

12. Johnson 1851, 21; Ruffin 1861, 173; North Carolina Land Company 1869, 70, 130; Coon 1908; Lilly 2003.

13. *Colonial Records* 9:411, 422, 425, 426, 445, 446, 523, 526, 542, 546, 548, 552, 585, 662; Ruffin 1861, 216; Janson 1935, 380; Forrest 1999.

14. Janson 1935, 381; Hyde County, Will of Hugh Jones, 19 Nov. 1824; Watson 1998, 44; Hyde County, NC, from H. S. Tanner's "A New Map of Nth Carolina" (1834–36), *Universal Atlas*, Philadelphia.

15. Hyde County, *History*, Fairfield, 18; Tazewell 1984; Marshall Parks (President, Fairfield Canal, New Bern and Beaufort Canal, Norfolk and Virginia Beach Rail Road), "Map of the Albemarle and Chesapeake Canal Connecting Chesapeake Bay with Currituck, Albemarle and Pamlico Sounds and Their Tributary Streams," Washington, DC, compiled and drawn by A. Lindenkohl, 16th ed., revised and corrected 1885 (originally prepared 1855).

16. Ruffin 1861, 220–21; Hyde County, *History*, Lake Landing, 8; Hyde County, *High Tides*, Fall 1983, 25–26; *Economist and Falcon* (Elizabeth City, NC), 9 Aug. 1895, 3; Hyde County, *History*, Fairfield, 55; *Washington Gazette* (Beaufort County, NC), 12 June 1884.

17. Lemmon 1988, 112, 128, 195, 236, 334; Watson 1998, 40.

18. *Washington Post*, 19 Jan. 1910; *Raleigh News and Observer*, 19 Jan. 1910; Wild-Ramsing 1992; see also permanent exhibit at Theatre Museum (Columbia, NC).

19. Lemmon 1971, 615.

20. Lemmon 1988, 84; Watson 1998, 32, 47, 51.

21. C. Olson 2006, 139–64.

22. Lemmon 1988, 459.

23. *Tar Heel* (Elizabeth City, NC), 20 Aug. 1909.

24. Ibid.

25. Meekins 2007.

26. Watson 1998, 40; Ruffin 1839, 698, 699.

27. Armstrong 1999, 1, 4, 6, citing H. M. Smith, "Report on a Collection of Fishes from the Albemarle Region of North Carolina," *Bulletin of the U.S. Fish Commission* 11 (1891): 185–200; Stewart and Roberson 2007, 199–207.

28. Peck 1984.

29. Hewitt 2003, 16; Armstrong and Hightower 2002; Maiolo et al. 2001, 29–45; Woodhouse and Overpeck 1998.

30. *Charlotte Observer*, 18 Dec. 1997 and 20 Dec. 1998; UNC-CH News Service, no. 510, 17 June 1998.

31. Tyrrell County, *Branches* 9 (Oct. 2004): 8.

32. *Hampton v. North Carolina Pulp*, 223 N.C. 535, 27 S.E.2d 538, U.S. District Court, E.D. North Carolina, Washington Division (1943) ("Can a private party maintain an action caused by a public nuisance?"); "Governor Declares January 18 'Weyerhaeuser Centennial Day,' Honoring Company's 100th Anniversary," Business Wire, 12 Jan. 2000; "Record of Decision, Remedial Alternative Selection, Weyerhaeuser Company Plymouth, Wood Treatment Site, Former Chlorine Plant Area, Operable Unit 3, Martin County, North Carolina," U.S. Environmental Protection Agency, Region 4, Atlanta, Georgia, Sept. 2003. This and other EPA publications relevant to pollution in the Albemarle-Pamlico region are available online at www.epa.gov and http://cfpub.epa.gov. See also www.weyerhaeuser.com.

8. *African American Experience*

1. Quinn 1991, 1:251, 252, 254, 2:722.

2. Fischer 2002, 27; Minchinton 1994, 5, citing *Albemarle Book of Warrants and Surveys*, 1681–1706.

3. Grimes 1910, 288 (William Simpson, John Philpott).

4. Powell 1989, 330, 333; Bassett 1896.

5. Fischer 2002, 27; Grimes 1910, 305, 309, 318, 326, 422; Sturman 2005, 270.

6. Quinn 1991, 1:114; Williams 1989, 9; Grimes 1910; North Carolina Colonial Court Records, 192 (Group 7, Misc. Papers); Garrow 1975; Bassett 1896.

7. Fischer 2002, 27; Minchinton 1994, 25. These statistics refer to importation by ship, based on maritime records. The same general pattern can be presumed for slaves imported by various land routes, but such records were not kept.

8. Numaoka 1998, 100; Minchinton 1994, 17, 40.

9. Warren 1885, 200; Sawyer 2004.

10. Steen 2003, 11; Redford 1988.

11. Smyth 1784, 2:100.

12. See, for example, Cecelski 1994a, 183–85; Cecelski 2001; Simpson 1998, 69–77; "The Great Dismal Swamp and the Underground Railroad," U.S. Fish and Wildlife Service, n.d., p. 2, www.fws.gov.

13. Cecelski 1994a, 188, citing *Laws of North Carolina, 1846–47*, c. 46; *1848–49*, c. 93.

14. Kaiser 2006, 2, 13, 14, 16.

15. I am grateful for the assistance of Chris Meekins, of the North Carolina Archives, for the following documents relating to the Polly Wynne murder: North

Carolina General Assembly, Session Records, Senate Committee Reports, Nov.–Jan. 1824, Box 4, 3 pages; Tyrrell County, Slave Records, Criminal Action Papers (1823).

16. Tyrrell County, Records of Slaves; Tyrrell County Court Minutes, Fall Term 1852; Cecelski 1994a, 177; Public Law 105-203, the National Underground Railroad Network to Freedom Act of 1998.

17. Lemmon 1988, 443.

18. Ibid., 163; Redford 1996.

19. *Dred Scott v. John F. A. Sandford*, 60 U.S. 393 (1857). The full opinion is available online at Cornell University Law School, Supreme Court Collection, www.law.cornell.edu/supct.

20. Henry Wadsworth Longfellow, "A Slave in the Dismal Swamp" (1842), Poems on Slavery 1842, Maine Historical Society, www.hwlongfellow.org.

21. Stowe 1856, 2:6, 11.

22. See, for example, Pelt 1996, 156.

23. Tyrrell County, Superior Court, Minute Docket, Mar. 1860.

24. *History of Macoupin County, Illinois* 1879, 187, Daniel B. Sawyer (1813–1881) (descendants of these Tyrrell County Sawyers still live in Macoupin County); "Memories of Ludford Tarkenton," *Independent* (Elizabeth City, NC), 27 Mar. 1936.

25. *Official Records—Naval*, series 1, vol. 6, 592; Barrett 1963, 95, citing J. M. Hough to W. Pettigrew, 18 Mar. 1862, Pettigrew Papers, Southern Historical Collection, University of North Carolina, Chapel Hill (excerpt quote, "In early March," reprinted in Tyrrell County, *Swamproots* [1984], 35); Jackman 1891, 35.

26. Major H. A. Gilliam to Hon. W. N. H. Smith, Williamston, 1 Apr. 1862, *Official Records of the Union and Confederate Armies*, series 2, vol. 3, 836.

27. African American Freedman's Savings and Trust Company Records, North Carolina, New Bern, NC. See Freedmen's Bureau Online, http://freedmensbureau.com/northcarolina; http://wiki.familysearch.org; and www.archives.org.

28. "Gov. Jarvis's Unsavory Record," *New York Times*, 14 Sept. 1880.

29. Sawyer 2007b.

30. *New York Times*, 19 Aug. 1947; *Washington Post*, 20 Aug. 1947; *Daily Advance* (Elizabeth City, NC), 18, 19, and 20 Aug. 1947; *Daily News* (Greensboro, NC), 19 Aug. 1947.

31. *New York Times*, 2 Sept. 1965.

32. Ibid.

33. *Washington Post*, 14 Nov. 1968. For further accounts of racial tension at this time see *New York Times*, 28 Aug. 1965; 2, 3, and 5 Sept. 1965; 29 Jan. 1966; 27 Apr. 1969; *Washington Post*, 12 and 14 Nov. 1968; Cecelski 1994b.

9. *Armed Conflict*

1. Carraway 2008, 166; Quinn 1991, 1:114.

2. *Colonial Records* 2:39–42, 45.

3. Butler 2000; Watson 2005, 52–56; North Carolina Maritime Museum, Beaufort, www.qaronline.org.

4. Dunbar 1958, 22 ("the British navy"), 39, 131; Tazewell and Fridell 2000, 45–58 ("by the desire" quote on 50).

5. Turks and Caicos Island Museum/Salt Industry, www.tcmuseum.org.

6. Quinn 1991, 1:436–37; Rountree 1989, 50, 62.

7. Morris 1958, 6–7 (quote); Sturman 2005, 287, 300; Kell and Williams 1975, 110.

8. Kell and Williams 1975, 13, 65, 113–34.

9. Keith 1952, 241, 249 ("Turks Island salt"), 454 ("I find that West India goods"), 571.

10. Ibid., 448 (quote); Tryon 1980–81, 2:668.

11. Kell and Williams 1975, 13, 113.

12. Kurlansky 2002, 260, 263.

13. North Carolina Maritime Museum, Beaufort, www.qaronline.org; Dunbar 1958, 22, 39, 131.

14. Yearns and Barrett 2002, 185–87, citing "Meeting the Salt Scarcity," in F. W. Johnston, *Papers of Zebulon Baird Vance* 1 (1963): 206–9.

15. Capt. Southam Hoffman to Headquarters, New Bern, 25 Aug. 1862, Civil War, Letters Received 1861–1863, Department of North Carolina (Union Military Campaign in North Carolina), Record Group 393, U.S. National Archives ("In the neighborhood"); Reed 1910, 68–69 ("17 horses"). See also Norris 1996; Hyde County Raid, 7–14 Mar. 1863, Hyde County Genealogical Society; McClees 2006, 2, 4; Pittman 1861–65.

16. Diary of Charles Lepley, Private, Co. E, 103rd Pennsylvania Volunteers, Plymouth, N.C., 27 Jan. 1864, Plymouth Pilgrims Descendants Society, Newsletter: *Voices from Plymouth* 8 (2003).

17. Meekins 2007; McClees 2002; Yearns and Barrett 2002; Jordan and Thomas 1995; Durrill 1990.

18. Mallison 1998, 139–46.

19. Sawyer 2009.

10. *Intracoastal Waterways*

1. Stick 1952, 193–208, 254.

2. Parkman 1983, 57; U.S. Army Corps of Engineers 1880.

3. *Washington Post,* 12 Nov. 1916.

4. "No Hope for Dismal Swamp Canal Route," *Independent* (Elizabeth City, NC), 18 Apr. 1919; State Ship and Water Transportation Commission 1924, 66; Hyde County, Deed Book 47:432–35; *United States of America v. Delilah Rose et al.,* Federal Court, Eastern District of North Carolina, Washington Division, Filed Hyde County, 15 Jul. 1924 (Compulsory Purchase Filed Hyde County Deed Book 47, 432–35); Harris 1995, 169; Swindell and Spencer 1973, 133–34.

5. Sawyer 2008b.

6. *Washington Post,* 12 Feb. 1928; *New York Times,* 5 Sept. 1928.

7. "Surveyors Work on Inland Waterway," *Daily Advance* (Elizabeth City, NC), 28 May 1935.

8. Hyde County, *Messenger* 13 (1) (Jan. 1936), 12 (7) (July 1935), 12 (9) (Sept. 1935); *Daily Advance* (Elizabeth City, NC), 30 May and 27 June 1935.

9. Sawyer 2008a; Carraway 2008, 161–65.

10. Barnes 2001, 70 (citing *Beaufort News* [Beaufort, NC], 21 Sept. 1933), 304; "Winds Estimated at Hatteras at 122 mph; Barometer Fell to 28.28—Lowest Known Locally," in C. J. O'Neal, *The Story of Ocracoke Island* (Swan Quarter, NC: Hyde County Bicentennial Project, 1976), 31.

11. The basis of the calculations in this paragraph is as follows: The length of the canal is approximately eighteen miles, and it is two hundred feet wide, and it is assumed the water height in the canal was increased during the storm by three feet, with four square miles of flood at an average depth of two feet at Gum Neck.

12. Dunbar 1958, 71, 73; Bureau of Sport Fisheries and Wildlife 1958–64, 13.

13. North Carolina Division of Water Quality, http://h2o.enr.state.nc.us.

14. Parkman 1983, 69; *Daily Independent* (Kannapolis, NC), 15 and 19 Aug. 1955; *Statesville Record* (Statesville, NC), 22 Aug. 1955; *New York Times*, 24 May 1956; Barnes 2001, 112; M. Berry 2006.

15. Richardson 1981; Madden 2005; Ferrell, Strickland, and Spruill 2007.

16. Baker, Baker, and Mann 1994, 4, 6; Fuss 2001; Madden 2005; Ferrell, Strickland, and Spruill 2007; www.invasivespecies.net.

17. Rose 2000, 261.

11. *Forests Then and Now*

1. Stahle, Cleaveland, and Hehr 1988; Stahle et al. 1998; "North Carolina Cypress Sets National Record," American Forest Organization, Washington, DC, May 2006, www.americanforests.org.

2. Tyrrell County, Will Book 1:138 (1783); Deed Book 50:7, 440.

3. Ruffin 1839.

4. Ibid., 728.

5. Hinesley 2002; North Carolina Division of Forest Resources, Urban and Community Forestry, Champion Big Tree Database, www.dfr.state.nc.us/Urban/nc_champion_big_trees_overview.htm.

6. *History of the Eleventh Pennsylvania Volunteer Cavalry* 1902.

7. Long 2001, 144; Timber Leases to Roper Lumber Company by local people in Washington County, NC, Deed Book AA:364 (1887); Book 50:50 (1905); Book 56:427 (1911); Book 65:238, 241, 244 (1915); *Independent* (Elizabeth City, NC), 18 Apr. 1919.

8. Ashe 1894, 29 (quote), 110.

9. Jones 1948; Ausbon 2007, 114; *Economist and Falcon* (Elizabeth City, NC), 22 May 1896 (quote).

10. *Atlanta Constitution*, 26 Dec. 1885.

11. Long 2001, 156.

12. *Dare County Times*, 28 July 1939.

13. *Virginian-Pilot* (Norfolk, VA), 2 Oct. 1994; Long 2001, 136–74; Tate 2000.

14. Ausbon 2007, 33, 34, 35, 63, 64, 236; RTS, 36 (WCB).

15. Tyrrell County, Deed Book 55:4 (1907); Book 54:592–93 (1907); Book 73:63 (1920). Pay slips for EPW from Richmond Cedar Works for Dec. 1946 and Jan. 1947 indicate that the net pay for two days, two hours was $11.53 and for five days, five hours was $32.32. Tyrrell County, *Tribune*, 15 May 1941; *Daily Advance* (Elizabeth City, NC), 11 June 1945.

16. RTS, 26 (EWAW).

17. RTS, 18F, 26, 76, 85, 198 (EPW); Dimple J. Taylor, personal communication ("kept employees"); Tennessee Ernie Ford, "Sixteen Tons," *Classic Country Album 1950–64*, www.cowboylyrics.com ("I owe my soul").

18. RTS, 90 (HMC); RTS, 35 (WCB); Ausbon 2007, 237; *Dictionary of American Naval Fighting Ships* 2004, s.v. "Lucille Ross."

19. Sharpe 1965, vol. 4; Fuss 2001, 24; RTS, 38, 39 (WCB).

12. Droughts and Forest Fires

1. North Carolina Division of Forest Resources, "Causes of Wildfire in North Carolina, 1970–2005," www.dfr.state.nc.us; Wade and Ward 1973; *New York Times*, 5 June 2008.

2. McAvoy and McAvoy 2003, 181; Whitehead 1981, 45; Woodhouse and Overpeck 1998.

3. Rountree 1989, 40.

4. *Daily Independent* (Kannapolis, NC), 5 Apr. 1955.

5. *Colonial Records* 24:861–62.

6. Lemmon 1971, 95.

7. Ibid., 98.

8. Janson 1935, 339.

9. Ruffin 1839, 733; Lemmon 1971, 384–85.

10. Lemmon 1971, 384–85 ("it was perhaps"); Ruffin 1839, 733 ("When at last").

11. Royster 2000, 414.

12. *New York Times*, 17 Apr. 1880; *Chester Daily Times* (Pennsylvania), 23 Apr. 1880; *Lake Superior News* (Michigan), 29 Apr. 1880; *Athens Messenger* (Georgia), 29 Apr. 1880; *Raleigh Farmer and Mechanic*, 29 Apr. 1880; Federal Census, Tyrrell County, 1880 Mortality Schedule, Alligator Township; White and Haire 2004, 82; *Tyrrell Tides* (Tyrrell County Genealogical and Historical Society newsletter) 15 (Mar. 2009): 3.

13. Sharpe 1965, vol. 4.

14. *New York Times*, 5 Apr. 1955.

15. *Statesville Record and Landmark* (Statesville, NC), 6 Apr. 1955 and 7 Apr. 1955 (quote); *Daily Independent* (Kannapolis, NC), 5 and 6 Apr. 1955.

16. *News* (Newport, RI), 6 and 7 Apr. 1955; *Bridgeport Post* (Bridgeport, CT), 7 Apr. 1955 (quote); RTS, 290.

17. *Coastland Times*, 28 Apr. and 5 May 1961; *Raleigh News and Observer*, 27 Apr. 1961.

18. *Los Angeles Times*, 8 Apr. 1985.

19. *Washington Post*, 9 Apr. 1985 (quote); *New York Times*, 13 Apr. 1985; *Philadelphia Inquirer*, 8 Apr. 1985; RTS, 143.

20. Poulter, Christensen, and Halpin 2006; Eastman 1994a, 6; 1994b, 56–63.

21. Wade and Ward 1973; *Charlotte Observer*, 5 Feb. 1986, 21 Mar., 19 June, and 10 Oct. 1987, and 23 June 1988; *Virginian-Pilot* (Norfolk, VA), 16 Sept. 1997.

22. U.S. Public Law 110-181, 28 Jan. 2008, Repeal of Authorization for Construction of Navy Outlying Landing Field, Washington County, NC; *Raleigh News and Observer*, 22, 23, and 27 Jan. 2008, 1 Feb. 2008.

23. No OLF Campaign, www.noolf.com; Virginians Against the OLF, www.novaolf.com.

24. North Carolina Division of Forest Resources, "Causes of Wildfire in North Carolina, 1970–2005," www.dfr.state.nc.us; *New York Times*, 5 June 2008.

13. From Peat Mining to Wildlife Refuges

1. E. Berry 1907; Madden 2005; Poulter, Christensen, and Halpin 2006.

2. Ruffin 1839, 728, 733; Ruffin 1861, 242; Lilly 1998, 2003.

3. Ruffin 1861, 240.

4. Poulter, Christensen, and Halpin 2006, 7; Kirk 1979, 14. For a general account of long-term variations of precipitation and temperature, respectively, see Woodhouse and Overpeck 1998, and DeGaetano and Allen 2002.

5. Carter 1975, 1978.

6. *Wall Street Journal,* 29 Aug. 1973; *Washington Post,* 29 Aug. 1973; *New York Times,* 8 May 1974; *Time,* 24 Apr. 1978.

7. Fuss 2001, 25.

8. Carter 1978, 33.

9. Ibid., 33, 34.

10. Gregory et al. 1984.

11. *New York Times,* 20 June 1983.

12. *National Wildlife Federation, et al., v. U.S. Army Corps of Engineers, et al.,* No. 83-1288-CIV-5, U.S. District Court, E.D. North Carolina, Raleigh District, 20 Dec. 1985; No. 87-3183, U.S. Court of Appeals, 4th Circuit, 13 Oct. 1988; *New York Times,* 10 Feb. 1984; *Charlotte Observer,* 31 Dec. 1985, 16 Aug. 1988.

13. McLean Industries, Inc., United States Lines, Inc., United States Lines (SA), Inc., and First Colony Farms, Inc., Debtors, Bankruptcy No. 86 B 12238-41, U.S. Bankruptcy Court, S.D. New York, 24 Nov. 1986, 3 Mar. 1987, 29 July 1987; *New York Times,* 17 Jan. 1987, 6 July 1988.

14. Richard King Mellon Foundation, "From Sea to Shining Sea: Richard King Mellon Foundation American Land Conservation Program, 1998–2002," Pittsburgh, PA, 2002, 45; *Charlotte Observer,* 4 Aug. and 19 Sept. 1989; *Fayetteville Observer,* 25 and 27 Aug. 1989; *New York Times,* 1 July 1990; *Pittsburgh Post-Gazette,* 11 July 2003, 27 Aug. 2006; *Raleigh News and Observer,* 14 Mar. 2004, 10 Apr. 2008.

15. *Virginian-Pilot* (Norfolk, VA), 28 Apr. 1990.

16. Anderson 1995; Michigan State University College of Law, Animal Legal and Historical Center, www.animallaw.info.

17. Rose 2000, 3–6, 7–9, 261–66; Baird 2006.

18. Baird 2006, 33.

19. *Raleigh News and Observer,* 10 Apr. 2008. See also Bryant 2007.

20. U.S. Fish and Wildlife Service, "Roanoke River National Wildlife Refuge," www.fws.gov/roanokeriver.

21. North Carolina Department of Environment and Natural Resources, Division of Coastal Management, 18 Mar. 2002 ("contains one of the largest"); *Raleigh News and Observer,* 10 Apr. 2008 ("The acquisition marks"). See also Fuss 2001.

14. Lost Heritage

1. *Daily Advance* (Elizabeth City, NC), 30 May 1935.

2. Ausbon 2007, 296, 298. See also ibid., 63, 296, 297, 300; *Raleigh News and Observer,* 10 Sept. 2006.

3. Ausbon 2007, 114.

4. Ibid., 115.

5. White and Haire 2004, 66. See also *Coastland Times,* 23 Sept. 1982.

6. Nowitzky 1888.

7. "Happy Bridal Couple," *Economist and Falcon* (Elizabeth City, NC), 9 Aug. 1895. For an excellent local account of the *Neuse* see Alexander 1954.

8. Lt. Commander George Gerrard to Col. William A. Howard, Commander Roa-

noke Island, 25 Aug. 1862, *Official Records—Naval*, Record Group 393; Col. Wm. S. Carter to Gov. Z. B. Vance, 28 Sept. 1862, in Hyde County Historical and Genealogical Society 1976, 74.

9. Hyde County Historical and Genealogical Society 1976, 15, 18–19; White and Haire 2004, 30–31, 95–96, 157–58; Ausbon 2007, 114.

10. Hyde County Historical and Genealogical Society 1976, 18.

11. Jones 1948.

12. Map of Upper Part of Alligator River, NC, from notes of survey made under the direction of Major W. S. Stanton, Corps of Engineers, USA, by 1st Lieut. E. W. Van C. Lucas, Corps of Engineers, USA, Nov. 1894, U.S. Engineer Office, Wilmington, NC, 26 Jan. 1895. Note: These maps are available at North Carolina State Archives, M.C. 325-A.

13. *New York Times*, 2 Nov. 1898, 18 Sept. 1933.

14. "Notice of Sale of the Steam Screw Vessel *Mamie G*," *Independent* (Elizabeth City, NC), 26 Feb. 1919; RTS (70, #1; 132, 206); "Lennie Christianson" (aged one hundred), *Scuppernong Reminder* (Tyrrell County, NC), 12 Feb. 2003.

15. Lowe 1984.

16. Bath, North Carolina, Historic Marker; *Our State* (Greensboro, NC), Apr. 2008, 160–64; Chesapeake Bay Floating Theatre, Inc., www.floatingtheatre.org.

17. RTS (WCB, 80); Ausbon 2007, 54; Ware 1961, 60 (quote).

18. Plaque on bridge at Northwest Fork of Alligator River: "Tyrrell County. State Project 1921. Federal Aid 1954"; *Daily Advance* (Elizabeth City, NC), 20 Sept. 1933 (quote).

19. Sawyer 2007a, 218; "Outer Banks Are in Business," *Washington Post*, 27 May. 1962.

15. *Urbanization and Depopulation*

1. Ewen and Hann 1998, 156 (translated from the diary of Rodrigo Ranjel, de Soto's private secretary).

2. Quinn 1991, 1:326; Sturman 2005, 301; Arthur Dobbs, London, to his son C. R. Dobbs, Carrickfergus, 16 Dec. 1752, Public Record Office, Northern Ireland, D/162/64.

3. Tryon 1980–81, 2:334, 360, 384–85, 388, 390, 768; Lemmon 1988, 317, 344, 398–99, 400, 403, 404, 407, 440, 480, 490, 501n.; Misc. Items, Heirs of Josiah Collins I, Josiah Collins Papers, North Carolina State Archives, A.B. 265.1–265.10.

4. Woodings 2001, 14–19.

5. "In Their Own Words: Tubize Artificial Silk Company," College of William and Mary, www.wm.edu/anthropology/hopewell.

6. Ibid.

7. Tyrrell County, *Times* 1 (Oct. 1995): 36–41 (quote on 37).

8. "In Their Own Words" (quote); Federal Census, Virginia, Prince George County, Hopewell: Employment: "Silk Plant," "Silk Mill"; *Daily Advance* (Elizabeth City, NC), 30 July 1934; Tyrrell County, *Tribune*, 28 Dec. 1939.

9. *Independent* (Elizabeth City, NC), 2 Sept. 1927, reprinted in Tyrrell County, *Swamproots*, Spring 1979, 42. Note: Years later this Scuppernong bridge was floated to Chowan County. See also Tyrrell County, *Enquirer*, 23 Nov. 1981.

10. *Independent* (Elizabeth City, NC), 2 Sept. 1927, reprinted in Tyrrell County, *Swamproots*, Spring 1979, 44.

11. Ibid.; Tyrrell County Road Commission, 31 Mar. 1928, Weekly Pay Roll, North Carolina State Archives, Roads, 096-925-3; Southern Historical Collection, Manuscripts Department, Library of the University of North Carolina, Chapel Hill, #3334, Elizabeth City Buggy Company, Account Books, 1927–1932.

12. Kirk, Cutter, and Morse 1936, 35.

13. *Daily Advance* (Elizabeth City, NC), 12 Dec. 1930.

14. Kirk, Cutter, and Morse 1936, 35, 42; *Daily Advance* (Elizabeth City, NC), 25 June 1934, 18 July 1935 (quote); Forrest 1999, 91–100; Civilian Conservation Corps, Enrollment & Discharge Records, Tyrrell County, NC.

15. *Daily Advance* (Elizabeth City, NC), 30 May and 15 June 1935.

16. *New York Times*, 21 Aug. 1938.

17. White and Haire 2004, 139 (quote); Wilson 1998.

18. Hyde County: http://www.ncgenweb.us/hyde/HYDE.HTM; Tyrrell County: http://www.ncgenweb.us/tyrrell/TYRRELL.HTM; Washington County: http://www.ncgenweb.us/washington.

Epilogue

1. Stahle, Cleaveland, and Hehr 1988; Stahle et al. 1998; Havholm et al. 2004. For a general account of long-term variations in precipitation and temperature, respectively, see Woodhouse and Overpeck 1998, and DeGaetano and Allen 2002.

2. Titus and Richman 2001; Titus 2002; Riggs and Ames 2003.

3. Historic Albemarle Tour, www.historicalbemarletour.org; Partnership for the Sounds, www.partnershipforsounds.org; Flood and Parker 2006; Ecotourism-Tyrrell County, including Inner Banks Xpeditions, www.columbianc.com; Red Wolf Coalition, www.redwolves.com.

4. McAvoy 1992; McAvoy and McAvoy 2003.

5. Chesapeake Bay Floating Theatre, Inc., www.floatingtheatre.org.

6. Thomas Hariot's "A Briefe and True Report," in Quinn 1991, 1:314–89.

7. The Lost Colony, www.thelostcolony.org (quote); North Carolina Estuarium, www.pamlico.com/nce.

REFERENCES

Alexander, J. W. 1954. "The Steamer *Neuse* on the North Carolina Sounds in the 1890's." Tyrrell County, *Times* 1 (2): 23–25.

Anderson, R. S. 1995. "The Lacey Act: America's Premier Weapon in the Fight against Unlawful Wildlife Trafficking." *Public Land Law Review.* Available online at www.animallaw.info.

Andrews, C. M. 1967. *Narratives of the Insurrections, 1675–1690.* New York: Barnes and Noble.

Armstrong, J. L. 1999. "Movement, Habitat Selection and Growth of Early-Juvenile Atlantic Sturgeon in Albemarle Sound, North Carolina." Master's thesis, Zoology Department, North Carolina State Univ., Raleigh.

Armstrong, J. L., and J. E. Hightower. 2002. "Potential for Restoration of the Roanoke River Population of Atlantic Sturgeon." *Journal of Applied Ichthyology* 18 (4–6): 475–80.

Ashe, W. W. 1894. *The Forests, Forest Lands, and Forest Products of Eastern North Carolina.* Raleigh: North Carolina Geological Survey, Bulletin Number 5, 1–128.

Ausbon, L. W. 2007. "Memories of Growing Up in Gum Neck, NC." Tyrrell County, *Times* 8 (2): 54–110.

Baird, S. 2006. "Great Dismal Swamp National Wildlife Refuge: Final Comprehensive Conservation Plan." U.S. Fish and Wildlife Service, Northeast Region, Hadley, MA.

Baker, P., S. Baker, and R. Mann. 1994. "Potential Range of the Zebra Mussel, *Dreissena polymorpha,* in and near Virginia." Gloucester Point: Virginia Institute of Marine Science, College of William and Mary.

Barnes, J. 2001. *North Carolina's Hurricane History.* 3rd ed. Chapel Hill: Univ. of North Carolina Press.

Barrett, J. G. 1963. *The Civil War in North Carolina.* Raleigh: Univ. of North Carolina Press.

Bassett, J. S. 1896. *Slavery and Servitude in the Colony of North Carolina: Electronic Edition.* Baltimore: Johns Hopkins Univ. Press. Available online at Documenting the American South, Univ. of North Carolina, Chapel Hill, http://docsouth.unc.edu.

Berry, E. W. 1907. "Pleistocene Flora of North Carolina." *Journal of Geology* 15: 338–49.

Berry, M. S. 2006. *History of Northeastern North Carolina Storms.* Hyde County Genealogical Society, North Carolina, www.ncgenweb.us/hyde/maps/HURICA NE.HTM.

Beyer, F. 1991. *North Carolina: The Years before Man.* Durham, NC: Carolina Academic Press.

Brickell, J. 1737. *The Natural History of North Carolina.* Dublin: printed for the author by James Carson. Available online at the Colonial Records Project, Historical Publication Section, Out-of-Print Bookshelf, Original Sources, North Carolina Office of Archives and History, Raleigh, NC, www.ncpublications.com/colonial/ Bookshelf.

Bryant, M. R. 2007. "Alligator River National Wildlife Refuge: Comprehensive Conservation Plan." U.S. Fish and Wildlife Service, Southeast Region, Atlanta.

Bureau of Sport Fisheries and Wildlife, North Carolina Wildlife Resources Commission, and Virginia Commission of Game and Inland Fisheries. 1958–64. "Back Bay–Currituck Sound Data Report: Introduction and Vegetation Studies." Available online at www.fws.gov/nc-es/coastal.

Burkholder, J. M., D. A. Dickey, C. Kinder, R. E. Reed, M. A. Malin, G. Melia, M. R. McIver, L. B. Cahoon, C. Brownie, N. Deamer, J. Springer, H. Glasgow, D. Toms, and J. Smith. 2006. "Comprehensive Trend Analysis of Nutrients and Related Variables in a Large Eutrophic Estuary: A Decadal Study of Anthropogenic and Climatic Influences." *Limnology and Oceanography* 5 (1, Part 2): 463–87.

Burkholder, J. M., E. J. Noga, C. W. Hobbs, H. B. Glasgow Jr., and S. A. Smith. 1992. "New 'Phantom' Dinoflagellate is the Causative Agent of Major Estuarine Fish Kills." *Nature* 358: 407–10; 360: 768.

Butler, L. S. 2000. *Pirates, Privateers, and Rebel Raiders of the Carolina Coast.* Chapel Hill: Univ. of North Carolina Press.

Byrd, W. 1728. "History of the Dividing Line." In *The Westover Manuscripts.* Petersburg, VA, 1841. Available online at Documenting the American South, Univ. of North Carolina, Chapel Hill, http://docsouth.unc.edu.

Carraway, D. C. 2008. *South River: A Local History from Turnagain Bay to Adams Creek.* Fayetteville, NC: GLORY! Marketing.

Carter, L. J. 1975. "Agriculture: A New Frontier in Coastal North Carolina." *Science* 189: 271–75.

———. 1978. "Peat for Fuel: Development Pushed by Big Corporate Farm in Carolina." *Science* 199: 33–34.

Cecelski, D. S. 1994a. "The Shores of Freedom: The Maritime Underground Railroad in North Carolina, 1800–1861." *North Carolina Historical Review* 71 (2): 174–206.

———. 1994b. *Along Freedom Road: Hyde County, North Carolina, and the Fate of Black Schools in the South.* Chapel Hill: Univ. of North Carolina Press.

———. 2001. *The Waterman's Song: Slavery and Freedom in Maritime North Carolina.* Chapel Hill: Univ. of North Carolina Press.

Clark, M. K, S. D. Lee, and J. B. Funderburg. 1985. "The Mammal Fauna of Carolina Bays, Pocosins and Associated Communities in North Carolina: An Overview." *Brimleyana* 11: 1–38.

Clark, M. K., M. S. Mitchell, and K. S. Karriker. 1993. "Notes on the Geographical and Ecological Distribution of Relict Populations of *Synaptomys cooperi* (Rodentia: Arvicolidae) from Eastern North Carolina." *Brimleyana* 19: 155–67.

Cloud, E. F. 1996. *Portsmouth: The Way It Was.* Ocracoke, NC: Live Oak.

Coker, R. E. 1906. "The Natural History and Cultivation of the Diamond-Back Terrapin, with Notes on Other Forms of Turtles." *North Carolina Geological Survey Bulletin* 14: 1–67.

Collins, J. 1991. "The Wild Boar in North Carolina." Species profile at North Carolina Wildlife, www.ncwildlife.org.

Colonial and State Records of North Carolina. Available online at Documenting the American South, Univ. of North Carolina, Chapel Hill, http://docsouth.unc.edu.

Columbus, Christopher. 1988. *Select Documents Illustrating the Four Voyages of Columbus.* 2 vols. Translated and edited with introduction and notes by Cecil Jane. New York: Dover Publications.

Combs, E. L., III. 2003. "Trading in Lubberland: Maritime Commerce in Colonial North Carolina." *North Carolina Historical Review* 80 (1): 1–27.

Coon, C. L. 1908. *The Beginnings of Public Education in North Carolina: A Documentary History, 1790–1840.* Vol. 2. Available online at Documenting the American South, Univ. of North Carolina, Chapel Hill, http://docsouth.unc.edu.

Cronin, T. M., B. J. Szabo, T. A. Ager, J. E. Hazel, and J. P. Owens. 1981. "Quaternary Climates and Sea Levels of the U.S. Atlantic Coastal Plain." *Science* 211 (4479): 233–40.

Culver, M., W. E. Johnson, J. Pecon-Slattery, and S. J. O'Brien. 2000. "Genomic Ancestry of the American Puma (*Puma concolor*)." *Journal of Heredity* 91 (3): 186–97.

Davis, D. E. 2006. *Southern United States: An Environmental History.* Santa Barbara, CA: ABC-CLIO.

Dawdy, S. L. 1995. "The Meherrin's Secret History of the Dividing Line." *North Carolina Historical Review* 72 (4): 386–415.

DeGaetano, A. T., and R. J. Allen. 2002. "Trends in Twentieth-Century Temperature Extremes across the United States." *Journal of Climate* 15: 3188–3205.

Dictionary of American Naval Fighting Ships. 2004. Washington, DC: Naval Historical and Heritage Command, www.history.navy.mil/danfs.

DiGiulio, R. T., and E. W. Ryan. 1987. "Mercury in Soils, Sediments, and Clams from a North Carolina Peatland." *Water, Air and Soil Pollution* 33: 205–19.

Downing, R. L. 1981. "The Current Status of the Cougar in the Southern Appalachians." *Proceedings of Nongame and Endangered Wildlife Symposium*, Athens, GA, 13–14 Aug. 1981, 142–51.

———. 1984. "The Search for Cougars in the eastern United States." *Cryptozoology* 3: 39.

Driscoll, N. W., J. K. Weissel, and J. A. Goff. 2000. "Potential for Large-Scale Submarine Slope Failure and Tsunami Generation along the U.S. Mid-Atlantic Coast." *Geology* 28 (5): 407–10.

Dunbar, G. S. 1958. *Historic Geography of the North Carolina Outer Banks.* Baton Rouge: Louisiana Univ. Press.

Durrill, W. K. 1990. *War of Another Kind.* New York: Oxford Univ. Press.

Eastman, J. M. 1994a. "The North Carolina Radiocarbon Date Study, Part 1." *Southern Indian Studies* 42: 1–63.

———. 1994b. "The North Carolina Radiocarbon Date Study, Part 2." *Southern Indian Studies* 43: 1–117.

Ellis, H. 2004. *Sweetness and Light: The Mysterious History of the Honeybee,* New York: Harmony Books.

Environmental Protection Agency. 1998. "What You Should Know about *Pfiesteria piscicida.*" Fact sheet. June.

Ewen, C. R. 1996. "Continuity and Change: De Soto and the Apalachee." *Historical Archaeology* 30 (2): 41–53.

Ewen, C. R., and J. H. Hann. 1998. *Hernando De Soto among the Apalachee: The Archaeology of the First Winter of Encampment.* Gainesville: Univ. Press of Florida.

Fay, C. W., R. J. Neves, and G. B. Pardue. 1983. "Alewife/Blueback Herring." Species Profiles: Life Histories and Environmental Requirements of Coastal Fishes and Invertebrates (Mid-Atlantic). U.S. Fish and Wildlife Service. FWS/OBS-82/11.9.

Fearn, M. L., and K. Liu. 1995. "Maize Pollens of 3500 B.P. from Southern Alabama." *American Antiquity* 60 (1): 109.

Ferrell, G. M., A. G. Strickland, and T. B. Spruill. 2007. "Effects of Canals and Roads on Hydrologic Conditions and Health of Atlantic White Cedar at the Emily and Richardson Preyer Buckridge Coastal Reserve, North Carolina, 2003–2006." Scientific investigations report 2007-5163. Reston, VA: U.S. Geological Survey.

Firestone, R. B., A. West, J. P. Kennett, L. Becker, T. E. Bunch, Z. S. Revay, P. H. Schultz, T. Belgya, D. J. Kennett, J. M. Erlandson, O. J. Dickenson, A. C. Goodyear, R. S. Harris, G. A. Howard, J. B. Kloosterman, P. Lechler, P. A. Mayewski, J. Montgomery, R. Poreda, T. Darrah, S. S. Que Hee, A. R. Smith, A. Stich, W. Topping, J. H. Wittke, and W. S. Wolbach. 2007. "Evidence for an Extraterrestrial Impact 12,900 Years Ago That Contributed to the Megafaunal Extinctions and the Younger Dryas Cooling." *Proceedings of the National Academy of Sciences* 104 (41): 16016–21.

Fischer, K. 2002. *Suspect Relations: Sex, Race and Resistance in Colonial North Carolina.* Ithaca, NY: Cornell Univ. Press.

Flanagan, L. 2000. *Ancient Ireland: Life before the Celts.* Dublin, Ireland: Gill and Macmillan.

Flood, J., and C. Parker. 2006. *Stakeholder Meeting on Red Wolf Ecotourism in North Carolina Report.* 10 May, Columbia, NC. Washington, DC: Defenders of Wildlife.

Forrest, L. C. 1999. *Lake Mattamuskeet: New Holland and Hyde County.* Charleston, SC: Arcadia.

Fox, G. n.d. *An Autobiography.* Available online at www.strecorsoc.org/gfox/title.html.

Franklin, W. N. 1926. "Agriculture in Colonial North Carolina." *North Carolina Historical Review* 3 (4): 539–74.

Fuss, D. J. 2001. "Restoration and Management Plan for the Emily and Richardson Preyer Buckridge Coastal Reserve, Tyrrell County, North Carolina." North Carolina Coastal Reserve Program, Division of Coastal Management, Department of Environment and Natural Resources, Raleigh.

Gardener, P. S. 1990. "Excavations at the Amity Site: Final Report of the Pomeiooc Project." Archaeological Research Report No. 7. Archaeology Laboratory, East Carolina Univ., Greenville, NC.

Garrow, P. H. 1975. *The Mattamuskeet Documents: A Study in Social History.* Raleigh, NC: Archaeology Branch, Division of Archives and History.

Gaskell, J. 2000. *Who Killed the Great Auk?* Oxford: Oxford Univ. Press.

Gay-Lord, J. H. 2001. *Albemarle Sound: The South Shore Settlements.* Plymouth, NC: Beacon Printing.

Glasgow, H. B., J. M. Burkholder, M. A. Mallin, N. J. Deamer-Melia, and R. E. Reed.

2001. "Field Ecology of Toxic *Pfiesteria* Complex Species and a Conservative Analysis of Their Role in Estuarine Fish Kills." *Environmental Health Perspectives* 109 (supp. 5): 715–30.

Goerch, C. 2003. "Excerpts from Carolina Chats." Tar Heel Gem & Mineral Club Web site, www.tarheelclub.org/octo3.doc. Newspaper excerpts taken from C. Goerch, *Carolina Chats* (Raleigh: Edwards and Broughton, 1944).

Gregory, J. D., R. W. Skaggs, R. G. Broadhead, R. H. Culbreath, J. R. Bailey, and T. L. Foutz. 1984. "Hydrologic and Water Quality Impacts of Peat Mining in North Carolina." Report No. 214. Water Resources Institute. Raleigh: North Carolina State University Technical Reports Repository, NC-WRRI-214.pdf (www.lib.ncsu .edu).

Grimes, J. B. 1910. *Abstracts of North Carolina Wills: Compiled from Original and Recorded Wills in the Office of the Secretary of State.* Raleigh, NC: E. M. Uzzell.

Haire, V. C., L. D. Hill, M. L. VanHorne, and G. A. White. 1996. *Bridging Generations: A History of Tyrrell County.* Tyrrell County Genealogical and Historical Society.

Harris, M. H. 1995. *Hyde Yesterdays: A History of Hyde County.* Wilmington, NC: New Hanover.

Harrison, G. B. 1941. *A Jacobean Journal Being a Record of Those Things Most Talked of during the Years 1603–1606.* London: Routledge.

Hayden, E. 1888. "The Great Storm of March 11 to 14, 1888." *National Geographic* 1 (1): 40–58.

Havholm, K. G., D. V. Ames, G. R. Whittcar, B. A. Wenell, S. R. Riggs, H. M. Jol, G. W. Berger, and M. A. Holmes. 2004. "Stratigraphy of Back-Barrier Coastal Dunes, Northern North Carolina and Southern Virginia." *Journal of Coastal Research* 20 (4): 980–99.

Heist, E. J., J. R. Bowles, and A. Woolf. 2001. "Record of a North American Cougar (*Puma concolor*) from Southern Illinois." *Transactions of the Illinois State Academy of Science* 94 (4): 227–29.

Hellgren, E. C., and M. R. Vaughan. 1989. "Demographic Analysis of a Black Bear Population in the Great Dismal Swamp (Virginia, North Carolina, USA)." *Journal of Wildlife Management* 53: 969–77.

Hellgren, E. C., M. R. Vaughan, and F. Stauffer. 1991. "Macrohabitat Use by Black Bears in a Southeastern Wetland." *Journal of Wildlife Management* 55: 442–48.

Hewitt, D. A. 2003. "Abundance and Migratory Patterns of Anadromous Fish Spawning Runs in the Roanoke River, North Carolina." Master's thesis, Fisheries and Wildlife Sciences, North Carolina State Univ., Raleigh.

Hinesley, L. E. 2002. "Research at N.C. State University Related to Regeneration of Atlantic White Cedar (AWC) and Baldcypress." U.S. Fish and Wildlife Service document.

Hinshaw, C. R., Jr. 1948. "North Carolina Canals before 1860." *North Carolina Historical Review* 25 (1): 1–56.

History of the Eleventh Pennsylvania Volunteer Cavalry. 1902. Franklin, PA. Preface signed by John L. Roper and others.

History of Macoupin County, Illinois. 1879. Philadelphia: Brink, McDonough & Co.

Hobbs, C. H., III. 2004. "Geological History of Chesapeake Bay, USA." *Quaternary Science Reviews* 23: 641–61.

Hodge, F. W. 1910. *Handbook of American Indians, North of Mexico, Part 2.* Bulletin 30, Bureau of American Ethnology, Smithsonian Institution. Washington, DC: U.S. Government Printing Office.

Hulton, P. 1984. *America 1585: The Complete Drawings of John White.* Chapel Hill: Univ. of North Carolina Press.

Hutchinson, D. L. 2002. *Foraging, Farming and Coastal Biocultural Adaptation in Late Prehistoric North Carolina.* Gainesville: Univ. Press of Florida.

Hyde County Historical and Genealogical Society. 1976. *Hyde County History: A Hyde County Bicentennial Project.*

Jackman, L. 1891. *A History of the Sixth New Hampshire Regiment in the War for the Union.* Concord, NH: Republican Press Association. Reprint, Earlysville, VA: Old Books, 1996.

Janson, C. W. 1935 (1807). *The Stranger in America, 1793–1806.* Reprinted from the London edition of 1807. New York: Press of the Pioneers.

Johnson, C. E. 1851. *An Address before the Medical Society of North Carolina, at Its Second Annual Meeting, in Raleigh, in May 1851. Seaton.* Raleigh, NC: Gales.

Jones, R. W. 1948. "An Autobiography, Written by Robert William 'Capt. Bob' Jones in 1948." Columbia, NC: Tyrrell County Genealogical Society. Available online at http://homepages.rootsweb.com/~gumneck.

Jordan, W. T., and G. W. Thomas. 1995. "Massacre at Plymouth: April 20, 1864." *North Carolina Historical Review* 72 (2): 125–93.

"Journal of a French Traveller in the Colonies, 1765, I." 1921 (1765). *American Historical Review* 26 (4): 726–47.

Kaiser, J. J. 2006. "Masters Determined to Be Masters: The 1821 Insurrectionary Scare in Eastern North Carolina." Master's thesis, History Department, North Carolina State Univ., Raleigh.

Keith, A. B. 1952. *The John Gray Blount Papers.* 4 vols. Raleigh: North Carolina State Department of Archives and History.

Kell, J. B., and T. A. Williams, eds. 1975. *North Carolina's Coastal Carteret County during the American Revolution, 1765–1785.* Greenville, NC: Era.

Kirk, J. S., W. A. Cutter, and T. W. Morse. 1936. "Emergency Relief in North Carolina." North Carolina Emergency Relief Administration. Raleigh, NC: Edwards and Broughton.

Kirk, P. W., Jr. 1979. *The Great Dismal Swamp.* Charlottesville: Univ. Press of Virginia.

Kurlansky, M. 2002. *Salt: A World History.* New York: Penguin Books.

Lawson, John. 1967 (1710). *A New Voyage to Carolina.* Edited by H. T. Lefler. Chapel Hill: Univ. of North Carolina Press.

Leary, W. J. 1915. "The Fisheries of Eastern North Carolina." *North Carolina Booklet* 14 (4): 174.

Lee, D. S. 1977. "The Status of the Panther in North Carolina." *Wildlife in North Carolina* 41 (7): 6–9.

——. 1979. "North Carolina State Museum's Panther Survey Program." *Eastern Cougar Newsletter,* ed. R. L. Downing, USDI, U.S. Fish and Wildlife Service, Department of Forestry, Clemson University, South Carolina.

Lefler, H. T. 1955. "A description of 'Carolana' by a 'Well-Willer'. 1649." *North Carolina Historical Society* 32: 102–5. Article printed originally in the *Moderate Intelligencer,* 26 Apr.–2 May 1649.

Lemmon, S. M. 1971. *The Pettigrew Papers, Volume I, 1685–1818.* Raleigh: North Carolina State Department of Archives.

——. 1988. *The Pettigrew Papers, Volume II, 1819–1843.* Raleigh: North Carolina State Department of Archives.

Leonard, J. A., R. K. Wayne, J. Wheeler, R. Valadez, S. Guillen, and C. Vila. 2002. "Ancient DNA Evidence for Old World Origin of New World Dogs." *Science* 298: 1613–16.

Lilly, J. P. 1998. "Washington County: Natural History and Historic Overview." In B. B. L. Modlin, F. B. Jones, and S. B. Phelps, eds., *Washington County, NC: A Tapestry*, 3–18. Winston-Salem, NC: Josten. Washington County Bicentennial Publication.

——. 2003. "Organic Soils." *A Century of Soil Science*. Soil Science Society of North Carolina. www.soil.ncsu.edu.

Linzey, D. W. 1995. *The Mammals of Great Smoky Mountains National Park*. Blacksburg, VA: McDonald & Woodward.

——. 1998. *The Mammals of Virginia*. Blacksburg, VA: McDonald & Woodward.

——. 2008. *A Natural History Guide to Great Smoky Mountains National Park*. Knoxville: Univ. of Tennessee Press.

Locat, J., H. Lee, U. Brink, D. Twichell, E. Geist, and M. Sansourcy. 2009. "Geomorphology, Stability and Mobility of the Currituck Slide." *Marine Geology*. doi:10.1016/j.margeo.2008.12.005.

Long, M. W. 2001 (1968). *The Five Lost Colonies of Dare*. Elizabeth City: Family Research Society of Northeastern North Carolina.

Lowe, P. W. 1984. "John Sewell Grew Up in a Hotel." *Hertford County Reflections*, a booklet published by the Hertford County Committee for America's 400th Anniversary: *State* (NC) 55 (6) (Nov. 1988): 10–13.

L.S. 1868. "The Pine Country." *Galaxy* (New York) 6 (4): 560.

Madden, S. 2005. "Evidence of Saltwater Intrusion at the Emily and Richardson Preyer Buckridge Reserve, Tyrrell County, North Carolina." Master's thesis, Nicholas School of the Environment and Earth Sciences, Duke Univ.

Maiolo, J. R., J. E. Whitehead, M. Mcgee, L. King, J. Johnson, and H. Stone. 2001. *Facing Our Future: Hurricane Floyd and Recovery in the Coastal Plain*. Greenville, NC: Coastal Carolina Press/East Carolina Univ.

Mallison, F. M. 1998. *The Civil War on the Outer Banks*. Jefferson, NC: McFarland.

Martof, B. S., W. M. Palmer, J. R. Bailey, and J. R. Harrison. 1980. *Amphibians and Reptiles of the Carolinas and Virginia*. Chapel Hill: Univ. of North Carolina Press.

McAvoy, J. M. 1992. *Clovis Settlement Patterns, Nottoway Survey, Part I: The 30 Year Study of a Late Ice Age Hunting Culture on the Southern Interior Coastal Plain of Virginia*. Special Publication Number 28. Archaeological Society of Virginia.

McAvoy, J. M., and L. D. McAvoy. 1997. *Archaeological Investigations of Site 44sw202, Cactus Hill, Sussex County, Virginia*. Research Report Series Number 8. Virginia Department of Historic Resources.

——. 2003. *The Williamson Clovis Site, 44dw1, Dinwiddie County, Virginia: An Analysis of Research Potential in Threatened Areas*. Research Report Series Number 13. Virginia Department of Historic Resources.

McClees, R. W. 2002. *Roll of Honor: Tyrrell County's Blue & Gray*. Tyrrell County, NC: privately published.

——. 2006. "Union Troops Visit Somerset: July 1862." *Tyrrell Branches* 11 (2): 1–6.

McPhee, J. 2002. *The Founding Fish*. New York: Farrar, Straus and Giroux.

Meekins, A. C. 2007. *Elizabeth City, North Carolina, and the Civil War: A History of Battle and Occupation*. Charleston, SC: History Press.

Meyers, J. M., and D. A. Pike. 2006. "Herpetofaunal Diversity of Alligator River National Wildlife Refuge, North Carolina." *Southeastern Naturalist* 5 (2): 235–52.

Minchinton, W. E. 1994. "The Seaborne Slave Trade of North Carolina." *North Carolina Historical Review* 71 (1): 1–61.

Morgan, M. H. 1995. *Hyde Yesterdays: A History of Hyde County.* Wilmington, NC: New Hanover.

Morris, W. S. 1958. *Ye Countie of Albemarle in Carolina: A Collection of Documents, 1664–1675.* Raleigh: North Carolina Department of Archives and History.

Norris, D. A. 1996. " 'The Yankees Have Been Here!': The Story of Brig. Gen. Edward E. Potter's Raid on Greenville, Tarboro, and Rocky Mount, July 19–23, 1863." *North Carolina Historical Review* 73 (1): 1–27.

North Carolina Land Company. 1869. *North Carolina: A Guide to Capitalists and Emigrants.* Raleigh: North Carolina Land Company. Available online at Documenting the American South, Univ. of North Carolina, Chapel Hill, http://docsouth.unc.edu.

Nowak, R. M. 2002. "The Original Status of Wolves in Eastern North America." *Southeastern Naturalist* 1 (2): 95–130.

Nowitzky, George I. 1888. *Norfolk: The Marine Metropolis of Virginia, and the Sound and River Cities of North Carolina.* Raleigh, NC: E. M. Uzzell.

Numaoka, T. N. 1998. "Josiah Collins III, a Successful Corn Planter: A Look at His Plantation Management Techniques." *Japanese Journal of American Studies* 9: 98–120.

Nuttli, O. W. 1973. "The Mississippi Valley Earthquakes of 1811 and 1812: Intensities, Ground Motion and Magnitudes." *Bulletin of the Seismological Society of America* 63 (1): 227–48.

Oaks, R. Q., Jr., and N. K. Coch. 1963. "Pleistocene Sea Levels, Southeastern Virginia." *Science* 140: 979–83.

O'Brien, S. J., M. E. Roelke, N. Yuhki, K. W. Richards, W. E. Johnson, W. L. Franklin, A. E. Anderson, O. L. Bass Jr., R. C. Belden, and J. Martenson. 1990. "Genetic Introgression within the Florida Panther *Felis concolor coryi*." *National Geographic Research* 6 (4): 485–94.

O'Brien, T. G., and P. D. Doerr. 1986. "Night Count Surveys for Alligators in Coastal Counties of North Carolina." *Journal of Herpetology* 20: 444–48.

Official Records of the Union and Confederate Armies. 1880–1901. Washington, DC: Government Printing Office. Available online at Cornell University, Making of America, http://digital.library.cornell.edu/m/moawar.

Official Records of the Union and Confederate Navies. 1894–1922. Washington, DC: Government Printing Office. Available online at Cornell University, Making of America, http://digital.library.cornell.edu/m/moawar.

Olson, C. 2006. "The *Curlew:* The Life and Death of a North Carolina Steamboat, 1856–1862." *North Carolina Historical Review* 83 (2): 139–64.

Olson, S. L. 1977. "A Great Auk, *Pinguinis* [sic], from the Pliocene of North Carolina." *Proceedings of the Biological Society of Washington* 90: 690–97.

O'Rourke, F. J. 1970. *The Fauna of Ireland.* Cork, Ireland: Mercer.

Otis, C. P. 1878. *Voyages of Samuel de Champlain.* Vol. 2. Boston: Prince Society. Available online at Wisconsin Historical Society, www.americanjourneys.org.

Palmer, W. M., and A. L. Braswell. 1995. *Reptiles of North Carolina.* Chapel Hill: Univ. of North Carolina Press.

Parkman, A. 1983. *History of the Waterways of the Atlantic Coast of the United States.* National Waterways Study, U.S. Army Engineer Water Resources Support Center.

Peacock, E., W. R. Haag, and M. L. Warren Jr. 2005. "Prehistoric Decline in Freshwater Mussels Coincident with the Advent of Maize Agriculture." *Conservation Biology* 19 (2): 547–51.

Pearce, J. D. 2000. "Lake Mattamuskeet." *Poor Town News* 87. Available online at www.poortown.com.

Peck, R. M. 1984. "Stone Fish Traps on the Pee Dee River in North Carolina." *Indian-Artifact Magazine* 3: 4–5, 58.

Pelt, M. R. 1996. *A History of Original Free Will Baptists.* Mt. Olive, NC: Mt. Olive College Press.

Petrie, S. A., and K. L. Wilcox. 2003. "Migration Chronology of Eastern Population Tundra Swans." *Canadian Journal of Zoology* 81: 861–70.

Pittman, T. M. 1861–65. *Thomas M. Pittman Papers,* Civil War, Correspondence, 1861–1865 (PC 13.16). Washington, DC: U.S. National Archives.

Poulter, B., N. L. Christensen Jr., and P. N. Halpin. 2006. "Carbon Emissions from a Temperate Peat Fire and Its Relevance to Interannual Variability of Trace Atmospheric Greenhouse Gases." *Journal of Geophysical Research* 111, D06301, doi:10.1029/2005JD006455.

Powell, W. S., ed. 1958. *Ye Countie of Albemarle in Carolina: A Collection of Documents, 1664–1675.* Raleigh: North Carolina Department of Archives and History.

——. 1973. "North Carolina Creatures." *North Carolina Historical Society* 50: 155–68.

——. 1989. *North Carolina through Four Centuries.* Chapel Hill: Univ. of North Carolina Press.

Quinn, David Beers, ed. 1991. *The Roanoke Voyages, 1584–1590: Documents to Illustrate the English Voyages to North American under the Patent Granted to Walter Raleigh in 1584.* 2 vols. New York: Dover Publications.

Radford, A. E., H. E. Ahles, and C. R. Bell. 1968. *Manual of the Vascular Flora of the Carolinas.* Chapel Hill: Univ. of North Carolina Press.

Rao, D. S., and N. Raghuramulu. 1996. "Food Chain as Origin of Vitamin D in Fish." *Comparative Biochemistry and Physiology Part A: Physiology* 114 (1): 15–19.

Ramsey, G. V. 2000. *Stone Milestones along the Dismal Swamp Canal.* Suffolk: Virginia Canals and Navigation Society.

Redford, D. S. 1988. *Somerset Homecoming: Recovering a Lost Heritage.* Chapel Hill: Univ. of North Carolina Press.

——. 1996. "The Slave Community at Somerset." *Carolina Peacemaker,* 14 Feb. Abstracted from North Carolina State Archives Web site.

Reed, J. A. 1910. *History of the 101st Regiment Pennsylvania Veteran Volunteer Infantry, 1861–1865.* Chicago: L. S. Dickey.

Richardson, C. J., ed. 1981. *Pocosin Wetlands: an Integrated Analysis of Coastal Plain Freshwater Bogs in North Carolina.* Stroudsbourg, PA: Hutchinson Ross.

Richmond, N. D. 1963. "Evidence against the Existence of Crocodiles in Virginia and Maryland during the Pleistocene." *Proceedings of the Biological Society of Washington* 75: 65–68.

Riggs, S. R., and D. V. Ames. 2003. *Drowning the North Carolina Coast: Sea-Level Rise and Estuarine Dynamics.* North Carolina Sea Grant Program, Pub. No. UNC-SG-03-04. Raleigh, NC.

Rogers, P. M., and D. A. Hammer. 1998. "Ancestral Breeding and Wintering Ranges of the Trumpeter Swan (*Cygnus buccinator*)." *North American Swans: Bulletin of the Trumpeter Swan Society* 27 (1): 13–29.

Rose, R. K., ed. 2000. *The Natural History of the Great Dismal Swamp.* Norfolk, VA: Old Dominion Univ. Publications.

Rountree, H. C. 1989. *The Powhatan Indians of Virginia: Their Traditional Culture.* Norman: Univ. of Oklahoma Press.

Rountree, H. C., and E. R. Turner III. 2002. *Before and After Jamestown: Virginia's Powhatans and Their Predecessors.* Gainesville: Univ. Press of Florida.

Royster, C. 2000. *The Fabulous History of the Dismal Swamp Company: A Story of George Washington's Times.* New York: Vintage Books.

Ruffin, E. 1839. "Jottings Down in the Swamps." *Farmers' Register* 7: 698–703, 724–33.

——. 1861. *Agricultural, Geological, and Descriptive Sketches of Lower North Carolina, and the Similar Adjacent Lands.* Raleigh, NC: Institute for the Deaf and Dumb and the Blind.

Russell, D. A., F. J. Rich, V. Schneider, and J. Lynch-Stieglitz. 2009. "A Warm Thermal Enclave in the Late Pleistocene of the Southeastern United States." *Biological Reviews* 84: 173–202.

Salter, B. B., and D. S. Willis. 1972. *Portsmouth Island: Short Stories and History.* Privately published.

Sawyer, R. T. 2004. "Dr. Edward Warren, C.S.A., Confederate Exile." In G. A. White and V. C. Haire, eds., *Heritage of Tyrrell County,* 119–20. Tyrrell County Genealogical and Historical Society.

——. 2007a. *A Life on the Alligator River: The Extraordinary Life of an Ordinary Woman.* Charleston, SC: privately published. Copies have been deposited with the North Carolina Collection, Joyner Library, East Carolina University, Greenville, NC, and with the Tyrrell County Genealogical and Historical Society, Columbia, NC.

——. 2007b. "Life on the Alligator River: World War I Comes to Gum Neck." Tyrrell County, *Branches* 12 (2): 21–48.

——. 2008a. "Life on the Alligator River: Hurricane of September 15–16, 1933, Highest Flood in Gum Neck in the 20th Century." Tyrrell County, *Branches* 13 (1): 1–29.

——. 2008b. "Life on the Alligator River: Inland Waterway Comes to the Alligator River, a Chronology." Tyrrell County, *Branches* 13 (1): 30–41.

——. 2009. "Life on the Alligator River: The Civil War, as Experienced by the People of Gum Neck." Tyrrell County, *Branches* 14 (2).

Scarry, J. F., and C. M. Scarry. 1997. "Subsistence Remains from Prehistoric North Carolina Archaeological Sites: Zooarchaeological Assemblage from the Coast Region." North Carolina Office of Archaeology, www.arch.dcr.state.nc.us.

Sentry, J. 2003. "Live Dunes and Ghost Forests: Stability and Changes in the History of the North Carolina's Maritime Forests." *North Carolina Historical Review* 80 (3): 334–71.

Sharpe, Bill. 1954–65. *A New Geography of North Carolina.* 4 vols. Raleigh, NC: Sharpe.

Short, F. T., L. K. Muehlstein, and D. Porter. 1987. "Eelgrass Wasting Disease: Cause and Recurrence of a Marine Epidemic." *Biological Bulletin* 173: 557–62.

Shurtleff, W., and A. Aoyagi. 2004. "History of Soybeans in North Carolina." Soy Info Center, www.soyinfocenter.com.

Simpson, B. 1997. *Into the Sound Country: A Carolinian's Coastal Plain.* Chapel Hill: Univ. of North Carolina Press.

——. 1998. *The Great Dismal: A Carolinian's Swamp Memoir.* Chapel Hill: Univ. of North Carolina Press.

Smith, H. M. 1907. *The Fishes of North Carolina.* Raleigh, NC: E. M. Uzzell.

Smith, H. M., M. J. Preston, R. B. Smith, and E. F. Irey. 1990. "John White and the Earliest (1585–1587) Illustrations of North American Reptiles." *Brimleyana* 16: 119–31.

Smith, J. 1612. "Captain John Smith's Summary: A Map of Virginia." In P. L. Barbour, ed., *The Jamestown Voyages under the First Charter 1606–1609*, vol. 2, 321–74. Cambridge: Hakluyt Society, Cambridge Univ. Press, 1969.

Smyth, J. F. 1784. *A Tour of the United States of America.* Vol. 2. London. Quoted in "The Great Dismal Swamp and the Underground Railroad," U.S. Fish and Wildlife Service, n.d., p. 2, www.fws.gov.

Stahle, D. W., M. K. Cleaveland, D. B. Blanton, M. D. Therrell, and D. A. Gay. 1998. "The Lost Colony and Jamestown Droughts." *Science* 280: 564–67.

Stahle, D. W., M. K. Cleaveland, and J. G. Hehr. 1988. "North Carolina Climate Changes Reconstructed from Tree Rings: A.D. 372 to 1985." *Science* 240: 1517–19.

State Board of Agriculture. 1896. *"North Carolina and Its Resources."* Raleigh, NC: State Board of Agriculture. Available online at Documenting the American South, Univ. of North Carolina, Chapel Hill, http://docsouth.unc.edu.

State Ship and Water Transportation Commission. 1924. *Report of the State Ship and Water Transportation Commission.* Raleigh, NC: Edwards and Broughton.

Steen, C. 2003. "Restoration Excavation at Somerset Place Plantation State Historic Site, 1994 and 2001." Archaeological Council Publication Number 28. Raleigh: North Carolina Department of Cultural Resources.

Stephenson, E. F. 1995. *Parker's Ferry, Hertford County, North Carolina.* Murfreesboro, NC: Meherrin River Press.

———. 2002. *North Carolina's Last Haul Seine: Williams Fishery.* Murfreesboro, NC: Meherrin River Press.

———. 2007. *Herring Fishermen: Images of an Eastern North Carolina Tradition.* Charleston, SC: History Press.

Stewart, K. G., and M. R. Roberson. 2007. *Exploring the Geology of the Carolinas: A Field Guide to Favorite Places from Chimney Rock to Charleston.* Chapel Hill: Univ. of North Carolina Press.

Stick, D. 1952. *Graveyard of the Atlantic: Shipwrecks of the North Carolina Coast.* Chapel Hill: Univ. of North Carolina Press.

———. 1987. *The Ash Wednesday Storm, March 7, 1962.* Kill Devil Hills, NC: Gresham.

Stith, P., J. Warrick, and M. Sill. 1995. "Boss Hog: North Carolina's Pork Revolution." *Raleigh News and Observer* 19, 21, 22, 24, and 26 Feb.

Stockton, R. P. 1986. *The Great Shock: The Effects of the 1886 Earthquake on the Built Environment of Charleston, South Carolina.* Easley, SC: Southern Historical Press.

Stowe, H. B. 1856. *Dred: A Tale of the Great Dismal Swamp.* 2 vols. Boston: Sampson. Available online at Documenting the American South, Univ. of North Carolina, Chapel Hill, http://docsouth.unc.edu.

Strachey, W. 1612. *The History of Travell into Virginia Britania.* London: Hakluyt Society.

Strommel, H. 1965. *The Gulf Stream: A Physical and Dynamical Description.* 2nd ed. London: Cambridge Univ. Press.

Sturman, J. P., ed. 2005. *Von Graffenried's Account of the Founding of New Bern in 1710.* Raleigh: North Carolina Historical Commission. Reprint of pages 224–320 from a publication of the same title by V. H. Todd., 1920.

Swindell, M. R., and R. S. Spencer Jr. 1973. *In Memory of . . . : An Index to Hyde*

County Cemeteries. Hyde County Historical and Genealogical Society.

Talwani, P., and W. T. Schaeffer. 2001. "Recurrence Rates of Large Earthquakes in the South Carolina Coastal Plain Based on Paleoliquefaction Data." *Journal of Geophysical Research* 106: 6621–42.

Tate, S. 2000. *Logs and Moonshine: Tales of Buffalo City, N.C., as Told by Former Residents.* Nags Head, NC: Nags Head Art.

Tazewell, C. W., ed. 1984. *Meet Marshall Parks: Founder of Virginia Beach.* Virginia Beach, VA: W. S. Dawson.

——. 1990. *Marshall Parks Scrapbook: Entrepreneur and Canal Builder.* Virginia Beach, VA: W. S. Dawson.

Tazewell, W. L., and G. Fridell. 2000. *Norfolk's Waters: An Illustrated History of Hampton Roads.* Sun Valley, CA: American Historical Press.

Titus, J. G. 2002. "Does Sea Level Rise Matter to Transportation along the Atlantic Coast?" *The Potential Impacts of Climate Change: Workshop,* 1–2 Oct. U.S. Department of Transportation.

Titus, J. G., and C. Richman. 2001. "Maps of Lands Vulnerable to Sea Level Rise: Modelled Elevations along the U.S. Atlantic and Gulf Coasts." *Climate Research* 18: 205–28.

True, F. W. 1887. "The Turtle and Terrapin Fisheries, Part XIX." In G. B. Goode, ed., "History and Methods of the Fisheries," *The Fisheries and Fishery Industries of the United States,* sec. 5, vol. 2, pp. 493–503. Washington, DC: U.S. Commission of Fish and Fisheries.

Tryon, William. 1980–81. *The Correspondence of William Tryon and Other Selected Papers.* 2 vols. Edited by William S. Powell. Raleigh: North Carolina Division of Archives and History.

Tyus, H. M. 1974. "Movements and Spawning of Anadromous Alewives, *Alosa pseudoharengus* (Wilson) at Lake Mattamuskeet, North Carolina." *Transactions of the American Fisheries Society* 103 (2): 392–96.

U.S. Army Corps of Engineers. 1880. "Improvement Albemarle-Dismal Swampland: Appendix I." Report. 46th Congress, 3rd Session (15 July).

USDA, Natural Resources Conservation Service. n.d. "Plants Database." http://plants.usda.gov/index.html.

VanDerwarker, A. M. 2001. "An Archaeological Study of Late Woodland Fauna in the Roanoke River Basin." *North Carolina Archaeology* 50: 1–46.

Wade, D. D., and D. E. Ward. 1973. "Air Force Bomb Range Fire." Research Paper SE-10 5. U.S. Department of Agriculture Forest Service, Southeastern Experiment Station, Asheville, NC.

Ward, H. T., and R. P. S. Davis Jr. 1999. *Time before History: The Archaeology of North Carolina.* Chapel Hill: Univ. of North Carolina Press.

Ware, C. C. 1961. *Albemarle Annual.* Wilson, NC: Atlantic Christian College.

Warren, E. 1885. *A Doctor's Experiences in Three Continents.* Baltimore: Cushing & Bailey.

Watson, A. D. 1998. "Sailing Under Steam: The Advent of Steam Navigation in North Carolina to the Civil War." *North Carolina Historical Review* 75 (1): 29–68.

——. 2005. *Bath: The First Town in North Carolina.* Raleigh: North Carolina Office of Archives and History.

Wellman, M. W. 1980. *Dead and One: The Stories behind Ten Famous Murders; Classic Crimes of North Carolina.* Chapel Hill: Univ. of North Carolina Press.

Whan, B., and G. Rising. 2009. "Trumpeter Swans Did NOT Breed in Eastern North America." Gerry Rising's Nature Watch Web site, www.acsu.buffalo.edu/~insrisg/nature/swans.html. Citing map of F. C. Bellrose, *Ducks, Geese and Swans of North America* (Harrisburg, PA: Stackpole Books, 1976).

White, G. A., and V. C. Haire, eds. 2004. *Heritage of Tyrrell County North Carolina.* Tyrrell County Genealogical and Historical Society.

Whitehead, D. R. 1965. "Prehistoric Maize in Southeastern Virginia." *Science* 150: 881–83.

——. 1981. "Late Pleistocene Vegetational Changes in Northeastern North Carolina." *Ecological Monographs* 51 (4): 451–71.

Wilde-Ramsing, M. 1992. "The Estelle Randall." *North Carolina Archaeological Society Newsletter* 2 (4): 1.

Williams, E. L. A. 1989. *In the Name of God, Amen! Abstracts of Hyde County, North Carolina Wills Probate 1709 through 1775.* Hyde County Historical and Genealogical Society.

Williamson, H. 1812. *The History of North Carolina.* Philadelphia: Thomas Dobson.

Wilson, C. N. 1998. *The Most Promising Young Man of the South: James Johnston Pettigrew and His Men at Gettysburg.* Abilene, TX: McWhiney Foundation Press.

Wilson, P. J., S. Grewal, I. D. Lawford, J. N. M. Heal, A. G. Granacki, D. Pennock, J. B. Theberge, M. T. Theberge, D. R. Voigt, W. Waddell, R. E. Chambers, P. C. Paquet, G. Goulet, D. Cluff, and B. N. White. 2000. "DNA Profiles of the Eastern Canadian Wolf and the Red Wolf Provide Evidence for a Common Evolutionary History Independent of the Gray Wolf." *Canadian Journal of Zoology* 78 (12): 2156–66.

Winkler, M. G., and C. B. DeWitt. 1985. "Environmental Impacts of Peat Mining in the United States: Documentation for Wetland Conservation." *Environmental Conservation* 12: 317–30.

Wolf, F. A., and S. G. Lehman. 1926. "Diseases of Soy Beans Which Occur Both in North Carolina and the Orient." *Journal of Agricultural Research* 33 (4): 391–96.

Woodhouse, C. A., and J. T. Overpeck. 1998. "2000 Years of Drought Variability in the Central United States." *Bulletin of the American Meteorological Society* 79: 2693–2714.

Woodings, C. R. 2001. "A Brief History of Regenerated Cellulosic Fibres." In *Regenerated Cellulose Fibres,* 14–19. Cambridge, UK: Woodhead.

Wright, A. H. 1911. "Other Early Records of the Passenger Pigeon." *Auk* 28: 427–49.

Yearns, W. B., and J. G. Barrett. 2002. *North Carolina Civil War Documents.* Chapel Hill: Univ. of North Carolina Press.

Zehmer, J. G., Jr. 2007. *Hayes: The Plantation, Its People, and Their Papers.* Raleigh: North Carolina Office of Archives and History.

Individual entries are grouped under general categories (e.g., "alligator" under fauna, or "Capt. John Smith" under "people, notable"). Boldfaced page numbers refer to illustrations.

earthquakes (*continued*)
  Specific examples: *AD 929*, 46; *1404*, 46; *1735* (Bath), 45–46, 217n4; *1811–12* (New Madrid), 46; *1886* (Charleston), 46; *1906* (San Francisco), 46
economy. *See* banking and barter; charges and prices; commerce and industry; companies; exports and imports; markets; tax and customs
Edenton: colonial capital of, 59; commerce in, 59, 61, 103, 115; communications in, 59, 104; earthquake felt in, 46; fisheries in, 90; forest fire in, 171; naturalist in, 17; royal customs in (Port of Roanoke), 59, 103, 139; steamboats in, 104, 112, 113, 115; Tea Party, 60–61. *See also* Chowan River
Edgecombe County, NC, Tarboro, 115. *See also* Tar River
Elizabeth City: agriculture in, 76, 193, 206; during the Civil War, 115, 143; commerce in, 76, 104, 110–13, 195, 205; Dismal Swamp Canal, 104, 105, 152; emigration to, 114–15, 201; mills in, 76, 205; newspapers in, 114–15, 195; shipbuilding in, 115; steamboats in, 35, 93, 110–13, 191–99; storms in, 52, 54; train in, 201; U.S. Coast Guard in, 139
energy and power: biofuel, 141; coal, 159, 177; crisis, 181; electricity, 40, 117, 203; gasoline, 202; methanol, 181; steam engine, 76, 96, 103, 112; water, 47, 70, 117; wind, 70, **71;** wood, 113, 141, 142. *See also* peat (organic soil)
environmental disturbances: bird populations and, 69, 74; carbon, 5, 177–78; crop diseases, 71–77; and the EPA, 118; erosion from mountains, 3; eutrophication, 96, 97; fishing practices, 91, 96; genetically modified crops, 76, 77; greenhouse gases, 178; of intracoastal waterways, 150–54; land clearance, 68; logging practices, **165;** oxygen, 96, 97, 177–78; peat oxidation, 177–78; in prehistory, 68, 69; slave labor and, 122; of water quality,

69, 171; wood consumption for fuel, 113, 141, 142. *See also* salinity
environmental pollution: and bellwether species (herring), 87, 97; chemical, 80, 81, 97, 118; erosion and siltation, 3, 54, 110; fish kills, 50, 80, 81; herbicides, 77, 175; hog waste and other agricultural, 80–81; litigation and, 98, 118, 182; from the Outer Banks, 98; from peat, 97, 178, 182; of shellfish, 98
exports and imports, 61, 193, 195; brandy, 104; farm produce, 193; feathers, 21, 22; honey and beeswax, 61, 103; Indian and prehistoric, 59, 98; logs, 159; rice, 74, 75; pork, 104, 140. *See also* marine stores

Fairfield (Hyde County, NC): agriculture in, 76; during the Civil War, 194–95; disease in, 149–50; fauna of, 42; roads and bridges in, 149–50, **149,** 198, 204; steamboats in, 112, 191–99
Fairfield Canal: during the Civil War, 111; construction of, 110–11, 196; as siltation free, 110; steamboat commerce on, 93, 110–11, 191–94. *See also* Alligator-Pungo Canal; Alligator River
famine, 62–66
fats (oils): bear, 33; eaten by Indians, 70; herring, 87; passenger pigeon, 70; soybean, 76
fauna: alligators, 4, 14, 15, 16–20, **17,** 94, 97, 128, 184, 214nn13–14; amphibians, northern limits of, 15–16; bats, Rafinesque's big-eared, 16; bats, Seminole, 16; bears, black, 31, 33–36, **34;** beavers, 38; bedbugs, 193; bison, 15, 25–26, 28, 215n35; bobcats, 38, 39, 42; chinch bugs (bedbugs), 193; chinch bugs (corn pests), 71–72; cladocerans, 87; clams, Asiatic, 153; clams, wedge, 153–54; conchs, 97; cooters, Florida, 15; copepods, 97; cougars (panthers), 36–43; coyotes, 31, 32, 216n68; crabs, blue, 51, 95, 99; deer, white-tailed, 28, 29, 30, 37, 38, 39–40, 168; dolphins (porpoises), 14,

forest fires (*continued*)
by military bombs, 175; land-drainage policy link to, 170, 172, 175–76;
peat fires, 174, 179; prehistory of, 167;
rains extinguished, 171, 172, 173;
trees adapted to, 168. Specific examples: Dare County (1957, 1971), 167,
175; Great Dismal Swamp (1799,
1806, 1930), 171–72, 179–80; Lake
Phelps (1791, 1806, 1955, 1961, 1985,
2008), 167, 170, 171, 172–74, 179. *See
also* drainage; logging; peat (organic
soil)
freezes and cold winters: *1596,* 45; *1703,*
45; *1707,* 70; *1780,* 45; *1816–17* (year
without summer), 45; *1857,* 45; *1892–
93,* 45; *1917–18,* 45

Gates County, NC: Merchants Mill
Pond, 19, 81, 184–85, 188; Sandbanks,
175
ghost towns: on Alligator River (list of),
205; Buffalo City, 160–61, 205; New
Holland (Lake Mattamuskeet), 109
Goldsboro (Wayne Co, NC), 113, 115,
118
Great Depression: in the Albemarle region, 202–4; and conservation, 184;
and employment, 163, 184, 202; government measures during, 149, 184,
203; and roads and bridges, 203–4
Great Dismal Swamp: agriculture in, 67,
74; drought in, 74; fauna of, 19, 25–
26, 29, 31, 33, 34, 35, 40, 71; forest
fires in, 171–72, 179–80; and Lake
Drummond, 5, 11, 97, 185; NWR,
185–86, 188, 189; peat in, 177, 179–
80; pollution in, 97; prehistory of, 67;
and slavery, 74, 123, 124, 125, 127–
28, 212; George Washington and, 6,
74, 189; water diversion in, 158–59,
185. *See also* Dismal Swamp Canal
Gulf Stream: and climate, 4, 7, 14; and
Spanish exploration, 56; and winter
storms, 53. *See also* climate change
Gum Neck: African Americans in, 131,
132, 134, 135; agriculture in, 62–66,
204; canal, 128; during the Civil War,

129, 130, 132, 145, 192, 194–95; disease and famine in, 62–66; economy
of, 65, 148–50, 160, 162, 192, 193,
203, 204, 205; fauna of, 35, 38, 41–42;
fisheries in, 92–94, 95, 118; floods and
dike in, 54, **55,** 175; forest fires in,
172, 173–74; Indians and Tramaskecook, 60, 205; landings in, 18,
19, 65, 93, 94, 95, 160, 175, 192–95,
197; logging in, 160, 161–64; and migration, 114, 148, 162, 201; plane
crashes in, 173, 175; post office, 206;
roads and bridges in, 38, 41, 198, 204,
206; settlement of, 65, 205; slavery in,
128–32; steamboats and water highway in, 112, 191–99, 204; storms in,
54, 150–54. *See also* Alligator-Pungo
Canal; Alligator River

Halifax County, NC: Roanoke Canal,
116, 117; —, Museum and Trail, 155;
Roanoke Rapids, 115, 117; Weldon,
85, 115, 116, 117
Hatteras: British attack on, 142; during
the Civil War, 143; earthquake felt at,
46; Gulf Stream and, 56; inlet, 50;
shipping hazards in, 147; storms at,
50, 52, 53. *See also* Ocracoke; Outer
Banks
Hertford County, NC: alligators in, 19;
herring fishery, 91; Murfreesboro, 91;
Riddicksville, 19; Williams Fishery, 91
hog(s): and acorns, 77, 79; barter of, 58;
Blackbeard and, 142; corporate farms,
79–80, 180; economic importance of,
79, 103; export of, 60, 77, 104, 140,
193, 194; fodder for, 70; foraging in
woods, 77, 78; Indians and, 58, 68; introduction of, 77; killing of, 79; military need for, 79, 142, 143; and
pollution, 79–81; predators of, 33,
35–36; and salt pork, 58, 60, 77, 79,
103, 104, 121, 140, 141, 143; slavery
and, 77, 121; storms and, 79; wild
herds of, 26–27, 77, 140
Hyde County, NC: African Americans
in, 135; agriculture in, 73, 76, 180; canals in, 108, 110, 111, 149–50,

Norfolk, VA: African Americans in, 124, 125, 134, 212; commerce in, 65, 94, 104, 110, 111, 191, 193; disease in, 150; Dismal Swamp Canal, 104, 111–12, 113, 139, 146, 147; earthquake felt at, 46; Elizabeth River, 104, 105, 152; forest fires in, 167, 171–72; logging in, 158, 160–61; market in (agriculture), 65, 94, 104, 110, 111, 191, 193, 206; market in (fisheries), 100, 193; migration to, 205; military in, 104, 136–37, 139, 146, 147, 205; salt penetration from, 152; slavery in, 124, 125, 212; steamboats in, 111–12, 113, 159, 193; tidewater, Virginia, 3. *See also* Albemarle and Chesapeake Canal; Dismal Swamp Canal

Northampton County, NC: enslavement of Indians in, 122; Roanoke Canal, 116, 117

North Carolina: agriculture in, 76, 79, 180; "Albemarle Countie," 59, 189; fisheries in, 90; during the Great Depression, 203; isolated communities in, 191, 204; Lords Proprietors, 58, 59, 61, 62, 77, 85, 140; Outlying Landing Field, 20, 24–25, 175, 183; pollution in, 80–81; Virginia, relations with, 90, 104, 115, 190; wildlife refuges, 184–89. *See also specific counties by name*
—agencies: NC Coast Federation, 182; NC Colonial Council, 122; NC Estuarium, 212; NC Department of Environment and Natural Resources, 187; NC Department of Transportation, 187; NC Division of Coastal Management, 187; NC Division of Marine Fisheries, 86, 91, 97; NC Division of Water Quality, 152; NC General Assembly, 107, 109, 123; NC Museum of Natural History, 40, 41; NC Power and Light Company, 118, 183; NC Provincial Congress, 141; NC Riverkeepers and Waterkeepers Alliance, 80; NC State Highway 64, 152; NC State Highway 90, 202; NC State Highway 94, 150, 204, 206; NC State Highway Commission, 204; NC State

University, 42; NC Supreme Court, 118; NC Underwater Archaeology, 112, 142; NC Wildlife Commission, 187

Nottoway River, 4, 9, 28, 84, 91, 99, 126, 156, 167

Ocracoke: British attacks on and occupation of, 139, 140, 142; piracy at, 138; shipping entrance ("the bar"), 59, 103, 104; Spanish attack on (1740s), 142. *See also* Hatteras; Outer Banks

Onslow County, NC: Camp Lejeune, 67; prehistory of, 67; slavery in, 124–25; White Oak River, 5

Outer Banks: Corolla (Whale Head), 142; fauna of, 26, 85, 184; fisheries, 85, 98; inlets changing in, 22, 50, 88; military in, 139, 142; Oregon Inlet, 50, 88; as physical barrier, 4; pollution from, 98; Portsmouth Island, 21, 46, 48, 142; prehistory of, 9; roads to, 198; salt factory in, 142; shipwrecks in, 139, 146; storms at, 22, 48, 50, 53, 54, 88, 146; tourism in, 98, 198, 209; Whalebone, 51. *See also* Hatteras; Nags Head; Ocracoke

Outlying Landing Field, 20, 24–25, 175, 183

Pamlico County, NC: Arapahoe, 16; fossil alligator in, 16; mammoth in, 16

Pamlico Sound: Croatan Sound, 46, 50, 91; drainage basin of, 4; fauna of, 23, 85, 86, 88, 101; Pamlico River, 4, 51, 86; pollution of, 80, 98, 182; Roanoke Sound, 88; salinity changes in, 51; shellfish in, 98, 99; steamboats on, 113; storms on, 48, 51; wildlife refuges, 184

Pasquotank County, NC, Nixonton, 61

Pasquotank River, 52, 104, 114, 149–50

peat (organic soil): forest fires and, 174, 179; mining, 181, 183; oxidation and soil loss, 178, 179; pocosins and, 5, 48, 176, 177, 178; pollution from, 96, 97, 178, 182. *See also* First Colony Farms

Pender County, NC, 156

sea-level changes (*continued*)
10. *See also* flooding and water control
shellfish: middens, 69, 98; oysters, 84, 95, 98; and pollution, 69, 98, 182; in prehistory, 69, 83, 97, 98; regional history of, 97–99; scallops, 97; shrimp, 84, 95, 99. *See also* fauna; fish; fisheries
shipping: agricultural, 112, 193; and bankruptcy, 180–83; British warships, 138, 140; disease spread by, 149–50; and freight charges, 146, 147, 182; and lighthouses, 46, 100, 164, 196; and logging, 159, 162; Ocracoke Inlet, 59; and piracy, 138; qualifications of captains, 195–96; and shipbuilding, 115, 156–57, 164; shipwrecks, 48, 55, 140, 146, 147; slave ships, 123, 138; and steamboat agents, 193, 194; and storms, 48, 55; and water highway, 191–99, 204; water in canals for, 185
ships and vessels, **148;** CSS *Albemarle*, 144; *Alma*, 93, 95, 191, 195; *Armeca*, 114; *Bravo*, 115; *Calypso*, 105; *Caroline*, 55; *Camden*, 123; *Curlew*, 113; *Currituck*, 147; *M. E. Dickerman*, 191, 194; *Dolphin*, 103; *Estelle Randall*, 112; *Elvira Jane*, 65; *Exxon Valdez*, 118; ferries, 150, 198, 206; *Fox*, 115; *Gibbins*, 140; James Adams Floating Theatre, 196–97, 212; *Jennett*, 123; *Lady of the Lake*, 111–12; *Lizzie Burrus*, 191, 194–95; *Lovely Peggy*, 102–3; *Lucille Ross*, 164; *Mamie G.*, 197; *Mary Steele*, 18; *R. L. Myers II*, **192;** *Nellie Prior*, 159; *Neuse*, 45, 112, 195, 228n7; *New Bern*, 112, 159; *Norfolk*, 112–13; *Pamplico*, 113; *Parrot*, 55; *Polly*, 123; *Post Boy*, 113; *Pungo*, 148; *Queen Anne's Revenge*, 138, 142; *M. E. Roberts*, 112; *Sally*, 103; *Schultz*, 115; *Snow Squall*, 143; *Soon Old*, 191, 195; *Susan*, 55; *Susannah*, 55
slaves and slavery: Albemarle history of, 31, 112–13, 114, 120–32, 138; bought and sold, 75, 77, 90, 121, 126, 129–30, 140; canals dug by, 104, 105–6, 107,

109, 110; during the Civil War, 131, 143; free colored, 96, 122, 130, 132, 160; labor, 39, 73, 74, 96, 100, 111; at local level, 128–32; sickness of, 75; Somerset Place, 123–24; Underground Railroad, 121, 123, 124, 125, 190, 212. *See also* African American(s); Somerset Place (plantation)
Somerset Place (plantation): agriculture at, 63, 72, 73, 75–76, 107, 143; during the Civil War, 143; Collins Canal (1788), 88, 106–7, 170; Lake Company and, 106; slavery at, 123, 126; soil subsidence at, 157, 178; and tourism, 212. *See also* Josiah Collins *under* people, notable
Southampton County, VA: Outlying Landing Field, 175; slave insurrection at, 126
storms: active periods, 62–66, 210; and agricultural pollution, 80–81; and crop failures, 61–64; geological impact of, 48; and herring migration, 88; and salt penetration, 150–54. Specific examples: 1587, 48; 1667–70, 48, 61–62; 1727–28, 62; 1731, 50; 1761, 48; 1769, 48; 1811, 50; 1828, 22, 50, 88; 1836, 109; 1842–43, 62–66; 1846, 48, 50; 1879, 48; 1888 (Great Blizzard), 55; 1889, 55; 1899 (San Ciriaco), 48, 52; 1933, 48, 52, 54, 150–52, 196, 198, 203, 210; 1944 (Great Atlantic Hurricane), 48, 52; 1945, 66, 88; 1954 (Hazel), 23, 47, 152–53; 1955 (Connie, Diane), 23, 47, 152–53; 1960 (Donna), 47; 1962 (Ash Wednesday Storm), 48, 53–54, 198; 1999 (Floyd), 48, 80–81; 2003 (Isabel), 32, 47, 81, 91; 2005 (Katrina), 151–52; 2005 (Ophelia), 153
swamps: draining of, 74, 178; as slave refuges, 123, 127–28

Tar River: agriculture on, **121;** antiquity of, 15; drainage basin, 4; fauna of, 17, 85, 86; floods on, 51; invasive species in, 153–54; pollution of, 80; steamboats on, 113, 115, **192;** Tarboro, 115.